PRAISE FOR *BUSINESS CONTINUITY MANAGEMENT*

T0295527

The second edition of *Business Continuity Management* provides an indispensable guide to navigating the complexities of organizational resilience centred around ISO 22301. James Crask's experience enables him to provide practical strategies for realizing effective resilience, empowering organizations to thrive in the face of adversity. Whether you're a seasoned professional or new to the field, this is essential reading for anyone committed to safeguarding their organization's future.
Oliver Gordon, Non-Executive Director, Institute of Strategic Risk Management

James Crask has managed to distil his expertise, broad perspective and years of deep thought into this essential guide to all things business continuity management. It provides a comprehensive understanding of what really matters and how to make it work. Using a combination of lessons well learned and recent relevant events as the basis, this guide really does deliver practical, clear and usable methodologies.
Mark Stringer, Director, EMEA Business Resilience, Salesforce

Instead of seeing operational resilience as another regulatory hurdle to overcome, firms should view it as a catalyst to drive change across the business, taking a long-term strategic view on the resilience and the technology that will allow them to thrive in a period of unprecedented uncertainty. The contents of *Business Continuity Management* provide a practical, easy-to-follow step-by-step guide for any practitioner keen to know where to start.
Sumaiya Khoda, Director, Group Operational Resilience Risk and Third Party Risk Management, London Stock Exchange Group

If there is one lesson the permacrisis has imparted, it is that the unlikely can – and very likely will – happen. With expert evaluation of the response to Covid and analysis of the impacts of global conflicts, this up-to-the-minute

second edition offers pragmatic approaches for resilience practitioners seeking to grapple with a multitude of simultaneous challenges, and to build a sound case to secure any investment needed for recovery."
Deborah Ritchie, editor and journalist

Business Continuity Management

A practical guide to organization resilience and ISO 22301

SECOND EDITION

James Crask

Publisher's note
Every possible effort has been made to ensure that the information contained in this book is accurate at the time of going to press, and the publishers and authors cannot accept responsibility for any errors or omissions, however caused. No responsibility for loss or damage occasioned to any person acting, or refraining from action, as a result of the material in this publication can be accepted by the editor, the publisher or the author.

First published in Great Britain and the United States in 2024 by Kogan Page Limited
Second edition 2024

2nd Floor, 45 Gee Street
London
EC1V 3RS
United Kingdom
www.koganpage.com

8 W 38th Street, Suite 902
New York, NY 10018
USA

© James Crask 2021, 2024

The right of James Crask to be identified as the author of this work has been asserted by him in accordance with the Copyright, Designs and Patents Act 1988.

ISBNs
Hardback   9781398614895
Paperback 9781398614871
Ebook   9781398614888

British Library Cataloguing-in-Publication Data
A CIP record for this book is available from the British Library.

Library of Congress Cataloging-in-Publication Data
A CIP record for this book is available from the Library of Congress.

Typeset by Hong Kong FIVE Workshop, Hong Kong
Print production managed by Jellyfish
Printed and bound by CPI Group (UK) Ltd, Croydon CR0 4YY

Kogan Page books are printed on paper from sustainable forests.

CONTENTS

ABOUT THE AUTHOR

James Crask has worked in the resilience field since 2003. He currently leads the Strategic Risk Consulting practice at Marsh, a global risk management advisory and insurance brokerage. His work here involves supporting organizations in numerous industry sectors to build their resilience arrangements. This includes working with some of the world's largest food and consumer goods companies, multinational financial services organizations, critical infrastructure operators and technology and media businesses to implement global resilience programmes.

Previous roles have included working as the head of risk management for the BBC and a similar role at the UK Nuclear Decommissioning Authority, which is responsible for the safe decommissioning of the UK's fleet of civil nuclear sites. He also spent many years working for PwC, leading the UK firm's enterprise resilience advisory services and advising companies in a wide range of industrial sectors.

Prior to his consulting roles, James worked in the UK Cabinet Office supporting government ministers and the British prime minister to prepare plans for national disasters. In this role he also supported the response to national crises as part of the UK Government's crisis response machinery known as COBR.

James also chairs the International Organization for Standardization (ISO) panel that is responsible for all global business continuity and organizational resilience standards. It is this committee that publishes ISO 22301, ISO 22313, ISO 22316 (organizational resilience) and other related standards.

01

Introduction

History is littered with organizations, governments and even civilizations that have failed to respond to disruptive events, were unable to adapt and as a result no longer exist. There are parallels here with ecology and the Darwinian concept of survival of the fittest. Animals that adapt well to their changing environments and are stronger and more resourceful in the face of adversity would likely be the ones to survive. Organizations share similar qualities. The pre-crisis health of an organization, along with its ability to adapt in the face of substantial change, will likely define how effective their recovery will be from a disruption. Weaker organizations, and those that are unwilling or unable to change, are unlikely to survive.

Evidence of this need for constant adaptation can be found in the history of some well-known global brands operating today:

- **Nokia** can trace its origins to the operation of paper mills until its transition into electronics and then the telecommunications industry.[1]
- **Toyota's** origins can be traced back to the manufacture of weaving machines.[2]
- **Wrigley** started life selling soap and baking soda until the individual running the business noticed the chewing gum it was offering to help sweeten the deal was becoming more popular than their original main product.[3]
- **Peugeot's** origins go back to operating a flour mill until the business began to mechanize and eventually evolved into an engineering, bicycle, and ultimately a global automotive business.[4]

These four organizations, and many more like them, succeeded because they saw a need to change and seized an opportunity to do something differently. This same mindset can be applied to resilience.

In the context of resilience, the need to adapt will be driven by different root causes than those driving Peugeot and Nokia to change, and the stimulus for change may at times be quicker to materialize than some of the timelines followed by the brands above. Those organizations that maintain a capability to spot a potential disruption, quickly respond to it, recover and then adapt are more likely to thrive in the longer term. While business continuity is not the only thing that contributes to an organization's resilience, it does play a highly important role in helping organizations to achieve an adaptive capacity when facing a need to change.

This book is intended to provide some practical guidance on how organizations can build their resilience. It has been written from many years of successes and personal mistakes made by the author in implementing business continuity, crisis management and more latterly operational resilience arrangements in government institutions, for multinationals, infrastructure businesses, charities, media and telecommunications, technology and financial services organizations.

The guidance this book provides is grounded in good practice enshrined within the International Standard ISO 22301 (for business continuity). However, the advice provided is not intended to be defined by the approach directed by the ISO. Instead it takes the good practice contained in ISO 22301 and seeks to explore a more pragmatic approach to implementing improvements to an organization's resilience – taking account of the need to adapt methodologies to fit the specific contextual and cultural nuances of each organization.

This book has also been written out of frustration over how dry most industry papers and discussions on business continuity have become. Too many business continuity and resilience programmes unquestioningly implement an ISO without pausing to ask whether it is appropriate for their organization. Too many practitioners have become dogmatic in their approach and inflexible to the demands of modern organizations.

At the heart of the concept of resilience is the ability of an organization and its people to constantly adapt. Yet if an organization's approach to business continuity and resilience stands still, the world and the people around it will move on and, over time, plans prepared to help manage a business disruption will become irrelevant and unhelpful to management when they are needed most.

The business continuity and resilience profession is one of only a small number that give individuals the chance to experience the full breadth of what an organization does and the opportunity to work at both the operational and strategic levels of a business. Few professional disciplines afford an opportunity for staff to operate from the boiler room all the way up to the boardroom on issues that matter to the success of the organization. It gives staff the chance to work with senior management when things are going wrong in the heat of a crisis, as well as when they are going right. Resilience professionals get to see the organization, and the people who work for it, in various states of stress; that in itself provides a huge opportunity to learn.

This book is for practitioners new and old to the profession. Most of all, though, it is for individuals who want to be informed by codified good practice but not to become defined by it. It is for individuals who want more out of their careers and are looking to challenge management and the leaders of their organizations to think slightly differently about business continuity and resilience.

This book does not provide all of the answers: none can. Instead, it offers advice on the practical steps that can be taken to implement an effective business continuity and resilience capability. It offers some tips, tools and templates, but these are shared in the knowledge that while they may offer a good place for readers to start, they are likely to need tailoring to meet the specific needs of the organizations they work for.

This is the overarching approach taken by this book. Every organization is different and every stakeholder a practitioner interacts with will have a different set of needs and values, and a different outlook on life. This requires practitioners to question every piece of advice and good practice received and tailor it to fit the highly specific needs of the organization they work for.

If a cookie-cutter approach is what a practitioner is looking for, they are in the wrong profession.

Business continuity and resilience

No conversation about business continuity can take place without a wider discussion on resilience. Business continuity is an important part of what makes an organization more resilient; however, it is not the only thing that helps to achieve this.

Discussions on the concept of resilience began accelerating after the 2008 financial crisis – driven, in part, by the crisis itself and the sense from myriad IT failures, mainly in the banking sector, that demonstrated there was more to resilience than having a business continuity plan. It has since evolved to become the focus of banking regulators and the basis for an international standard.

The intention of this book is to put business continuity into a wider business resilience context. It does not seek to provide an academic analysis of what organizational resilience is and how it can be achieved. Instead, it seeks to provide some insights into what resilience might mean for different types of organization, how the concept can be utilized to improve an organization's preparedness for disruption events, and some challenges and pitfalls when implementing it.

The terms 'business continuity' and 'resilience' are at times used interchangeably throughout this book, but in general:

- **Business continuity** is used to describe the capability of an organization to continue or recover operations following a disruptive incident.
- **Organizational resilience** is a concept that has become the focus of banking regulation and current academic discourse. The term is used to describe an integrated approach to delivering business continuity alongside aspects of what many organizations would consider operational risk management.
- **Resilience** is used to describe the outcome provided by good business continuity, along with a broad range of other risk

management activities that when combined help organizations prepare for, respond to and recover from disruptive events.

An introduction to business continuity

Returning to the main focus of this book: business continuity

Under normal circumstances, organizations would typically be able to operate in a value-creation mode – driving towards the delivery of their business plan and strategy. This could be considered a 'business as usual' state. Following a disruption, however, the organization will enter into a value-protection mode, which seeks to focus efforts on either recovering or maintaining the delivery of the most critical parts of the organization before a full recovery can be achieved. This switch between value creation to value protection and then back to value creation again is at the heart of what business continuity provides.

The plans developed as part of the business continuity process set out the procedures for management to follow to get an organization back on its feet again. These plans are designed to provide the capability needed to help an organization to recover critical processes and activities to pre-agreed levels and within a pre-agreed timeline as set by management.

The delivery of a business continuity capability involves:

- identifying the processes and activities that are critical to an organization's ability to deliver its products and services and meet its objective and therefore should be prioritized for recovery following a disruption;
- understanding the resources that will be needed to deliver these critical processes and activities and then implementing recovery strategies and solutions for use following a disruption;
- developing and then maintaining a comprehensive set of business continuity, incident management and crisis management plans to help the organization respond to a full range of impacts arising from a disruption or a larger crisis;

- providing training to staff involved in delivering and then maintaining business continuity capabilities so that they are competent to do so;

- running regular exercises to rehearse teams and plans and to validate the organization's response and recovery plans – an essential step in the process to ensure that plans will actually work when they are most needed;

- operating a process of continuous improvement to ensure business continuity capabilities remain up to date and relevant for the organization.

As the list above suggests, business continuity takes a lifecycle approach to delivery. This process is designed to ensure that recovery arrangements are continuously improved and always remain fit for purpose and up to date for the organization should they need to use them.

There are five steps to the business continuity management life-cycle, as described in Figure 1.1.

FIGURE 1.1   Business continuity management lifecycle

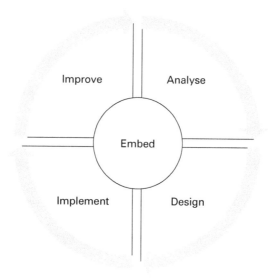

1 **Analyse:** a crucial step in the lifecycle and the first place to start if business continuity is being delivered from scratch. It is at this stage that the business impact analysis is undertaken to identify the organization's critical processes and activities and determine the priorities for recovery. Mistakes at this crucial stage, either in the form of processes or activities being missed or where their criticality is incorrectly assessed, are likely to result in recovery plans that are ineffective.

2 **Design:** this stage involves the development of recovery strategies and their associated solutions for the resources needed by the critical processes and activities for their delivery. For example, these resources could be the trained staff needed to perform a particular role, a computer system, data, a third-party supplier or a specific building. The recovery strategies and solutions developed here form the basis of what will be documented in recovery plans (which come next) and should ensure all critical processes and activities can be recovered within agreed timeframes and to the capacities expected.

3 **Implement:** it is only at this stage that a business continuity plan begins to take shape. The outputs from the first two steps of the lifecycle provide much of the detail that will be needed to develop the plan. While there will be a temptation to skip to this step, without undertaking the earlier analysis and design steps, the plans developed will likely be ineffective.

4 **Improve:** continuous improvement mechanisms will include management reviews, audits, post-incident debriefs and of course exercises designed to validate the effectiveness of the business continuity plans. Each time an improvement is identified through any of these means the processes implemented at this stage ensure the organization's arrangements are updated to reflect the latest learning and good practice.

5 **Embed:** this step focuses on the provision of training to staff to ensure they are able to effectively deliver their business continuity duties, but also includes raising awareness among the broader population of staff. While not all staff will need a detailed

knowledge of business continuity, they will, however, need to understand their role both in supporting the development of plans and what is expected from them when a disruption occurs.

This five-step lifecycle will help to deliver business continuity plans that meet the organization's recovery requirements to help provide an effective response to a business disruption. In order to ensure a smooth delivery, the process requires some form of programme management to help deliver it. This would typically involve a delivery plan setting out the milestones and activities needed and an agreed set of resources to oversee the implementation process. This will all need to be supported by a governance and reporting structure to ensure the programme stays on track.

While this lifecycle provides a consistent and repeatable approach to plan development, practitioners must be prepared to adapt established methodologies to suit the particular needs of the organization they are working with. Individuals following a too rigid approach to business continuity will often find it harder to motivate colleagues to support delivery and maintenance activities, particularly if suggestions of different ways of doing things from colleagues are being ignored. An overly dogmatic approach to delivery, combined with a lack of listening, will likely undermine the sustainability of any capabilities that are put in place.

The personality and skillset of an effective resilience professional

No business continuity and resilience capability can be implemented without competent staff to oversee delivery. Having the right personal qualities, skills and experience will be critical for the success of the programme. As with any role, a poorly performing business continuity or resilience manager will be unlikely to succeed in implementing an effective recovery capability. But what does good look like?

First and foremost, resilience professionals must be good at dealing with uncertainty. This has become particularly critical in the face of a string of recent global crises including the Covid-19 pandemic, the wars in Ukraine and the Middle East and the ongoing disruption to global supply chains.

Wherever there is complexity in an organization or where people are involved, things always have the capacity to go wrong or result in unanticipated outcomes. The programme approach to delivering business continuity, and the plans themselves used to recover a business following a disruption, may not work entirely as anticipated by planners. There will always be challenges along the way that will need to be overcome. Being inquisitive, seeking to understand problems and thinking logically about how to overcome them will be the best approach to keep the programme on track.

This means practitioners will need to adapt to their circumstances and adjust plans and approaches to fit new and evolving situations. The worst approach to these challenges would be to blindly carry on along the same path as before or even to throw in the towel and declare the cause lost. At the heart of the role of a resilience professional is the ability to face uncertainty and seek solutions to new problems.

The ability to analyse data, spot patterns and identify vulnerabilities that others may have missed will also be important. At the root of many disruptions will be a small failure or a risk that has been missed by others. Being able to spot these vulnerabilities so they can be addressed before they have the chance to lead to a major disruption will be important. And if this skill does not come naturally, individuals should instead keep asking probing questions. Practise by asking colleagues why things are done in a certain way and how tasks get delivered. By asking lots of questions and seeking to understand how an organization and its networks and dependencies work, a practitioner will be better able to build a picture of where there might be unmitigated vulnerabilities and what could be done about them.

Resilience professionals also need to be good at working with people and communicating. Emotional intelligence is at times just as important as, if not more so than an individual's technical expertise. Being able to persuade reluctant colleagues to write a recovery plan they think they will never need is a highly valuable skill and often an undervalued one. So too is being able to alter the style of communication to allow a resilience manager to relate to a broad range of staff, from operational employees working on a factory floor through to the executive directors in the boardroom. This means holding a solid understanding of people's personal motivations, their goals and aspirations, and adapting communication methods to complement these. A practitioner will also need a good level of verbal and written communication skills. Risks, issues and the finer complexities of a business continuity programme will need to be explained using language that colleagues will understand. That means avoiding jargon wherever possible, and relating what is being communicated back to the individual receiving the message to ensure the right approach and content is being used. Written forms of communication are also very important, particularly when preparing papers for leadership committees. The preparation of business reports that seek to persuade a senior decision-making body to take a particular course of action, or make a major investment in resilience, is a skill that few will learn at college or university. Practice is key – a poorly structured and written report will likely fail to achieve its primary goal.

Taking the first steps

In many cases an organization will already have implemented a large amount, if not all of the business continuity lifecycle set out above. This means a practitioner will not be starting completely from scratch. There may well be steps of the lifecycle that have been implemented well, and in other areas the process followed might have resulted in a poor level of capability. Or indeed the organization may have changed significantly since the planning cycle was last followed.

Before starting the process of rebuilding, replacing or renewing any existing arrangements, it will be important to conduct an initial review and gap analysis to establish the health and completeness of current capabilities.

If it is not entirely clear whether capabilities already exist, the following five questions provide a useful place to start:

1 Is a member of senior management accountable for business continuity and resilience?

2 Has the organization responded to a significant disruption in the recent past?

3 Are critical processes and activities clearly understood, and have these been documented anywhere?

4 Have any business continuity plans been drafted in the past and are these up to date?

5 Have exercises been performed in the past to practise the response to a disruption?

The answers to these questions will help to establish the existence and validity of any business continuity arrangements. The absence of positive responses to these questions might suggest the lack of any current business continuity arrangements and the possibility that the delivery process will need to start from scratch.

Where arrangements are already in place, it will be necessary to establish their completeness and effectiveness. A basic gap analysis against the main clauses contained within ISO 22301 will be a good place to start or, alternatively, using some of the assurance techniques discussed in later chapters of this book.

The results of the initial assessment can then be used to build a delivery programme setting out clear milestones, tasks and resource requirements focusing on the areas of the lifecycle that require particular attention. Such information will also be useful to support the development of any business cases needed to obtain investments – either in the recruitment of competent staff needed to run the programme or tools and other resources needed for delivery. There will be a temptation, including pressure from some stakeholders, to jump straight into delivery as soon as possible. However, time will be needed to properly plan the programme and a failure to do so will make delivery harder to achieve in the longer term.

Above all of this pre-preparation, the delivery of business continuity and resilience will take an inquisitive mind, persistence and an objective, logical approach to problem-solving. Tackled in the right way, the delivery of business continuity and resilience can be enormously rewarding to individuals who choose to take this career path.

Reading this book will help practitioners to take those first steps in delivering a business continuity programme that achieves quality results. It has been structured into three parts to help put business continuity into its broader business resilience context, to provide guidance on the steps that will need to be followed to implement an effective recovery capability, and provide some tools and tips that will aid in that process:

1 **Part One** sets out some of the concepts that underpin business continuity and resilience and includes an analysis of the lessons emerging from how organizations responded to the Covid-19 pandemic in 2020/21 and the war in Ukraine.

2 **Part Two** sets out common approaches to implementing business continuity and resilience, built around the business continuity lifecycle and the 'plan, do, check, act' model as described in the International Standard for Business Continuity ISO 22301 (requirements) and ISO 22313 (guidelines).

3 **Part Three** provides some templates and tools for use by practitioners when implementing business continuity and resilience arrangements.

Notes

1   Nokia (nd) Our history, https://www.nokia.com/about-us/our-history/ (archived at https://perma.cc/MVB9-S67X)

2   Toyota (nd) History of Toyota, https://www.toyotauk.com/about-toyota/history-of-toyota.html (archived at https://perma.cc/G4PH-J8ZC)

3   Clayman, A (nd) Wm Wrigley Jr Company, est 1891, Made in Chicago Museum, https://www.madeinchicagomuseum.com/single-post/wrigley/ (archived at https://perma.cc/7WJB-VRCC)

4   Peugeot (nd) Peugeot's history and achievements, https://www.peugeot.co.uk/peugeot-history/ (archived at https://perma.cc/HC4S-45GZ)

PART ONE

Core principles

02

The evolution of resilience

Resilience has now become a firmly established concept within most organizations. Its recent evolution has been helped in part by a string of global crisis events, from Covid-19, to the conflicts in Ukraine and the Middle East, to the omnipresent threat of supply chain failures. Some commentators have characterized this recent experience as a *permacrisis* where citizens, governments and organizations are waging a constant battle against the effects of one crisis after another. The effect of this experience has been to push the concept of resilience firmly onto the agenda of most boards. Whereas in the past resilience professionals may have struggled to sustain interest from senior decision makers, now there is a constant demand for assurance over an organization's preparedness to weather the next crisis.

Whilst this book's primary focus is business continuity management, it cannot ignore the wider concept of resilience. Of course the concept has not come from nowhere; resilience has been the focus of academic papers, articles from industry, and professional bodies and regulators for many years. This chapter explores its origins, what it means, challenges to implementing it and how the concept can be best used alongside an already established, or maturing, business continuity programme.

The debate about what organizational resilience actually is has been raging for many years. It has attracted a wide range of responses, from highly vociferous, almost evangelical support to individuals that shout 'heresy' and label it as the next management buzzword created to help consultancies to sell their services. To some extent the debate has been quietened by our collective experience of having lived through so many global crisis events. The emergence of more regulation focused in this area, and the publication of resilience strategies by governments has also helped practitioners to coalesce around a common understanding of what organizational resilience is.

That does not mean that full consensus has been achieved. There are still many vested interests within organizations vying for influence and control. Risk managers, business continuity managers and security professionals, to name a few, could understandably feel threatened by the concept. In organizations that have achieved resilience in one particular way for years, or where individuals have long-established ways of working, it is not surprising to see people getting defensive. However, organizations that were significantly impacted by Covid-19, or any of the other recent global crises, have lived experience that tells them that resilience takes a collective effort with input from a wide variety of internal and external stakeholders. It is clear to most that organizational resilience is a shared responsibility.

Organizational resilience is a concept that builds upon existing risk management disciplines and processes; it does not seek to replace them. If anything, the resilience evangelists would argue, the concept gives greater credence to business continuity by making it more of a board-level conversation and by providing the glue that binds all the different risk management-related disciplines together.

The limitations of business continuity and the birth of resilience

To understand why organizational resilience matters, we must explore the limitations of business continuity and the reasons why the concept has become a focus for regulators and other external stakeholders.

Despite investments in business continuity, organizations still fail

There are plenty of examples of organizations that have suffered a major disruption or crisis and not lived to tell the tale. Many of these will have had business continuity plans, but they still failed. This suggests either that their business continuity arrangements were ineffective (which may certainly be possible) or there are other reasons why organizations catastrophically fail.

Three recent case studies can be used here to explore this point further: Home Depot's cyber-attack in 2014, the impact of the Japanese earthquake and tsunami on Nissan in 2011, and Woolworths' demise in 2005.

We will start with Woolworths, an example from the United Kingdom of a business that failed as a result of a string of circumstances unrelated to business continuity.

WOOLWORTHS

Woolworths was omnipresent on UK high streets from the time its first retail store opened in 1909. The company, selling a wide range of household and giftware at affordable prices, would have been well known to anyone growing up in the UK from the 1950s onwards. Most would remember a favourite Woolworths children's toy, eaten from one of their dinner plates or sampled the ubiquitous pick and mix confectionery.

Sadly their long history came to an end when the company entered administration in 2009 and was then formally wound up in 2015, owing £385 million to creditors and leaving 27,000 staff out of work.[1] But what went wrong? Their demise was not a result of a fire or a flood or a general failure of business continuity planning. Instead, their failure was a result of a combination of issues, including fierce competition from supermarkets, an over-reliance on selling physical forms of music at a time when CDs and DVDs were being replaced by online purchases, and a delayed start to meeting the demand for internet-based shopping. These much more strategic issues were what eventually killed Woolworths.[2]

There are actually very few examples of organizations that have catastrophically failed as a result of a poor business continuity response to a business disruption. Instead, the reasons tend to be more poor business planning and flawed strategic decision-making. However, a poor response to a crisis or disruption unrelated to any of these more strategic weaknesses will likely further compound the rot.

The argument here is that while experiencing a crisis or a disruption and handling the response badly might not ordinarily cause a failure, it could be just enough to tip an organization suffering from more systemic weaknesses over the edge of a cliff. The human immune system is analogous to this. While influenza is a nasty virus and kills a great many people each year, many more will make a full recovery. However, if your immune system has already been weakened – perhaps through age or as a result of another infection such as HIV – the chances of survival are much less.[3] A combination of a poorly functioning immune system, in this case systemic organizational weaknesses, and a poor response to a disruption or a crisis, can spell disaster.

The reverse of this also appears to be true. Organizations with a healthier immune system are more likely to ride out the storm of a major disruption or crisis and emerge on the other side. A good business continuity capability will of course help, but often there are stronger forces that influence this success.

HOME DEPOT

The US-based home renovation store Home Depot's experience of a cyber-attack that took place between April and September 2014 can be used to demonstrate this. The attack resulted in costs nearing $200 million,[4] but despite this experience, the company's share price still outperformed its peers in the immediate aftermath of the event. A Marsh and Cranfield University study[5] in 2018, which explored the impact of crises on share performance of 70 companies that had suffered some kind of major and very public crisis event, showed that Home Depot did relatively well out of their experience.

Of course, no board wants to see $200 million leave the business in avoidable costs and fines, but if Home Depot's response is judged on the impact it had on its share performance, they appeared to do well. The analysis from Marsh and Cranfield University showed the company was left with a 7.89 per cent increase in share performance 250 days post-crisis when compared with peers.

On the face of things Home Depot's response appears to have been well orchestrated. They went public relatively quickly (once they knew of the hack) and they published results from an internal investigation, giving confidence to stakeholders that they were in command of the situation. It is also worth considering that the attack occurred at a time when major cyber hacks were still relatively novel, meaning it would have received much wider publicity than a similar attack might do today.

So can their increase in share performance be attributed solely to a good crisis response? Not entirely. According to their 2014 annual report, that year the business recorded an increase in sales of $4.4 billion, or 5.5 per cent[6] – something was going well.

At the time of the hack, Home Depot was benefitting from a rebounding US housing market, which had been in decline since the 2008 financial crisis. Figure 2.1, taken from the US Department of Housing and Urban Development's Office of Policy Development and Research National Housing Market Summary for 2014, shows that the number of homeowners with equity in their homes was steadily growing, and the number that were being lifted out of negative equity was falling.

The confidence this gave to property owners appears to have led to an increase in home improvements, which perhaps had been put off while times were bad. And where did homeowners buy the hardware supplies needed for their do-it-yourself projects? Home Depot.

The effects of a good crisis response on an organization's ability to survive and then go on to thrive post-event cannot be decoupled from other underlying organizational and contextual characteristics that might be driving success. Yes, in the case of Home Depot the organization appeared to deliver an assured response to their hack, but the influence of the economic context the business was operating in at the time of the event cannot be ignored. Perhaps if there is one lesson from the Home Depot experience, it is to ensure that, if a crisis is to occur, make sure it happens when the business is doing well.

FIGURE 2.1   Chart showing US homeowners with equity in their homes vs. those in negative equity (referred to here as being 'underwater')

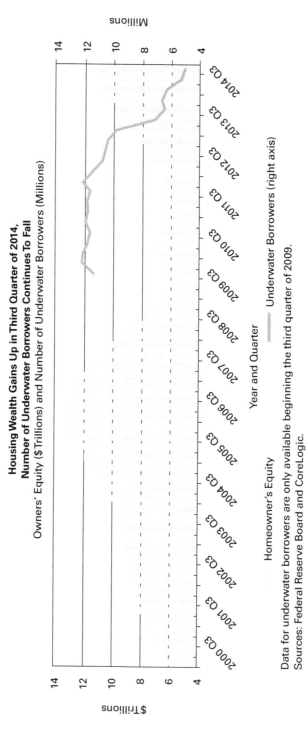

**Housing Wealth Gains Up in Third Quarter of 2014,
Number of Underwater Borrowers Continues To Fall**
Owners' Equity ($Trillions) and Number of Underwater Borrowers (Millions)

Homeowner's Equity ———— Underwater Borrowers (right axis)

Data for underwater borrowers are only available beginning the third quarter of 2009.
Sources: Federal Reserve Board and CoreLogic.

This chart was originally published by the U.S. Department of Housing and Urban Development, Office of Policy Development and Research, and is reproduced here with the Department's permission.[7]

NISSAN 2011

In 2011 Japan was rocked by a magnitude 9 earthquake, causing massive damage; this was followed by a huge tsunami. A combination of the two events killed close to 20,000 people, caused an explosion at the Fukushima nuclear power plant and led to economic costs in the region of $360 billion.

Nissan, like many businesses in Japan, was heavily impacted by the disaster. In addition to physical damage to plant and other assets, the disruption to supply chains and the local workforce, many of whom were facing their own personal crises, resulted in widespread disruption. Nissan's factory in Iwaki was particularly impacted. The plant, which pre-crisis produced 370,000 Infiniti and Nissan engines yearly, was extensively damaged and out of action for several months.[8] Later that year flooding experienced in Bangkok, Thailand – another major global car production hub – caused the industry further disruption at a time when production capacity was still recovering in Japan.

Nissan, Honda and Toyota were all impacted by the 2011 earthquake and Bangkok floods in similar ways. These three Japanese car manufacturers can be used as useful comparisons when exploring how a similar set of impacts can have very different outcomes.

Table 2.1 shows Nissan had fully recovered its lost production by the end of 2011 and was left with the smallest recovery bill out of the three manufacturers and a slightly higher share performance relative to its peers.

So what contributed to Nissan's ability to recover more quickly?

Nissan's own reports suggest that a combination of investments in earthquake protection at key plants helped, along with the speed and concerted way in which their crisis management teams began putting the business back together again. These measures do not happen by accident; they take planning and preparation, suggesting that a good business continuity and crisis management capability will have certainly aided Nissan. However, in many of the public reports exploring how Nissan handled the crisis, one topic is raised time and again: supply chain resilience.[11,12] Nissan, it appears, had a more flexible and agile supply chain, allowing the organization to quickly

TABLE 2.1   Japanese automotive manufacturers' recovery from the 2011 earthquake and tsunami

	Lost output	Net units lost output	Recovery costs*	Share performance (250 days post-earthquake)
Toyota	980,000	370,000	$3.26 billion	+0.8%
Honda	446,000	100,000	$889.3 million	−0.89%
Nissan	At least 55,000**	Recouped	$732.5 million	+3.98%

* Combines charges for fiscal year ended March 2011, and the fiscal year ending March 2012.
** Nissan provided lost production only for 03/2011, no figures for lost output since 04/2011. But full, unrestricted production was restored in September 2011.
SOURCE Adapted from Auto News[9] and Marsh[10]

adapt supply strategies and operations and enabling them to restore production more quickly than many of their competitors.[13]

The Woolworths, Home Depot and Nissan examples all demonstrate that a wide range of capabilities, decisions, behaviours and organizational characteristics come together to influence resilience. Business continuity and crisis management, while an important part of the equation, only provide half the answer.

Instead, resilience is achieved through a complex interplay of highly structured processes (such as business continuity) and less visible organizational characteristics. These have been well summarized in the 2016 International Standard for Organizational Resilience (ISO 22316[14]).

ISO 22316 uses a broad definition to define resilience as the 'ability of an organization to absorb and adapt in a changing environment' and sets out seven of what it calls principles that contribute towards an organization's resilience:

1 Alignment of staff behaviours with a shared vision and the organization's overall purpose, to help drive consistent decisions that contribute to an organization's purpose rather than running counter to it.

2 An accurate and up-to-date understanding of the organization's context, providing the intelligence needed to inform investments in resilience and adaptation requirements.

3 The ability to absorb, adapt and respond to change, as a measure of an organization's capacity to evolve itself to maintain relevance in a changing world.

4 Good governance and management, as a means to ensure effective and disciplined decision-making at all levels of an organization.

5 Diversity in skills, leadership, knowledge and experience, as a way to capture a wide variety of approaches to tackling problems and seeking innovation.

6 Coordination between management disciplines (such as business continuity, security and risk management) with contributions from technical and scientific areas of expertise, to provide a joined-up approach to the management of risk.

7 And all underpinned by the effective management of risk throughout the organization.

The principles are further explored with a set of what the Standard refers to as 'attributes' of an organization that either enhance resilience or erode it. The concept being, though perhaps not perfectly articulated in the document, that if an organization understands the relationships between these attributes and its resilience, it can begin to measure how much of these attributes it has. And once something can be measured, it can then be managed and in this case enhanced.

Many of the attributes mentioned in the Standard have very little to do with business continuity, and some are very difficult to visualize and measure. This makes practical implementation of the Standard a real challenge for practitioners. The resilience benefit of having an empowered and effective leadership or a shared vision and a clarity of purpose for an organization are difficult to argue against at a conceptual level. However, this grand view of resilience touches almost every corner of an organization and crucially would need a skillset and knowledge to implement it that is just not available in most organizations.

The concept of resilience as described in ISO 22316 is all about achieving an adaptive capacity. This definition suggests an organization can only be more or less resilient at any given point in time and against a specific set of defined situations. Organizations therefore can never claim to be completely resilient – there is no end to the journey. This, combined with the difficulties associated with visualizing what a resilience outcome looks and feels like, the limited availability of appropriate skills and knowledge needed to implement it and the pervasive nature of the concept, makes the guidance available in ISO 22316 difficult to implement. While the Standard provides a hugely helpful set of foundations for how to think about resilience, it provides little guidance on how to actually achieve it.

Regulators have recognized the importance of resilience: the experience from the UK banking sector

In 2012 the Royal Bank of Scotland (RBS), a UK-headquartered bank, suffered a major IT disruption resulting in 6.5 million customers experiencing weeks of disruption to their banking services. The failure prevented customers from accessing basic banking services, with many not being able to find out what money they had in their accounts. RBS for a short period of time stopped being a bank. The official regulatory fine was set at £56 million,[15] but of course the final bill to include compensation payments to affected customers and the resulting improvements needed to IT systems ran into the hundreds of millions.

The RBS experience demonstrated how interconnected the banking system had become and how highly dependent the industry was on technology. Many years of acquisitions, consolidations and expansion had created highly complex systems that were poorly integrated and not well understood by management. This RBS incident was the catalyst for what was already a growing area of concern for UK banking regulators.

The regulator's response was what they called a 'Dear Chairman' exercise, or DCE-1 as it became known – essentially a formal letter from the regulators to the chair of each bank asking for assurance on a range of issues arising from the RBS experience. The purpose of the exercise was to understand the extent of any similar risks present in other banks and to establish whether another RBS could be possible. The results of the first exercise found that there were issues for concern:

- insufficient oversight of technology at board level;
- weaknesses in the banks' three lines of defence models and IT risk management arrangements;
- weaknesses in banks' disaster recovery capabilities.[16]

Essentially boards did not hold a sound understanding of technology risk, these risks were poorly controlled, and the banks' ability to recover following a disruption of critical IT was questionable.

In response to the concerns raised by the DCE-1, a second exercise was run (DCE-2) in 2015. While some improvements were noted on the themes arising from the first Dear Chairman letter, six further areas of improvement were identified:

1 **Board accountability for critical infrastructure:** a general lack of board-level ownership for IT risk.

2 **IT expertise on the board:** limited subject-matter expertise at board level. Essentially boards had plenty of bankers, but few technologists.

3 **IT risk appetite:** weaknesses in the way risk appetite was being applied and a lack of comprehensive mapping of resilience requirements needed to support critical customer functions.

4 **Maturity of the three lines of defence** remained relatively weak, with a poor delineation between first-line and second-line activities. Many banks had become highly reliant upon audit and external expertise to perform assurance activities of their technology risk controls.

5 **Resilience scenarios** were not far reaching enough to capture high-impact events, or to reflect concentration risk and dependencies on shared industry infrastructure (such as key payment systems).

6 Contractors: weaknesses in the banks' oversight of third-party IT providers, despite the growing reliance upon external IT vendors to support critical technology services.

The two Dear Chairman exercises demonstrated that technology risk was systemic, poorly controlled and had the potential to cause widespread disruption and harm to consumers and the economy.

The case for a change in the way resilience was being achieved in the UK financial services sector was further strengthened by a string of IT failures, each impacting on customers:

- **2014** – the failure of the Real Time Gross Settlement (RTGS) system at the Bank of England – ordinarily processing over £100 trillion of payments a year and which particularly inconvenienced consumers waiting to transfer funds to buy a new house on the day of the failure. According to an independent review performed by Deloitte, the failure was caused by a combination of poor root-cause analysis, change management, weaknesses in system robustness, governance failings and issues with how the bank responded.[17] Following this failure, a further technical issue was experienced in 2023, leading to more delays to house purchases.

- **2015** – HSBC experiences technical issues preventing 275,000 payments from business clients. While numbers affected were much smaller than other examples here, the incident occurred the day before a holiday weekend, meaning some employees who were expecting a salary payment were left without.

- **2016** – Tesco Bank experiences a cyber-attack exposing sensitive personal information of card holders and resulting in criminals netting £2.4 million, plus an eventual fine from the regulators of £16.4 million.[18]

- **2017** – online banking systems for Nationwide, a UK-based building society, are disrupted for several hours.

- **2018** – approximately 1.8 million customers are locked out of their accounts at TSB bank due to a failed system upgrade.

- **2018** – a hardware failure at a Visa data centre prevents some 'chip and pin' payments across Europe, disrupting 5.2 million card payments.[19]

- **2023** – a processing failure at The Clearing House impacts customers of several of the largest banks in the United States, including JP Morgan Chase & Co, Citigroup Inc., Wells Fargo & Co and Bank of America.

The results from the DCE letters and the string of IT failures experienced in the years after RBS's outage demonstrated that many of the approaches being taken to deliver operational resilience were insufficient at protecting banks and consumers from disruption. Limited end-to-end resilience planning, a poor understanding of technology risks and weak governance controls had left blind spots and capability gaps. This was despite heavy investments in the sector on business continuity planning.

This gave the world the concept of operational resilience, which the Bank of England began to consider as important to the sector as financial stability had become in the world after the 2008 financial crisis. In 2018 the Bank published its discussion paper on operational resilience,[20] positioned as a consultation exercise.

The 2018 discussion paper sought to drive a more strategic view of resilience and drive banks to:

- Build a clear understanding of the organization's important business services (including their supporting systems and processes) that would, if they were to be disrupted, have a significant negative impact on consumers and the market as a whole.

- Define the organization's tolerance for disruption impacts as an expression of the maximum amount of disruption that could be tolerated before consumer and market impacts become intolerable.

- Maintain knowledge of how a failure of an individual activity, process or system could impact the provision of an overall business service providing an end-to-end resilience capability.

- Assume that failure will occur, and actively consider alternatives for key processes and systems should they become disrupted.

- Undertake more comprehensive scenario testing to validate plans using a range of scenarios, including extreme (low-probability, high-impact) events.

For many practitioners the description above reads like business continuity, but delivered well. In fact, most of the capabilities needed to implement the regulator's vision were already in place within many of the organizations that were subject to their focus. However, there were two important differences:

1 **much closer integration** between business continuity and operational risk teams, with risk information being used to inform the definition of the organization's tolerance of disruption impacts and the development of the scenarios needed to validate their resilience capabilities;

2 **elevating the discussion** to the executive and board level to drive greater ownership and oversight for the resilience of important business services and to obtain strategic-level input into which investments should, and should not, be made to control disruption risks to a level acceptable to the business and consumers.

The core components of the operational resilience process being driven in the banking sector were not necessarily new. Many of the concepts and capabilities draw heavily from business continuity. However, the approach being taken was different, requiring more collaboration between teams and with a renewed mandate to get things done.

Much can be learned from the UK's banking experience with resilience for other sectors. The disconnection between customer outcomes from resilience capabilities, a lack of joined-up thinking and an insufficient level of challenge provided by scenario testing are all lessons that apply to any industry.

However, where there is a heavy interest from regulators, resilience practitioners should be mindful of the limitations of their motivations. The mandate of most regulators is to represent the consumer or to maintain the stability and safety of an industry or market. They are not necessarily interested in the commercial health of individual entities (or, using the language of the regulator, market participants). This means that some of the measures suggested in the requirements and guidance provided by regulators only cover a part of what is likely to be needed.

Taking the banking example further, the regulators will be keen to ensure that the definition of impact tolerance puts customers and market stability first. They are less interested in issues that might damage a bank's commercial interests – such as the ability to launch a new mortgage product into the market. For the regulator, so long as there is sufficient capacity in the wider market for new mortgage products, the fact that one firm has been disrupted will likely be of only marginal concern. The moral of the story here is to ensure that scoring and grading mechanisms used to identify and prioritize business services should include commercial impacts as well as those the regulator might be expecting to see.

Global spread of regulation

The concept of resilience is not just a UK phenomenon. Other national regulators including in the US, Europe, Singapore and Hong Kong have been taking a similar path, each following a slightly different approach. However, most are underpinned by a common set of principles focusing on protecting critical business processes, safeguarding sensitive data and maintaining customer service during periods of disruption. These common themes will make it slightly easier for international organizations operating across multiple regulatory regimes to implement a common framework tying them all together.

The journey and challenges to achieving resilience nirvana

This chapter has already explored some of the challenges of implementing organizational resilience (as envisaged by ISO 22316), or the more tangible operational resilience outcomes expected by banking regulators in the UK. But what should most organizations be aiming for, and what are the challenges to reaching this nirvana?

In a perfect world, implementation would begin with a blank sheet of paper. Unfortunately this experience will be unlikely for many practitioners and so the resilience journey will start not at the beginning, as logic would suggest, but somewhere along the way. The exception to this would be implementing resilience in a brand-new organization from the ground up, where there are no existing governance and risk management regimes to work within and where staff are not carrying any 'baggage' or preconceived ideas from previous projects related to resilience. The reality for many, though, will involve building upon existing structures, working to break down barriers that have built up between disciplines and to encourage collaboration, and tackling what are sometimes very strongly held beliefs of what resilience is and how to achieve it.

This reality will force many practitioners to take a slower and more considered approach to building resilience. This slow and steady approach will be essential for three reasons:

1 Staff will need to be encouraged to buy into the resilience way of thinking, to adapt their previously held beliefs and understand that the process does not necessarily pose a threat to their existence, or the normal way of doing things. This will involve a significant amount of socialization of the concept, giving staff the time they need to understand and begin to support it.

2 Basic building blocks will be required to provide the strong foundations needed to implement a more integrated form of resilience. This means mature business continuity arrangements and a risk management process that is embedded within the organization.

3 Time will be needed to establish what resilience means for the organization. This involves understanding how the industry sector and other external influencers will affect the type, focus and amount of resilience that will be needed. Given that resilience requires a substantial amount of very senior management input, getting this step right could be the difference between achieving a sustainable capability and falling at the first hurdle.

The final point above is worth pausing on for a moment. An organization's resilience outcome will be specific to them and relative to the overall purpose that the organization fulfils, the industrial sector they operate in, their internal culture and any previous disruption and crisis experiences they may have had. Understanding how these factors will influence the focus and eventual outcome of a resilience programme will be very important.

This can be further explored by making some basic comparisons between different organizational characteristics and their potential influence on resilience (Table 2.2).

TABLE 2.2   The relationship between organizational characteristic and resilience

Characteristic A	Influence on resilience		Characteristic B
Highly innovative organization, regularly exploring new ways of doing things	Failure may be expected, even encouraged in order to innovate	Failure may be less tolerated, control is key	Traditional delivery approach, limited organizational change
Significant regulatory scrutiny	Compliance focus with limited deviation from what the regulator expects to see	Increased freedom to adapt resilience arrangements	Low levels of external scrutiny
Operating in high-risk environments	Low-risk appetite, high degree of focus on prevention	Greater focus on 'what-if' recovery planning	Generally low-level risk activities
Highly collaborative internal culture	Easier to implement an enterprise-wide approach to resilience involving input from multiple disciplines	More time needed to build the internal consensus needed to affect change; implementation may be a significant challenge	Closed culture, limited interaction

TABLE 2.2   *continued*

Characteristic A	Influence on resilience		Characteristic B
Public-facing services where a disruption would have immediate impacts	Reputation will be key and a sure-footed, speedy response to a disruption will be important	Revenue drivers may be stronger than reputation concerns with end consumers	**Several steps away from end consumers, time available to respond**
Products and services are purchased for their reliability and safety	Quality management, prevention and disciplined innovation will be a focus, low tolerance to disruption	Higher tolerance to disruption, increased willingness to try new things	**Low levels of reliability expected/focus on consumables**

Below are a few different organizational types as examples to explore how different characteristics influence the approach taken to deliver resilience:

- **Pharmaceutical company:** highly regulated with innovation delivered in a highly controlled and rigorous way. The focus of resilience may be skewed towards maintaining safety and quality and preventing crises from occurring. The focus of resilience will extend throughout the organization's supply chain to ensure the raw materials needed for drug manufacturing are always available and supplied to the right standards.

- **Manufacturing:** a focus on safety, quality and efficiency will often be key here. The need for efficiency and margin pressures will cast a significant influence on the amount of resilience the organization is willing to maintain on its balance sheet. Supply chain resilience is also important here, along with a focus on the locations and assets used for production.

- **Fast-moving consumer goods:** efficiency and margin pressures are probably most acute in this sector owing to fierce competition.

- **Financial services:** highly regulated with a strong focus on preventing individual firms from harming consumers or undermining the stability of the wider market. These organizations also typically have a high degree of dependence upon technology, meaning resilience activities can be skewed towards IT resilience considerations and take a compliance-based approach to delivery as a reflection of the significant interest from regulators.

- **Professional services firms:** reputation matters to these organizations – without it the business will be unlikely to survive. Second to reputation are the people whose knowledge the organization is selling to its clients. In these organizations the resilience of physical assets and buildings is less of a focus. Instead, technology resilience to allow mobile working, looking after sensitive data and its people will be the main considerations.

- **Technology start-ups:** innovation is king here; without it these organizations will not succeed. With innovation comes the risk of failure and disruption and for some start-ups this will be expected, even encouraged in order to push the boundaries of what it means to innovate. In these organizations ideas matter, so people and the knowledge they hold will be the focus. Given the expectation that failure will happen at some point along the journey, these organizations can be some of the hardest to persuade to implement a structured resilience regime. As these organizations grow, the challenge will be switching from a start-up mentality to a culture where reliability is more important to the customers they serve.

Knowing what is driving an organization's particular focus and interest in resilience matters. This allows a practitioner to follow a path of least resistance by implementing a programme that is the best fit for the organization's culture and context. Other approaches are of course possible, but they will likely come with more pain and effort. It is a bit like stroking a cat from its tail to head – it might sit there happily the first time it is done, but eventually it is going to stick its claws in and draw blood.

Knowing how much resilience is enough for the organization and then measuring whether that outcome has been achieved presents further challenges. For traditional forms of business continuity and even operational resilience discussed above, the process is relatively straightforward. In these areas there are processes that can be checked, standards and guidelines that can be referred to and tangible outcomes that can be tested. For the more esoteric elements of resilience, including some of the principles and attributes described in ISO 22316, measurement is much more of a challenge.

These issues are explored in more detail in Chapter 14. However, it is worth reflecting here on the nuances of a broader approach to resilience and how they influence the measurement of performance.

Defining how much resilience is enough relies upon a solid understanding of what resilience means for the organization, as set out above. This provides the means needed to identify what resilience outcomes are required by the organization. Recovery planning for an important fixed asset critical for a production process will look quite different from increased inventory held at a distribution centre or deeper capital reserves and insurance coverage needed to pay for a resilience risk that materializes. The trick here is to define a resilience requirement that is realistic, achievable and easily understood by decision-makers and then to use existing performance measures where these are available.

This approach can be strengthened at a later date when further buy-in and support has been achieved for the programme, and as more decision-makers understand what resilience is and what the target outcomes are. It is at this point that practitioners will be given greater freedom to operate and the organization will be ready to receive a more complex vision for resilience.

TABLE 2.3   Chapter checklist

☐	Identify what resilience means for your organization.
☐	Identify the key internal stakeholders that would be needed to implement a broader approach to resilience.
☐	Establish whether the building blocks are already in place upon which resilience can be developed.

☐	Expect some level of challenge from colleagues, but listen to their ideas and concerns; they may have different (maybe even better) ways of solving the problem.
☐	Build a realistic, achievable and easily understood vision and delivery plan for resilience.
☐	Take a gradual approach, building maturity slowly so that colleagues come along on the journey.
☐	Ensure the performance management regime reflects the overall maturity of the organization's approach to resilience; use existing metrics and performance measures where these are available.

Notes

1 BBC (2018) What has happened to Woolworths' stores 10 years after closure, 19 November www.bbc.co.uk/news/business-46259048 (archived at https://perma.cc/XF69-KE9N)

2 The Woolworths Museum (2017) A potted history of Woolworths stores www.woolworthsmuseum.co.uk/aboutwoolies.html (archived at https://perma.cc/8RTA-S6WY)

3 Cromer, D, Jan van Hoek, A, Jit, M, Edmunds, J, Fleming, D and Miller, E (2013) *The Burden of Influenza in England by Age and Clinical Risk Group: A statistical analysis to inform vaccine policy*, Elsevier, Amsterdam

4 Seals, T (2017) Home Depot to pay $27.25m in latest data breach settlement, *Info Security*, 13 March www.infosecurity-magazine.com/news/home-depot-to-pay-2725m/ (archived at https://perma.cc/2EPR-UFNH)

5 Crask, J and Stark, D (2019) To Survive or Thrive: How crises impact company value, Marsh, November https://www.marsh.com/content/dam/marsh/Documents/PDF/UK-en/Exploring%20the%20Effects%20of%20Organisational%20Crises.pdf (archived at https://perma.cc/N725-HD6D)

6 Home Depot (2015) 2014 annual report, 26 March https://ir.homedepot.com/~/media/Files/H/HomeDepot-IR/reports-and-presentations/annual-reports/annual-report-2014.pdf (archived at https://perma.cc/J8KF-HNAU)

7 US Department of Housing and Urban Development (2015) National housing market summary, March www.huduser.gov/portal/periodicals/ushmc/pdf/NationalSummary_4q14.pdf (archived at https://perma.cc/4LLB-YMY5)

8 Nissan (2011) Nissan recovery stories, 29 June, https://www.nissan-global.com/EN/REPORTS/2011/06/110629.html (archived at https://perma.cc/5GGX-PLTT)

9 Greimel, H (2012) Auto News – Tsunami: The aftermath, 12 March, https://www.autonews.com/article/20120312/OEM01/303129960/tsunami-the-aftermath (archived at https://perma.cc/CY3C-AXMS)

10 Crask, J and Stark, D (2019) To Survive or Thrive: How crises impact company value, Marsh, November https://www.marsh.com/content/dam/marsh/Documents/PDF/UK-en/Exploring%20the%20Effects%20of%20Organisational%20Crises.pdf (archived at https://perma.cc/N725-HD6D)

11 Pierce, F (2020) Nissan stays ahead of the supply chain curve, Supply Chain, July www.supplychaindigital.com/logistics/nissan-stays-ahead-supply-chain-curve (archived at https://perma.cc/V8ZC-3MQB)

12 Nissan (2011) Nissan recovery stories, 29 June, https://www.nissan-global.com/EN/SUSTAINABILITY/LIBRARY/SR/2012/ASSETS/PDF/SR12_E_P008.pdf (archived at https://perma.cc/5GGX-PLTT)

13 Construction News (2011) Japan quake: Nissan leads Japanese plant recovery, Construction Week, 21 March www.constructionweekonline.com/article-11499-japan-quake-nissan-leads-japanese-plant-recovery (archived at https://perma.cc/Q54T-VA62)

14 ISO (2016) ISO 22316 – Organizational Resilience Principles and Attributes, Geneva

15 BBC (2014) RBS fined £56m over 'unacceptable' computer failure, 20 November www.bbc.co.uk/news/business-30125728 (archived at https://perma.cc/6H62-F6RR)

16 FCA (2015) Letter from the acting CEO of the FCA to the chair of the UK Parliament Treasury Committee, 19 October, www.parliament.uk/globalassets/documents/commons-committees/treasury/Correspondence/Letter-from-Tracey-McDermott-FCA-to-Treasury-Chair-19-10-15.pdf (archived at https://perma.cc/4RCB-DMWV)

17 Deloitte (2015) Independent review of RTGS outage, 23 March, www.bankofengland.co.uk/-/media/boe/files/report/2015/independent-review-of-rtgs-outage-on-20-october-2014.pdf (archived at https://perma.cc/4NRD-7D4U)

18 FCA (2018) Press release – FCA fines Tesco Bank £16.4m for failures in 2016 cyber-attack, 1 October www.fca.org.uk/news/press-releases/fca-fines-tesco-bank-failures-2016-cyber-attack (archived at https://perma.cc/Y42Q-2WX8)

19 Visa (2018) Letter from the VISA CEO to the chair of the UK Parliament's Treasury Committee, 15 June www.parliament.uk/globalassets/documents/commons-committees/treasury/Correspondence/2017-19/visa-response-150618.pdf (archived at https://perma.cc/XZW6-EHSJ)

20 Bank of England (2018) Discussion Paper – Building the UK financial sector's operational resilience, July www.bankofengland.co.uk/-/media/boe/files/prudential-regulation/discussion-paper/2018/dp118.pdf?la=en&hash=4238F3B14D839EBE6BEFBD6B5E5634FB95197D8A (archived at https://perma.cc/6TGH-RAV3)

03

What can we learn from international standards?

The first formal standard created by the world's first national standards body was published by the British Standards Institution at the turn of the 20th century and focused on steel sections for tramways.[1] Since then many thousands of national, and later international standards have been published on a wide range of issues including food safety, quality management, consumer products, sustainability and of course business continuity and organizational resilience. Standards have an important role to play in making consumer products safe for us all to use, promote best practice in thinking, and drive consistency in the way certain products are made and processes delivered. The products we all touch every day – whether a tin of baked beans, the computer we work from or the brakes on our cars – are all subject to standardization in some form.

Some of their titles and the numbering systems they use can make it hard for the novice to understand. And the topics covered range from the dull to the outright bizarre: for example ISO/TS 20224-7 discusses methods of detecting animal-derived materials in foodstuffs. Or, as the title summarizes it, the 'Donkey DNA detection method'. Given the UK's 2013 experience of finding horsemeat in ready meals available in British supermarkets, such a standard would appear to be a particularly important one, despite its amusing title.

Standards can be categorized by the topics they cover and their intended purpose and focus.

Purpose:

- **Guidelines:** These standards are designed to provide advice and guidance on a topic based upon internationally recognized best practice. They can generally be spotted by the number of 'should' statements contained within them. The term 'should' in standards parlance is intended as a suggestion and not a firm instruction, and so there is more room for interpretation in how these standards are applied by the reader.

- **Requirements:** These standards provide an auditable framework that organizations can obtain independent certification against. They are categorized by the use of 'shall' statements, which are intended as an instruction to the reader. The shall statement, for example, could be used to specify the exact thickness of a drain cover to be used on the highway, or a particular step in a process that must be followed for an intended outcome to be realized.

Focus:

- **Process and concepts:** These standards set out a predetermined and repeatable way of delivering some kind of outcome. Many of the management system standards fall into this group, including ISO 22301 for Business Continuity.

- **Products:** These are less relevant for this book. Generally speaking they are very specific to a particular 'thing' – for example, the drain cover discussed above, an important medical device such as a pacemaker, or a doctor's gown.

Short history of resilience standards

Standards on business continuity have a more recent history

The most influential country-level standards that pre-date ISO 22301 and ISO 22313 have been those published in the United States (NFPA 1600, first published in 1995), the UK (with PAS 56 in 2003, followed by BS 25999 in 2007) and in Singapore (SS540, published in 2008). There have been many more originating from the national standards bodies of other countries; however, these three appear to have had the most significant impact on global thinking. While many source materials were used in the drafting of ISO 22301, it was BS 25999 from the UK that had the most influence on the world's first international standard on the subject. Since their original publication in 2012, both ISO 22301 and ISO 22313 were reviewed and republished in 2019 and 2020 respectively.

Organizational resilience standards followed later and have so far had a much smaller impact on international discourse. The UK published BS 65000 on Organizational Resilience in 2014 (and again in 2022), providing a mixture of operational and strategic considerations relating to resilience. The International Standard ISO 22316 followed in 2017 after a long drafting process.

The amount of time taken to publish ISO 22316 was due in part to the nature of the international standards development process. The drafting process requires a high degree of consensus before publication can be achieved. Documents published by national standards bodies apply the same consensus-driven approach to development, where a document cannot be published until there is strong consensus for its contents. However, the job of reaching consensus is a little easier at a national level on the basis that international standards have to apply to a much broader range of cultures and languages.

The delays can also be attributed to ISO 22316 being ahead of its time

When the project began, there was limited international consensus on what resilience was, or how to achieve it; it took several years for the international community of resilience professionals to agree. The resulting standard provided a landscape document setting out the core principles underpinning resilience and what the main attributes or characteristics of a more resilient organization were. In reaching consensus, however, some of the more innovative ideas were lost on the cutting room floor. The resulting document struggled to satisfy practitioners who were at the vanguard of resilience thinking and knew more could have been achieved, or the traditionalists who felt resilience was just another business buzzword that would soon be forgotten. As a result, when it was first published, the document made minimal impact. However, it was the catalyst that started a much wider discourse.

The concept of organizational resilience is now much more widely debated and has become the subject of regulatory guidelines (such as the operational resilience focus of the Bank of England for the financial services industry in the UK), academic research, and initiatives such as the Resilience Alliance, which brings together four highly respected global professional services organizations: Airmic (risk management and insurance), ASIS (security), the BCI (business continuity) and IWFM (facilities management).[2] Several years ago, the suggestion that four different professional disciplines would all be aligned on the importance of resilience and what it meant for organizations would have been unheard of.

Management system standards

Ever wondered why ISO 22301 and ISO 22313 both cover business continuity?

The answer is that the ISO 22301 is a management systems standard providing a specification that can be used to inform an accredited certification process and a supporting guidance document (ISO 22313). ISO 22313 contains the guidelines that cannot be included in the requirements document, which itself is primarily intended to inform an auditing process. ISO 22313 provides the 'how' and ISO 22301 sets out the 'what'.

Management systems are an important group of standards for the resilience practitioner to understand. ISO defines a management system as '…the way in which an organization manages the interrelated parts of its business in order to achieve its objectives'.[3] They set out a repeatable process that can be applied by any organization and, if followed correctly, will deliver a consistent outcome each time. One way of understanding how management systems are differentiated from guidelines or guidance-based documentation is that they concentrate on the enablers to success. They look for evidence of leadership commitment: are policies and governance structures in place and has a process been clearly defined and documented to drive the delivery of the intended outcome?

Business continuity management is not the only area covered by a management system standard. Quality Management (ISO 9001) and Environmental Management (ISO 14001) are two of the most well-known and successful management system standards currently in circulation. In organizations that already have a well-established management system covering any of the 95 ISO management system standards currently in circulation,[4] the process of implementing another one can be a much smaller step relative to the first. This is because some of the core principles that underpin all management system standards deliver structures and processes that can be applied to a variety of topics.

The cycle of 'plan, do, check and act' (PDCA) provides a common structure for many management systems. The process, also referred to as the Deming Cycle (named after its originator, US engineer and management consultant William Edwards Deming), provides a structured way of implementing and continuously improving a process.

The PDCA cycle provides a philosophy that is central to implementing business continuity. At its heart is the concept of continuous improvement, an essential component of an effective resilience capability where constant adaptation is needed in response to changes in an organization's context and lessons learned from live incidents and crises.

The PDCA cycle for business continuity can be described as follows:

Plan: Establishing the business continuity policy, objectives, controls and processes needed to improve the organization's business continuity arrangements. This first step focuses on setting the governance structures and processes needed to implement and improve an organization's business continuity arrangements.

Do: Implementing and then operating the business continuity policy, controls and processes. The second step is where the bulk of the planning and implementation activities take place.

Check: Monitor and review performance against the policy and objectives and identify areas that need further improvement. The check stage is a vital component of the process, providing the structures needed to monitor performance and spot possible issues that need to be addressed.

Act: Maintain and improve the business continuity management system, taking corrective action where results of reviews and other sources of data suggest that improvements are needed. The final step takes the outputs from the check stage to implement actions that deliver a sustainable improvement to an organization's business continuity arrangements.

Management system standards also include a standard set of components:

- a **policy** that sets out the organization's intent and commits the organization to delivery;
- **people with defined responsibilities** covering implementation and management of the management system;
- **management processes** relating to the development, maintenance and continual improvement of:
  - policy
  - planning
  - implementation and operation
  - performance assessment
  - management review
  - improvement
- a set of **documents** and records that provide evidence of the organization's management system, including its approach to continuous improvement;

- any **specific** management system processes relevant to the organization.

It is a combination of the PDCA cycle and the common management system components set out above that makes implementation of additional management systems easier to achieve once an initial system has been created. While having a formal management system is not essential to the delivery of an effective business continuity plan, it will help strengthen it by providing strong governance and the process foundations needed to implement and continuously improve.

Many organizations successfully implement highly effective business continuity management capabilities without a formal management system. However, most will have inadvertently implemented core components of the management system without realizing. This is because implementing a sustainable process requires:

- senior management commitment;
- policy direction to the business;
- a set of common processes to drive consistency;
- information to identify areas for continual improvement.

All of these items are requirements of a management system, and those organizations that skip these steps will be unlikely to have a capability that is either effective or self-sustaining.

Seeking accredited certification

Accredited certification is only available for standards that are written as requirements documents, such as ISO 22301.

Accredited certification is subtly different from other certification processes. Technically speaking, any individual or organization can design their own 'certification' process involving some form of review and the issue of a certificate at the end of the process to show conformity against a particular way of doing things.

ISO DEFINITION OF CERTIFICATION AND ACCREDITATION[5]

Certification – the provision by an independent body of written assurance (a certificate) that the product, service or system in question meets specific requirements.

Accreditation – the formal recognition by an independent body, generally known as an accreditation body, that a certification body operates according to international standards.

To be an accredited certification body the bar is set much higher. The process can only be delivered by an organization that holds the authority to issue a certificate – usually referred to as an accredited certification body. These organizations must comply with strict rules designed to ensure the certification process they oversee is delivered to a high set of exacting standards. Its purpose is to ensure that interested parties can place reliance on the certificate in providing a trustworthy assessment of the organization's approach.

The availability of accredited certification is critically important where a high degree of reliance is placed upon the quality of a process or product. For example:

- to provide confidence over the quality of medical devices used in surgery – knowing that the instruments being used by the surgeon meet strict requirements set by an international standard will help to reduce the risk of poor-quality materials being used in medical settings;

- demonstrating that safety-critical parts being used in a car have been designed and tested to exacting standards.

For organizations involved in delivering these kinds of products and services, accredited certification has become a significant part of the organization's business model. Many would not be able to trade without it. For business continuity the drivers for accredited certification are less compelling for many organizations. The cost of obtaining a certificate, and then maintaining it with regular audits, can tip the cost-benefit analysis towards seeking other forms of assurance.

However, in the right setting there are good reasons why organizations choose to go through an accredited certification process. These include:

- Where an organization wants to demonstrate to a customer that the processes it has in place are robust – being certified against ISO 22301 can in some circumstances act as a competitive advantage when bidding for new work, particularly where reliability is of critical importance to the organization buying the services.

- Where an organization is looking to reduce the burden of requests for assurance from third parties – organizations that form part of the supply chain of many different organizations can often be subject to numerous requests for information about their business continuity arrangements. These due diligence exercises often come in the form of questionnaires, each asking similar questions and each taking management time to respond to. Showing customers a certificate against ISO 22301 could help to reduce the number of questions that will need to be answered.

- Where an organization wants to lead by example – perhaps they are an industry leader, deliver a critical part of national infrastructure or are a public sector organization that is keen to promote improved resilience of businesses in the wider economy. In this situation, being certified helps to show strong leadership and is an opportunity to practise what they preach.

Before embarking upon a process of accredited certification, a strong business case will need to be made to management for the investment needed to work through the process, and then maintain the certificate. This business case will need to include:

- **benefits:** a clear description of measurable benefits of going through the process;
- **costs:** what the cost of first achieving the certificate and then maintaining it will be to the organization;
- **resources:** what resources are needed to achieve certification and then to maintain it, including the time needed by departments to

support the collation of documentation needed for future audit processes;

- **scope:** the area or areas of the organization that will be covered by the certification process (more on this below);
- **roadmap:** a well-structured, fully resourced plan to achieve certification and the benefits set out above.

The cost and effort involved in achieving accredited certification can be controlled by carefully defining the scope of which areas of the organization will be covered by the process. For example, it is possible to define a scope covering the most critical or customer-facing areas of the organization and excluding less critical functions.

How the scope is defined will determine the ultimate cost of the process to achieve the certificate and then to maintain it. The scope will be clearly referenced on the certificate at the end of the process, so getting it right is crucial.

Most organizations will want to concentrate the scope in areas that are of greatest significance to the business and will be most likely to help achieve the benefits of certification as set out in the business case. However, the scope will need to be carefully challenged to ensure that it will lead to an accurate assessment of the organization's business continuity arrangements and deliver the planned benefits. Excluding highly critical parts of an organization, including functions and processes that other areas are highly dependent upon, will not be appropriate.

The scope may include:

- **high-revenue-generating areas** of the business, a disruption to which would have a material impact on the organization's profitability;
- **departments, assets or individual processes critical to supporting customers,** for example a call centre or online e-commerce and banking platforms – disruptions to these functions will likely be noticed by customers, quickly resulting in brand damage;

- **high-profile departments,** as distinct from customer-facing areas of a business – for example, the security function of a global credit card payments business may seek certification as a means to demonstrate to the industry and wider consumers that security and resilience are taken seriously.

The scope can sometimes exclude:

- **back-office functions not directly critical to customer-facing activities** – however, if critical areas of the business are highly dependent upon the processes delivered by these back-office functions, it is likely they will need to be included in the scope of the certification process.

The certification bodies will scrutinize the proposed scope very carefully before starting the auditing process, so big mistakes at this stage are unlikely. However, testing the proposed scope against the anticipated benefits will help (see Table 3.1).

TABLE 3.1   Certification benefits and their implications for scope

Targeted benefits of certification	Implications for the scope
Provide customers with confidence over service quality and reliability.	- customer-facing functions and processes - delivery functions responsible for producing/delivering the products and/or services to customers
Demonstrate to supply chain clients that the services provided to them are reliable.	- production/service delivery functions specific to client needs - purchasing, supply chain and logistics processes
Give a regulator confidence over the quality of resilience arrangements.	- regulated areas of the organization
Show industry leadership.	- areas of the organization that define the business for what it is - customer-facing processes and activities

The accredited certification process

There are a wide variety of accreditation bodies available to choose from. Not all are able to offer business continuity accreditation, so it is worth checking, and not all have a global footprint, which may make running an auditing process across multiple geographies for larger organizations a challenge.

They all tend to follow a three-step process:

1 **Pre-assessment:** involves meetings to discuss the certification process and to agree the scope of the audit. This initial step also allows the accreditation body to give an opinion on the organization's readiness for undertaking the certification process. If at this stage major gaps in the organization's business continuity approach are found, it is likely the certification body will suggest these are remedied before starting the full assessment.

2 **The assessment:** usually conducted as a series of visits to review documentation and interview staff. This is a detailed audit, with the length of time needed determined by the overall scope of the process agreed earlier and the size of the organization.

3 **Post-assessment:** an initial assessment is usually provided setting out any major gaps that need to be addressed before a certificate can be issued. Upon receipt of the evidence, the certification bodies will need to satisfy themselves that an improvement action has been closed. The certificate can then be issued.

The effort and cost involved in preparing for this process makes a pre-certification gap analysis a useful additional step. This could be conducted by the organization's own staff, a peer organization, or with the involvement of a third party. While this process will not result in an accredited certificate, it will help to identify any major flaws that need to be addressed before the auditors come in. This step is particularly useful when the scope of a certificate is broad, meaning the scale and cost of the audit and the potential for issues to be found will be greater.

The common pitfalls of standards

For all their benefits, there are also some flaws with standards. These do not make the documents any less useful, but they should be understood by practitioners seeking to implement them.

The first is in the way they are written. Standards bodies develop documents by building a consensus. This means that members of a standards committee will need to agree before a document can be finalized for publication. The benefits of this are that the standards it delivers represent national or international consensus on what best practice looks like at that point in time. This has significant benefits in building uniformity in the way certain processes are applied. However, it can also present challenges.

A consensus-driven approach to developing a document sometimes means that more radical, and at times more advanced, thinking is filtered out of the debate. Newer ideas that ISO committee members have very limited experience or knowledge of will need to be more carefully explained and defended during the drafting process. The standards development process does allow for this in the way that comments on approved drafts are addressed. However, at times, because of the need for progress in drafting, an issue that becomes lost in translation or is poorly argued can often find itself being left out of the draft. That means that some standards, particularly international ones that require an even higher level of consensus to be reached, may not at times reflect the best international thinking on a topic.

It is therefore perfectly OK, even sensible, to consider standards as a source document to build from rather than the only way of doing things. Standards are not always superlative.

The actual approach employed to achieve a business continuity capability may deviate slightly from the guidance contained in the standard. This is entirely sensible as it allows adjustments to be made to fit the organization or allow more innovative approaches to be employed which may not have made it into the standard. This statement applies mostly to a guidelines standard, which contains guidance on a certain way of doing things. Guidelines are always open to interpretation and will need to be tailored to fit the particular needs of individual organizations.

Specification standards, however, are different. As set out above, these standards provide a common set of requirements that must be followed to demonstrate conformity. The 'shall' statements in these standards leave little room for interpretation. However, as has already been covered above, the way in which these documents are structured, including ISO 22301, provides some flexibility as the requirements are separate from the guidance covering 'how' to achieve them.

The second common pitfall of standards is linked to the issues set out above but centres around how practitioners choose to apply them and communicate their approach to decision-makers.

Dealing with communication first, the majority of executive- and board-level directors have very little, if no, interest in what an ISO standard says. Instead, they tend to be more concerned about managing risk to the achievement of their objectives. The fact that a management system has been implemented and plans have been written to align with ISO 22301 will do little to interest this group of stakeholders. They will want to know if the plans will work and if the capability delivers a meaningful reduction to disruption risks relative to the cost involved in implementing them. Yet typically many senior management briefings fall into the trap of putting a standard centre stage of the discussion. Before the debate can really start, the argument has already been lost. Business continuity and resilience is not about a standard; they may be very important tools to guide an organization through the implementation process, but they are poor vehicles for seeking engagement from decision-makers.

The way practitioners speak about standards can further compound this issue. It would be completely understandable for a business continuity manager new to the profession to assume the ISO is the *only* way of doing things. After all, a standard sounds official and gives business continuity credibility. However, it would be a mistake to become too dogmatic in the way the standard is applied and how it is reflected in discussions with senior decision-makers. Instead the two most important skills of a resilience professional are listening and problem-solving:

- **Good listening skills** are needed to understand the nuances of the organization's requirements for resilience, the way its culture, structure and appetite for risk all interplay to influence the focus of planning activities.

- **Problem-solving** is needed to adapt best-practice approaches to fit common methodologies to the very particular requirements of the organization.

A failure to listen leads to a failure to understand, and this in turn makes it impossible to see a different, and sometimes better, way of doing things. Taking a particular approach just because it is the way the standard says it should be done can disengage colleagues and unknowingly contribute to a compliance culture where a process is blindly followed because the policy says it should be. In organizations that suffer from these issues, resilience capabilities can often be poorly embedded in the business, staff have very little buy-in to the process, and plans are ultimately unlikely to be useful when they are needed most.

How should standards be used?

This chapter has argued for the important role standards play but also identified some pitfalls for practitioners to be aware of. These pitfalls can be avoided by applying five principles:

1 Standards should be considered as an authoritative voice providing a best-practice approach to building resilience, but should not become the only source of guidance used by the organization in directing business continuity and resilience.

2 Organizations should not become too dogmatic in their implementation of the guidance provided by standards. There is always a need for tailoring – a point made several times in ISO 22313.

3   Standards should be seen as a tool to help along a journey, not to become the journey itself. Most decision-makers will not be motivated by the idea of tracking progress against a standard. The exception of course will be those organizations that have chosen to obtain accredited certification.

4   When seeking buy-in from colleagues, including senior decision-makers, the standard should not be presented as the focus of, or the end of, the process.

5   Practitioners should welcome challenge and new ways of doing things, even in situations where the individual might have decades of experience of one particular way of implementing business continuity.

TABLE 3.2   Chapter checklist

☐	Read ISO 22301, ISO 22313, BS 65000 and ISO 22316 to gain a rounded understanding of business continuity and resilience standardization.
☐	Establish whether any existing management systems are already in place and could be leveraged.
☐	Decide whether accredited certification is really needed, and if the answer is 'yes', prepare a strong business case to get the buy-in needed.
☐	Take an objective view of standards. Take the best bits from each but tailor the approach to the unique circumstances facing the organization.

Notes

1   BSI (2020) Our history, www.bsigroup.com/en-GB/about-bsi/our-history/ (archived at https://perma.cc/BE54-WPNL)

2   Airmic (2020) Press release: Resilience Alliance launched to enhance industry collaboration, 9 October, www.airmic.com/news/guest-stories/resilience-alliance-launched-enhance-industry-collaboration (archived at https://perma.cc/8U5R-RMK2)

3   ISO (2020) What is a management system? www.iso.org/management-system-standards.html (archived at https://perma.cc/GQ69-BJ5P)

4 ISO (2020) Management System Standards list, https://www.iso.org/
management-system-standards-list.html (archived at https://perma.cc/GS9X-
4HU3)

5 ISO (2020) Certification, www.iso.org/certification.html (archived at
https://perma.cc/7HJB-GD68)

04

How business continuity and resilience differs between industries

The core concepts and processes underpinning business continuity and resilience are common between industries. However, that is not to say the approach is the same everywhere – in fact each industry and organization will have its own characteristics driven by the context it is operating in. These characteristics can subtly influence and alter the focus of business continuity, the drivers and motivations for building resilience and the focus of where investment in resilience will be made.

On first look these differences can be hard to spot to the untrained eye. Understanding how organizational characteristics can influence the approach to delivering business continuity will make the implementation of plans and other resilience capabilities much more efficient, and a less painful experience for the practitioner.

Of course, for every generalization there is always an exception, or an outlier that challenges the norm. This chapter does not argue that all banks are the same, for example, or that all manufacturing organizations take the same approach to delivering business continuity. Instead it is intended as a guide to the main differences between how organizations approach resilience. It provides guidance on how to spot the organizational characteristics that drive different 'flavours' of business continuity and includes some practical advice on how to use these to achieve improved resilience outcomes.

Organizational characteristics

This chapter explores seven different types of organizational characteristics, each with their own influence on the approaches taken to deliver business continuity:

1 **Technology or data-driven business:** where technology is a core enabler or a significant differentiator for the business, or where the creation and commercialization of large volumes of data are central to the business model. Examples would include banking organizations and software companies.

2 **Office-based:** where the majority of the organization's activity is delivered primarily from an office environment. Examples could include most professional City-based firms including large parts of the public sector, auditors, legal advisers and most headquarters-based roles in any organization.

3 **Regulatory scrutiny:** where an organization is heavily regulated, including enhanced scrutiny of safety, security and resilience activities. Examples include infrastructure providers, banking organizations and elements of public sector activities.

4 **High-hazard environments:** where the organization's business model includes processes that are high risk or expose employees and the business to increased levels of safety risk. Examples include agriculture, chemical mining, and oil and gas businesses.

5 **Production environments:** where the organization is focused on the design, manufacture and/or maintenance of consumer products for sale. Examples include car manufacturers, food producers and hi-tech manufacturing.

6 **Service delivery organizations:** where the business delivers services to other businesses, often on an outsourced basis. Examples include security and facilities providers and IT service companies.

7 **Public sector or charity:** where the organization's focus is non-commercial, funded by state support or through donations. These organizations can also exhibit many of the other characteristics above but are worthy of a special focus here.

These seven characteristics are not mutually exclusive. Organizations can exhibit several of these at once, each with their own influence on business continuity. This of course presents an additional challenge to designing the most appropriate approach to delivering business continuity, as awareness of how each of these characteristics influences the approach will be needed.

So, what influence do these characteristics have?

Technology- or data-driven

All organizations are dependent upon technology in some form – no modern business can operate without IT. However, for some organizations their entire business model is built around data and technology – either because they sell these as services to customers, or because they are heavily dependent on technology and data themselves.

Examples would include a software company or a bank. While the link to technology and data is an obvious one in the case of a software company, the latter example is less clear without further explanation. Modern banking operations are impossible to deliver without highly complex and interconnected technology to process the huge amounts of data they manage. In these environments a disruption to technology services critical to a bank's operations can be catastrophic, both to the bank's own commercials and to consumers and markets. It is as a result of these market-wide impacts arising from banking disruptions, and recent experiences of system failures that prevent consumers from accessing basic banking services, that regulators have become interested in resilience.

We can use RBS, the UK-headquartered bank, as an example here. In 2012, the bank experienced a major IT outage disrupting 6.5 million consumers, amounting to 10 per cent of the UK population.[1] The outage, caused by a failed software upgrade, led to retail and commercial banking customers being unable to access banking systems, preventing payments and cash withdrawals from being made. This example provides a demonstration of how important technology has become to global banks. Their business models have become entirely dependent upon the availability of IT systems and the data they process, with limited manual workarounds available should a disruption occur.

To provide further context of the scale of the challenge, in 2022 the US Federal Reserve processed over 18 trillion transactions.[2] That equates to approximately 2,300 transactions for every human living on earth. With such massive volumes, there are no human manual workarounds that could replace the power of the computer.

In technology-rich environments a resilience professional must have a strong grasp on technology risk issues and be capable of translating what are often highly technical issues into a language that decision-makers will understand.

The traditional sequence of planning involves the setting of technology and data recovery requirements through the business impact analysis (BIA). This ensures IT continuity arrangements are aligned with the recovery requirements defined by the business. However, in technology- and data-rich environments, where technology systems are fundamental to the success of an organization's business model, the process can sometimes work in reverse. The size, complexity and ultimate cost of implementing resilience for these meta-systems can drive a separation in business continuity roles. It is common for technology teams to maintain the responsibility for defining the requirements, and implementing resilience arrangements, for critical systems in these environments. This can leave the business continuity team as an internal 'customer' of technology colleagues with little influence over the definition of technology and data recovery requirements.

Collaborative working is essential. Business continuity and IT continuity teams must work together to ensure the processes used to analyse the impacts of business disruptions are consistent across the organization. Discrepancies between the recovery requirements set by the business and the actual IT continuity capability implemented by technology teams need to be identified and debated in order to ensure there are no gaps left in the organization's resilience arrangements.

Office-based

An event that damages or denies access to a building that staff are highly familiar with from their daily routine is much easier for people to visualize than many other disruption events. A fire or severe weather is relatable to individuals.

It is why in organizations that are new to resilience planning, their first focus is often on making arrangements for alternative premises in the event of a denial of access to a primary location. While these arrangements are essential to the resilience of an organization, plans must stretch beyond a focus on buildings to capture other critical resource dependencies.

Organizations that are reliant upon office-based working have additional options that may not be readily available to other groups, particularly when compared with production and manufacturing environments. The main difference is the availability of remote working and the possibility of transferring processes delivered in one office environment to another location. These strategies can involve the same individuals performing the processes they would normally be delivering in their primary location, but elsewhere, or can involve the process itself being transferred to a totally different team with the same skillset. The larger an organization's property footprint, the more recovery options they may have open to them.

However, with increased choice comes complexity. Accommodating very large numbers of staff in a recovery location somewhere can be costly – either because other, less critical teams will need to be displaced, or leases will need to be agreed on recovery centres that may sit idle until they are needed. This means strict prioritization is likely to be needed through the BIA process to ensure only those individuals who need the space are granted a seat in a recovery location. The remainder may be expected to work from home, or even asked to temporarily stop working altogether.

The group working from home also poses some challenges. Cloud-based computing and remote access to company systems from any location has increased recovery options and resilience tremendously. Yet in all organizations there are still individuals, as identified through our experience with Covid-19, who have limited means to access company systems from home. If any of these individuals perform critical roles for the organization, they must have the right technology available at home to allow them to continue working.

In organizations that make use of in-house or third-party-provided recovery locations, it is important to coordinate access to avoid the facility becoming over-subscribed. Whilst the rise of home working has drastically reduced the space needed at recovery centres, where they are used sufficient care is required to avoid the three most common reasons for the plan to fail:

1 a department that assumes it can use office space currently inhabited by another team but fails to check that this is possible;

2 seats in recovery centres becoming 'double booked', which would be no problem in a disruption that only impacts upon one area of the business but will cause issues if a disruption causes wider impacts to other teams;

3 technology and other resource needs specific to individual teams are overlooked in planning, meaning these are not readily available in the recovery location when they are needed.

Finally, in environments that are highly focused on office recovery planning, dependencies on technology can be overlooked. It is essential for business continuity professionals to test with IT colleagues the circumstances under which a disruption to a building might impact on company IT systems.

Servers, communication and switching rooms may be physically located in the same building that is the subject of recovery planning. This means there may be scenarios where a denial of access event could in itself disrupt IT. And if that IT is critical to supporting operations in other locations, including recovery centres and homeworkers, the organization's entire resilience capability is undermined.

THE IMPACT OF COVID-19 ON OFFICE RECOVERY STRATEGIES

Until 2020 recovery solutions for many office-based organizations would involve moving staff to a temporary location, to work remotely, or transferring processes to an entirely different team already working elsewhere.

Covid-19 challenged our reliance on these strategies and opened our eyes to other possibilities.

Pre-pandemic, the idea that an entire office-based workforce could work from home for an extended period of time, and during that period continue to work productively, would have been unheard of in many organizations. But crises have a habit of driving more rapid advancement of change. So when governments began asking, and sometimes instructing, organizations to send colleagues home, business leaders moved from a position of 'it is impossible' or 'it will never happen', to 'we have to'.

The pandemic challenged our assumptions about macro risks that impact upon an entire global enterprise at the same time. Almost overnight, well-crafted and exercised strategies for moving groups of staff from one location to another had been challenged. Groups of people could no longer work together, save for under a set of very small exemptions. For many employees, working from home became the solution. Yet until that point most organizations had not properly planned a mass transition to remote working.

In very short order, organizations had to make plans for:

- shipping IT equipment to staff who needed it, particularly individuals with no home computer or who were sharing a laptop with a family member;

- finding ways to manage staff performance in a world where most line managers had very little experience of supervising remote workers;

- managing increased risk of information security breaches as a result of staff working in a less secure environment, or perhaps in a household that included staff from competitor organizations;

- ensuring staff were properly cared for at home, from the set-up of home offices to prevent muscular and skeletal conditions arising from sitting for long periods on inappropriate furniture, to spotting and treating an increase in mental health problems.

These challenges were more keenly felt in regulated businesses with roles that were either unused to working remotely, or pre-Covid were prevented from doing so by regulators. Extra screens for traders, recorded telephone lines for supervised roles and super-fast internet access for staff requiring rapid access to large volumes of data were needed.

Very few had planned for this and many were caught unprepared. And because most office-based organizations were in the same position, backlogs developed with IT hardware providers unable to cope with the increased demand.

POST COVID-19

The pain organizations went through during the early stages of the pandemic to ensure staff could work remotely has had significant benefits to their ongoing resilience.

Home working is now a more firmly established recovery option for most organizations, and crucially staff have the experience of making this work. However, leaders have realized that remote working for lengthy periods of time has its drawbacks. Managing staff performance, training new recruits and delivering tasks that require in-person collaboration mean some degree of face-to-face interaction is essential. Slowly staff began to return to their normal places of work and by May 2023, 70 per cent of companies had mandated staff to return to the office.[3] While home working still provides significant resilience benefits, there is a trend towards bringing critical teams back together again in person to manage the complexities of a crisis event. So while we may not see a return to the use of large-scale recovery centres, it is likely that more organizations will opt for a hybrid approach where less critical staff, or colleagues delivering tasks that do not require so much face-to-face interaction can work from home as their recovery option. This hybrid approach provides the best of both worlds – increased resilience for the majority of staff who can work remotely, a central location(s) for critical teams to work in person when they need to, and a less expensive work area recovery solution that saves the organization money.

Regulatory scrutiny

Regulators have become increasingly interested in the health of an organization's resilience. The wide-scale impacts of a failure of critical infrastructure, including energy, water and banking systems, have the potential to significantly harm consumers and damage economies. High-quality business continuity arrangements are considered by some regulators as a useful means to ensure consumers are not unduly harmed by a lack of preparedness for disruptions.

Organizations in highly regulated industries tend to focus a substantial amount of time on compliance activities, seeking to demonstrate that business continuity controls are meeting regulatory expectations.

The focus on compliance can sometimes come at the cost of the effectiveness of the plans themselves, particularly if the regulator's approach is immature in its thinking, or the organization has failed to understand the difference between the societal interests of the regulator versus the commercial interests of the business. Regulations will typically be skewed towards maintaining stable markets and preventing consumers from experiencing harm. To the regulator, a failure of one organization in an industry with plenty of spare capacity would not necessarily be a major problem. For the individual organization, it could be the difference between survival and total failure.

With the bulk of management information and reporting concentrating on tracking compliance against external regulation, it is possible for these organizations to lose sight of the reasons why they are implementing business continuity. A balance needs to be struck between maintaining compliance with external regulations and ensuring the commercial interests of the organization are safeguarded in the event of a disruption to their business.

The regulatory scrutiny has some positive side effects too. In these organizations it is usually much easier to obtain and maintain senior management support for business continuity. This is particularly true where regulators have substantial powers to impose sanctions for poor performance.

High-hazard environments

In these organizations, resilience can quite rightly become skewed towards preventing incidents from happening, and building rapid response arrangements to manage them should they occur. A failure of prevention and response controls could have catastrophic effects, not just on the commercial interests of the organization but on the people working for and living in the vicinity of the organization's premises, as well as the wider natural environment.

These organizations are often subject to increased regulation and substantial sanctions should controls be deemed ineffective, or an accident results in harm to people and the environment. The ever-present threat of these sanctions, which can *in extremis*, include the loss of the organization's licence to operate, means it can be easy for business continuity discussions to be drowned out by a focus on safety and security. Without a strong senior-level sponsor, it can be a challenge to build interest in the need for business continuity and secure the necessary investments needed to maintain it.

In addition, these organizations often have well-established emergency and incident management teams whose primary focus has traditionally been on prevention and emergency response. Business continuity can be a relatively new consideration for this team, and a topic they may have very limited personal experience in. However, the existence of emergency management skills can also be a positive in that the organization will be experienced in performing risk assessments, preparing plans, and delivering training and exercises. While the processes are different from those used to deliver business continuity plans, the familiarity with some of the core principles of preparedness and response will likely make delivery less of an uphill struggle.

Production environments

Modern production environments are well-oiled machines. Every area for possible efficiency will have been scrutinized to ensure a smooth production process.

Just-in-time manufacturing techniques ensure supplies of materials needed for a production process arrive at a factory just before they are needed, and finished outputs are completed to closely match the exact customer demand at that moment in time. This method helps to limit the amount of cost held in the production system, keeping the process lean and efficient.

Just-in-time production processes will have very little inventory of parts and other materials, and a small stockpile of finished products ready for sale. The rationale here is that the more stock and finished products are held in store, the more working capital that needs to be held and the less revenue that can be realized. But with every efficiency gained, an element of resilience is often lost. Spare parts, extra raw materials and an inventory of finished products can be useful to absorb the effects of a disruption to production processes. But the cost to do so could be too great for the business to bear.

Between January and July 2020, Toyota produced just over four million cars globally.[4] A rough calculation, assuming a seven-day-a-week production process, means that just under 18,000 vehicles rolled off a Toyota production line somewhere in the world each day. For the sake of argument, imagine a critical part that is needed for all 18,000 vehicles is disrupted and the business holds approximately four hours of inventory of that part at most major production locations. Holding more of that stock could cost many hundreds of millions of dollars, but each day of disruption that cannot be recovered could cost the business $630 million (assuming a $35,000 average vehicle ticket price). While this rather basic example is of course flawed, it makes the point that a disruption lasting longer than a few minutes or hours in many production environments can be hugely damaging.

The major benefit of implementing business continuity and resilience into a production environment is that they are often run by engineers who hold a good understanding of cause and effect. Educating staff in these environments of the importance of business continuity, by showing the relationship between a disruption and a damaging outcome, can be relatively easy in comparison with other organizational types.

However, there will likely be significant challenge from staff for any measures that lead to increased cost and inefficiency being introduced into the production process, even if it is for the benefit of resilience. To counter this, business continuity professionals need a good understanding of the economics of the organization's business model in order to make the case for investment in more resilience. The BIA process, and in particular the risk assessment element of it, can be a huge benefit here. Showing the relationship between a cause (in this case a disruption to business operations) and an effect (a delay to production) can be used to help justify any investments needed in recovery.

Returning to the Toyota example above, if the organization determines that anything more than a four-hour disruption is intolerable to the business, recovery strategies will need to be capable of resuming production within that timeframe. This might mean spare production capacity being available somewhere, switching to other types of production activity, or holding increased inventory. All of these recovery strategies come with a cost. And this is where the economics comes into play. By showing the delta between the cost of the resilience measures and the anticipated cost of a disruption, it becomes easier to justify the investments needed in resilience. A good-quality BIA and risk assessment process will provide the data needed to have this conversation.

A second significant benefit associated with production environments that make recovery planning a little easier is that the business model and supporting processes are generally pretty straightforward to understand. Raw materials are sourced, transported, stored and processed into a product, before being shipped to customers. Conceptually it is much easier to visualize how a disruption may occur along that chain and what its impacts might be when compared with other, more complex environments, such as in public sector organizations, where there are often multiple different products and services being delivered, even different business models being used.

Service delivery organizations

These organizations can provide a wide range of services, including cleaning, security, facilities management and IT services, to other businesses, usually on an outsourced model. They typically operate with small group functions and hold hundreds, if not thousands, of contracts with individual customers. It is often at the customer site where the bulk of the organization's employees work on a daily basis.

These organizations are typically categorized by low margins, with contracts designed to be highly competitive. There can also be a significant amount of churn in new contracts as new deals are struck with customers, making the pace of change quite high.

Business continuity in these environments is typically focused on protecting critical group-level services that are essential to the delivery of contracted activities. This makes them similar in nature to many office-based organizations, however, often with an increased focus on cost-effectiveness.

Resilience arrangements for the services that are being provided to customers will be driven by the nature of the services delivered and the requirements set out in their contracts. Service-based contracts where the organization is providing people to deliver security or cleaning services, for example, will have a different focus than a technology outsource provider. Recovery strategies and solutions for these two broad types of contract typically cover:

- Resource-based contracts (e.g. cleaning, security):
  - staff scheduling to allow flexibility in how resources are used;
  - cross-training staff to allow them to provide support to multiple customers;
  - contracts with third parties to provide surge capacity of appropriately qualified individuals when human resources are constrained.
- Technology-based services (e.g. managed IT services):
  - focus on IT continuity and resilience;

  o increased focus on technical resilience as dictated by the service level agreements set out in customer contracts.

In these environments, resilience professionals must be capable of delivering business continuity arrangements both for office-based activities and via a contract vehicle. This means holding a good understanding of contract management processes and how contract risk is managed.

Public sector or charity

Public sector organizations are some of the most complex to understand. Civic authorities, for example, often provide myriad services to citizens – from schools, transportation and social care through to police, fire, health services and even refuse collection. Resilience professionals in these organizations have some of the toughest jobs going.

Many of these functions provide critical services to citizens, who would have very little consumer choice by way of alternatives should the authority fail. As an added complication, public and voluntary sector budgets in most jurisdictions are always under pressure: efficiency is king.

This context means that the public and voluntary sectors share some of the characteristics of other organizational groups set out above:

- the constant pressure on keeping costs down from production companies;
- the external scrutiny from citizens is similar to the regulated group;
- providing support essential to life, safety and security draws parallels with the high-hazard group.

These characteristics combine to make a highly complex environment within which to deliver business continuity and resilience. The challenges are further compounded by the lower wages that staff in this sector are typically rewarded with, making it harder for public authorities and voluntary organizations to compete with the higher wages offered in other industries.

Persuading staff with limited budgets and competing delivery priorities to dedicate time to business continuity is hard. In these environments it is easy for business continuity tasks to be deprioritized. However, there are some characteristics of public and voluntary sector organizations that do help:

• The public-spirited nature of staff and their dedication to helping citizens, particularly those that are more vulnerable, are strong motivations to support business continuity efforts.

• For many societal risks, including major civil emergencies such as disease outbreaks, flooding or wildfires, the public and voluntary sectors are the last line of defence for citizens. If these organizations fail, the most vulnerable members of society will pay a heavy price. This can help to build a strong business case for effective business continuity and resilience.

Business continuity and resilience activities in the public sector need to demonstrate value for money and a strong link to efforts that allow the organization to continue serving its communities, even under extreme pressure. This means making a sound business case for resource investments linking resilience outcomes to citizens.

Getting started

The seven characteristics explored here are not mutually exclusive. An organization can exhibit many of these characteristics at once. This places an extra burden on business continuity and resilience professionals to take a sufficient amount of time to understand the particular context for their organization, its culture and the expectations of internal and external stakeholders.

One size does not fit all, meaning it is OK to adapt what is considered common or best practice. In organizations new to business continuity and resilience, and at least to start with, practitioners should not be afraid of following the path of least resistance. If the organization's focus is squarely on technology resilience or recovery planning for premises, start with these topics and build out from there. It may be better to capitalize on the immediate interests of stakeholders than spend significant time and effort educating them on the 'right' way of doing things.

Be prepared to adapt, try new approaches. It is OK to fail – so long as we continue to learn.

TABLE 4.1   Chapter checklist

☐	Get to know your organization – what does it do? Why does it do it? What is its culture like?
☐	Understand the needs of different stakeholders and the reasons why they might be motivated to view things a certain way or take a certain course of action.
☐	Don't assume that nothing can be learned from other industries. Be ready to take the best from all sectors.
☐	Be prepared to adapt, try new things and learn from failure.

Notes

1 FCA (2014) Final notice for Royal Bank of Scotland Plc, National Westminster Bank Plc and Ulster Bank Ltd, 19 November, https://www.fca.org.uk/publication/final-notices/rbs-natwest-ulster-final-notice.pdf (archived at https://perma.cc/J9MM-QH4W)

2 Federal Reserve Board (2023) Commercial automated clearinghouse transactions processed by the Federal Reserve – Annual Data, www.federalreserve.gov/paymentsystems/fedach_yearlycomm.htm (archived at https://perma.cc/JZ4J-TPND)

3 People Management (2023) Seven in 10 companies globally have mandated return to the office, study reveals, https://www.peoplemanagement.co.uk/article/1824486/seven-10-companies-globally-mandated-return-office-study-reveals (archived at https://perma.cc/JW3V-D4WH)

4 Toyota (2020) Toyota's global sales and production recovers to 90 percent of previous year's level in July 2020, 28 October, https://global.toyota/en/company/profile/production-sales-figures/202007.html (archived at https://perma.cc/AD8N-CZCR)

05

Comparing incident management, crisis management and business continuity

Being clear on the meaning of terms and definitions is highly important when planning for and responding to a business disruption. Any ambiguity at a critical moment of an organization's response to a disruption could damage its ability to recover effectively. Of particular importance is a consistent understanding held by all staff involved in preparing for or responding to an event of the key differences between what constitutes an incident, crisis and business disruption.

We can look to international standards as a good source of reference to help in our understanding of these terms. However, since the finer details of what constitutes a crisis and an incident will be different between organizations, standards can only help at a conceptual level. An incident for one organization (for example a hospital dealing with a traumatic death) would be a crisis for another. So knowing the different characteristics of what constitutes an incident or a crisis for each individual organization will be essential to help ensure plans deliver the response that is needed, and to ensure staff understand their roles.

Definitions from the International and European Standards

Incident: an incident is described in ISO 22301 as an 'event that can be, or could lead to, a disruption, loss, emergency or crisis'.

Business continuity: is defined in ISO 22301 as the 'capability of an organization to continue the delivery of products and services within acceptable timeframes at a predefined capacity during a disruption'.

Disruption: the ISO 22301 definition for disruption focuses on the effects an incident may have on an organization's objectives: 'incident, whether anticipated or unanticipated, that causes an unplanned, negative deviation from the expected delivery of products and services according to an organization's objectives'.

Crisis: the ISO for Crisis Management, ISO 22361, suggests a crisis is an 'abnormal or extraordinary event or situation that threatens an organization or community and requires a strategic, adaptive and timely response in order to preserve its viability and integrity'.

Another way to define an incident versus a crisis or a business disruption is to understand the nature of how an organization would typically respond to them.

Figure 5.1 describes the amount of management input and effort that is generally needed to manage an event and the time it takes for an organization to get back to a normal level of operation. This can be a useful way of visually exploring the difference between how incident, crisis and business recovery activities will be managed.

Figure 5.1 shows that:

- **An incident response** is typically a fast-paced situation requiring a more immediate and highly operational response designed to contain the issue and manage immediate impacts.

- **A crisis response** requires a more strategic level of decision-making input as a result of the scale of the event, the potential damage it may have on the organization or the requirement for significant resource requirements to manage it.

FIGURE 5.1 Expected management effort versus time involved in managing an incident, crisis and business continuity event

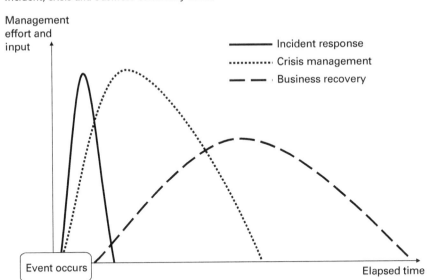

- **The business recovery phase** helps to restore the organization back to normal as a result of the disruptive impacts of an incident or crisis. This is where business continuity plans come into play.

It is possible for all three of these response types to be operating in parallel to address different impacts arising from the same event. An incident that causes a business disruption and also requires an element of crisis decision-making is possible and would need significant coordination between response teams to manage.

It is also possible for individual response types to be active but the others to remain absent from the process. An incident may be of such a low level of severity that it has no wider impact on business operations, or the need for crisis decision-making. Occasionally an organization could be facing a crisis but without an incident or business disruption to manage (for example a fraud or instance of bribery and corruption). However, business disruptions are the exception. Most business disruptions will, at their heart, be caused by an incident or will require an element of incident response decision-making.

Some of these nuances are explored in more detail below.

Defining an incident

An incident is defined as an event that could lead to a disruption, loss, emergency or crisis (ISO 22301). The definition implies that an incident can escalate into a much more significant business impact if it is not actively managed and contained. It also implies that an organization has an opportunity to do something about the incident before it evolves into something more significant. As an example, a fire breaking out in a wastepaper bin could develop into an emergency or a full-blown crisis, both of which would lead to some kind of loss for an organization. The existence of a smoke detector, fire extinguishers, an evacuation plan and the presence of staff trained in how to use them are all measures that have been consciously put in place to prevent the incident from developing into an emergency or a crisis.

The reason for using this example is to demonstrate that understanding the relationship between an incident, crisis and business disruption will allow an organization to better target their planning efforts and to implement response procedures that:

- identify the potential for an incident occurring – in the example given this would be the wastepaper bin as a source of fuel and perhaps the use of routine building surveys designed to identify fire risks like this one;

- provide triggers that help management to deliver a response that will help to prevent an incident from escalating into something more significant – this would be the smoke alarm, fire extinguishers, an evacuation plan and trained staff;

- provide criteria for determining when an incident has developed into something more significant, and escalation mechanisms to invoke a wider response – in the example this could be an onsite trained fire service and a crisis management team and business continuity plan that would begin the process of managing the longer-term impacts caused by the fire.

When does an incident become a crisis?

This is harder to define, as one organization's incident may be a crisis for another. There are, however, some helpful questions to ask that will help to determine when an incident is approaching a full-blown crisis:

1 **Can the incident be managed by local management and operational staff using well-established plans and procedures** (e.g. a property engineer responding to a lift fault with staff trapped inside)? If the answer is yes, it is likely this is not a crisis, as the resources to manage this event are well established and have the devolved authority to get on with managing the issue themselves.

2 **Will the incident require decisions to be taken that are out of the ordinary?** Particularly incidents that require sustained senior management input and decision-making relating to resource allocation, spending money or crafting external communications. An incident that falls within these criteria might push it into a crisis for many organizations.

3 **Does the incident threaten the viability of the organization?** Could the event result in sustained shareholder concern and share price volatility? Would the effects of the incident threaten the organization's reputation and ability to continue as a going concern? A yes to any of these questions for most organizations would be a sure sign of a more existential crisis.

Using recent examples of corporate crises can also be a helpful means of understanding what a crisis looks and feels like.

VW emissions

In 2015 Volkswagen admitted it had been manipulating emissions testing results for some of its vehicles in an effort to generate lower carbon emissions readings during laboratory tests.[3] The issue was first reported by the US Environmental Protection Agency (EPA), whose study suggested certain cars had been fitted with software that was capable of sensing when a vehicle was being tested for emissions in the laboratory and could reduce engine power output in order to limit emissions.[4] This, the EPA suggested, was in violation of the US Clean Air Act and resulted in some cars under-reporting their emissions by up to 40 times the standard.

The revelations resulted in significant global media and regulatory scrutiny, a backlash from customers, and class action lawsuits and criminal cases, which by 2020 in the US alone had resulted in $9.5 billion in compensation payments to affected consumers.[5]

There is no question that VW's experience was a crisis for the organization. What is interesting about this event is that there was no physical incident that required an operational response, and there was no immediate business disruption that needed the recovery of resources and activities. Production was unaffected. Instead, the event was a crisis that went right to the top of the business, involving senior executives having to make public statements about how the situation was being managed. It proves that crises can occur without much pre-warning and without the traditional escalation route from lower-level incidents, such as a fire or supply chain failure.

Facebook and Cambridge Analytica

In 2018 the social media giant Facebook was implicated in the compromise of millions of personal records of some of its users involving UK-based consulting business Cambridge Analytica. It was discovered that Cambridge Analytica had been harvesting personal data from millions of Facebook users without their express permission and using it, among other things, to support political campaigning for Donald Trump's run for the US presidency in 2016.[6]

Like the VW example, there was no traditional incident that escalated into this crisis, yet the impacts were profound for both organizations. There was significant media interest and, given the subject of the scandal and the open values that Facebook had previously been keen to demonstrate, the company experienced major political scrutiny, which culminated in the CEO, Mark Zuckerberg, testifying in front of the US Senate.[7]

Equifax cyber-security

In 2017, Equifax, a global consumer credit reporting agency, suffered a hack of their IT systems that resulted in more than 140 million customer records being stolen.[8] At the time the data breach was one of the largest in corporate history. In addition to the scale of the breach, what made it stand out further is that Equifax's purpose as a business relies upon the secure storage of some very personal information. For any business, a data breach of this scale, involving this type of sensitive information, would undoubtedly be a crisis; for Equifax, whose business model is built on managing highly personal data, the potential reputational effects were much more severe.

These three examples have one thing in common: they all escalated into a full-blown corporate crisis very quickly. In both the VW and Facebook examples, their crises appeared to members of the public as if from nowhere. While with hindsight there were some signs – indicated by an earlier cyber-attack[9] – that Equifax cyber-security may not have been as strong as it should have been prior to the 2017 attack, it too would have appeared like a bolt from the blue for many of its customers.

Feta cheese shortages

Some 40 per cent of soft cheeses produced in Greece come from one region, Thessaly.[10] In 2023, the area suffered widespread flooding leading to the deaths of an estimated 80,000 goats, the main source of the milk used to make Feta cheese.

The loss of such a large number of animals reduced the availability of raw material needed for cheese production. These effects were further compounded by many local dairies in the region suffering from damage from the flooding themselves leading to shortages of Feta and price increases for consumers.

Whilst for the average consumer, shortages of one type of soft cheese may not register as a crisis, for the farmers and the large dairy businesses reliant upon goat milk, the impacts were catastrophic. The crisis was fuelled further by many breeders of goats suggesting they would be unlikely to re-enter the industry.

In examples where an entire industry, or region has been impacted by an event, a full recovery is likely to require some form of external stimulus (as seen in many countries in response to COVID-19). In this case help came in the form of Government aid and funding from the European Union.

These examples prove that crises do not always give plenty of warning. There is sometimes no smouldering wastepaper bin about to burst into a major fire. It means that organizations need a crisis management capability that is able to very quickly begin making strategic decisions to take control of the situation.

So in summary, a crisis can typically be categorized as requiring:

- Sustained executive and board-level input and decision-making – however, it is important not to conflate crisis decision-making with the need to report updates about an incident to an executive team or board. Most incidents will require some level of reporting to senior management, but crises will likely need them to actively make decisions.

- Significant internal and external communications are likely to be needed to manage staff morale and the organization's external reputation.

- Major investment decisions in resources (both people and assets) to manage and overcome the event may need to be brought in, or reprioritized.

- A concerted effort to manage the concerns and interests of external stakeholders, including shareholders, regulators and supply chain partners, is likely to be needed, particularly if there is substantial media interest in the event.

Defining a disruption

Now we turn to the final definition of the trio considered in this chapter: disruption. It was defined earlier as an 'incident, whether anticipated or unanticipated, that causes an unplanned, negative deviation from the expected delivery of products and services according to an organization's objectives' (ISO 22301). In essence, a disruption results in stoppages and delays to the delivery of an organization's products and services. Not all disruptions will result in a crisis, but typically most disruptions at their root are the result of an incident.

It is worth keeping in mind that it is not an organization's products and services that are directly disrupted – instead, it is the disruption to the resources that these products and services rely upon that are for whatever reason unavailable. This is an important distinction, as business continuity plans are built around the recovery of critical resources should they be disrupted. The reasons why these resources have been disrupted are to a certain extent irrelevant to the planning process. This allows the development of scenario-agnostic plans that are capable of recovering key resource dependencies in the face of a much broader range of events than would be possible if concentrating on building procedures for individual scenarios.

ISO 22301 provides a useful framework to help consider which resources are of importance in the context of recovery and resilience.

People

Until artificial intelligence is born, an organization cannot exist without people. However, to paraphrase a well-known 20th-century author, some people are more important than others, and in the context of an organization that has suffered a disruption, this is particularly true. While all staff are needed to keep a business functioning well during normal operations, following a disruption an organization will need to prioritize the recovery of tasks, starting with those that are most important to the objectives contained within their business plan and the interests of stakeholders. This means deciding which roles, and therefore which people, will need to be the priority and focus for any recovery efforts.

Technology and data

Organizations have become so dependent upon technology, and the data that it processes, that no resilience capability will be complete without including information technology (IT) as an important part of the scope for business continuity and resilience. Technology and data have become fundamental to the way society and citizens go about their daily lives to the extent that any disruption to technology can have major widespread consequences.

For example, think of a failure of an air traffic control system or the computer systems that control traffic signals. Cities, regions and entire countries could grind to a halt. Now think of a bank's payment systems. No money can be deposited, no cash taken from cash machines and no mortgage payments can be processed. Now consider these scenarios lasting not just a few hours, but days.

According to the UK Finance 2019 payment markets report, in the UK alone in 2018, 34.9 billion consumer payments were made (debit and credit cards, direct debits, etc) and 4.4 billion from businesses.[11] All of these transactions need to be processed, not by humans but by machines. Disruption to the technology that underpins these payments would be catastrophic – even short delays would generate such enormous backlogs that banks would struggle to catch up.

But it is only money. One might argue that no one is directly physically harmed by a bank's systems being disrupted. Yet critical technology and the data it processes are everywhere; with us if we are unfortunate enough to find ourselves in a hospital operating theatre, operating our power stations and water treatment plants, and keeping us safe when driving or getting a train or aeroplane.

The importance of technology and data cannot be ignored by a resilience programme. Put simply, a business continuity plan that makes no provision for critical technology is likely to be a complete waste of paper.

Property

Most organizations have some kind of physical environment where work is undertaken. While technology is making it easier for employees to work outside a traditional office environment, there are still many industries where a physical location is needed. A factory making confectionery needs a factory, and a laboratory manufacturing pharmaceuticals needs a laboratory. Scenarios that envisage disruption to these locations are often the easiest to engage senior executives with. It is relatively straightforward to imagine a fire or a flood impacting on their premises. These scenarios feel more real and are perhaps more relatable.

Third parties

Whether they are outsource providers, suppliers, service providers or consultants, all organizations will rely upon third parties to some degree. Disruption to this group of resources can be difficult to manage for two simple reasons.

First, the risks that third parties are exposed to are not necessarily directly visible to the organization itself. Think of a warehouse operated by a third party that is used to store critical parts for the organization's production process. The fact that the fire has happened, though not immediately visible to the organization, will be reported at some point. However, even if the fire was reported immediately, it is unlikely that the organization would have had a detailed understanding of the fire risk at the warehouse, or the health of the controls that were in place to manage it.

This invisibility of the risks, and the measures in place to manage them, has two very important consequences:

1 It denies the organization time to react and to take action to minimize some of the impacts of the fire on their operations before they materialize in a disruption to their manufacturing process.

2 It prevents the organization from encouraging the third party to do something about the level of fire risk before it is too late.

Second, the resources needed to respond to third-party risks are not necessarily under the direct control of the organization. This is particularly true for businesses that have outsourced large functions from their own business to a third party – for example a call centre, logistics operations or an HR and payroll function. Where these functions are run in-house, it is under the direct control of the executive and board to do something about a disruption to the resources needed to deliver these activities. In a third-party relationship, this is not necessarily the case. It is rare for an organization to be able to directly control staff working for a third party without working through some form of contract.

During normal operations this should not be an issue, as contracts and performance measures are used to ensure the third party delivers to the standards that are expected and have been agreed. However, during a disruption, when a quicker pace of decision-making is required and action needs to be taken outside normal ways of working, the relationship between organization and third party can become more strained. The solution to this is to ensure that contracts and performance measures make provision for how the two organizations will operate together in the event of a disruption.

Assets

Referenced separately here to IT, data assets and property – to reflect the broader range of other asset types that an organization may rely upon. All organizations will be dependent to some extent on people, IT, premises and third parties; however, certain industries need to pay extra attention to other types of specialist assets, plant and machinery. A disruption to these assets can have a significant impact on the business.

An example could be the 'rolling road' of an automotive manufacturer. Used to calibrate vehicles before they pass a final quality inspection test, a 'rolling road' is not an asset that can be easily replaced or worked around. Critical assets like this appear in many manufacturing environments. They are often single points of failure owing to the high cost of maintaining redundant machinery that is set aside for when primary assets are faulty. The resilience for these assets may be less about recovery planning and more about prevention through maintenance and regular checks. This is where business continuity and risk management begin to overlap.

Scanning the horizon for potential incidents, crises and disruptions

If you take a pure business continuity approach to resilience, plans will be built around the resource dependencies explained above. However, as discussed throughout this book, to be fully effective, a business continuity capability must operate in parallel with an enterprise-wide approach to risk management. This is to ensure an organization is able to spot the risks of disruption, prevent or minimize them where it can, and recover business operations should these risks materialize.

To do this effectively organizations need the capability to scan the horizon to monitor for emerging risks that may later impact on the organization. An early warning of these risks buys an organization time to prevent it from happening, minimize its impacts, or to prepare for consequences through business continuity planning and other means such as financial provisioning and insurance.

There are a number of useful information sources available through which to get this early warning:

1 **Risk reports** such as those written by the World Economic Forum (WEF) – these provide a helpful summary of key emerging global risks.

2 **Peer group:** keeping an eye on competitors, tapping into industry groups and attending conferences can all help in gathering useful insights into the risks that other organizations are concerned about. What other organizations publicly state as their most important risks in their annual reports can also provide some insights into what others are facing.

3 **Professional advisers:** auditors, accountants, insurance brokers, legal counsel and other professional service providers can all provide insights from what they are seeing from how other organizations they may be working with are approaching the management of a specific risk or issue.

Individuals from risk management, marketing, supply chain, strategy, and internal audit and finance teams will also be useful sources of insights gathered from their own work in managing various forms of risk. While a highly structured horizon-scanning process and a formal team may not be appropriate for most organizations, simply getting these individuals together on a regular basis to share insights on possible emerging risks and to review the materials gathered from the sources identified above will provide some helpful information to support resilience planning.

TABLE 5.1   Chapter checklist

☐	Carefully define how the terms incident, crisis and disruption will be used in the organization, documenting this in the business continuity framework.
☐	Train staff involved in the planning process and the response on the meanings of these terms.
☐	Ensure there are individuals and teams in place with specific roles to support incident, crisis and business recovery activities. Document these in plans.
☐	Be sure to cover all resource dependencies when building business continuity plans to manage a disruption event.
☐	Build a mechanism that is capable of providing a periodical review of emerging risks, feeding outputs into the planning process.

Notes

1 BBC (2020) London firms sending staff home amid coronavirus fears, 26 February, www.bbc.co.uk/news/business-51643621 (archived at https://perma.cc/J828-47SZ)

2 Reuters (2020) Chevron employee in London tested negative for coronavirus, 29 February, https://www.reuters.com/article/us-china-health-chevron-workers-idUSKBN20N0L8/ (archived at https://perma.cc/2S66-GNLA)

3 BBC (2015) Volkswagen: The scandal explained, 10 December, www.bbc.co.uk/news/business-34324772 (archived at https://perma.cc/U8W6-CMNM)

4 United States Environmental Protection Agency (2018) Learn about Volkswagen violations, https://www.epa.gov/vw/learn-about-volkswagen-violations (archived at https://perma.cc/9VU4-QXKN)

5   Keating, D (2020) After five years, Europe's 'Dieselgate' victims have still not been compensated, 17 September, https://www.forbes.com/sites/davekeating/2020/09/17/five-years-on-dieselgate-victims-still-not-compensated/#2e515d53734b (archived at https://perma.cc/J7LP-9FED)

6   Cadwalladr, C and Graham-Harrison, E (2018) Revealed: 50 million Facebook profiles harvested for Cambridge Analytica in major data breach, 17 March, www.theguardian.com/news/2018/mar/17/cambridge-analytica-facebook-influence-us-election (archived at https://perma.cc/M8V9-VQ4H)

7   New York Times (2018) Mark Zuckerberg testimony: senators question Facebook's commitment to privacy, 10 April, www.nytimes.com/2018/04/10/us/politics/mark-zuckerberg-testimony.html (archived at https://perma.cc/57QY-6MER)

8   Bernard, T, Hsu, T, Perlroth, L and Lieber, R (2007) Equifax says cyberattack may have affected 143 million in the US, 7 September, www.nytimes.com/2017/09/07/business/equifax-cyberattack.html (archived at https://perma.cc/7XQZ-MD77)

9   Hern, A (2017) Equifax: credit firm was breached before massive May hack, 19 September, www.theguardian.com/technology/2017/sep/19/equifax-credit-firm-march-breach-massive-may-hack-customers (archived at https://perma.cc/E2HH-EAZF)

10   Financial Times (2023) Greek feta producers real from historic floods, https://www.ft.com/content/f08ed798-8c9e-4500-b830-8c694e523fc1 (archived at https://perma.cc/K9LY-VMRP)

11   UK Finance (2019) UK payment markets summary 2019, June, www.ukfinance.org.uk/sites/default/files/uploads/pdf/UK-Finance-UK-Payment-Markets-Report-2019-SUMMARY.pdf (archived at https://perma.cc/5EEN-5C6M)

06

Good practice in crisis response

Hope for the best and plan for the worst. If there was one phrase that neatly summarized the role of the resilience professional, this would be it. The role involves thinking of all the bad things that could happen, and then making sure an organization and its staff are prepared to face them should they occur. At the extreme end of all of the issues that resilience professionals are expected to deal with is a crisis. These situations represent an existential threat to an organization and will require a substantial amount of effort to prepare for and respond to. Put simply, a poor crisis response can result in irreparable damage to an organization and the careers of the people that work for it.

The main differences between an incident and a full-blown crisis are covered in more detail in Chapter 5. To paraphrase what is captured earlier in this book: a crisis will be an 'abnormal or extraordinary event or situation that threatens an organization or community and requires a strategic, adaptive and timely response in order to preserve its viability and integrity' (ISO 22361).

Expanding this definition further, an event is likely to be categorized as a crisis if:

- it cannot be readily managed by business-as-usual arrangements or by lower-level, more operational incident response teams;
- the response will require strategic decision-making and the commitment of substantial organizational resources, including finance;

- the situation threatens the viability of the organization and a lack of strategic action would result in substantial damage, even failure.

Of course we all hope that a crisis does not arise, but if it does, an organization's plans need to work and the people tasked with responding need to know what to do. But what does good look like? What separates a good crisis response from a poor one? And why does a good response matter?

This chapter explores these questions and seeks to explain what good looks like at each step of the way.

Why does a good crisis response matter?

The answer would seem to be pretty obvious, in that a major crisis by definition presents an existential threat to an organization's future survival. Put simply, a poorly handled crisis can destroy businesses and the reputations and careers of individuals involved in responding to them. The benefits of a good crisis response are not just anecdotal; they can be measured objectively. A Marsh and Cranfield University study in 2018 found that organizations that delivered an assured response to a crisis were rewarded on average with a 5 per cent increase in their share performance relative to peers.[1] The same study found that organizations that delivered a poor response to their crisis lost on average 12 per cent of share performance relative to peers (Figure 6.1). This study is not an isolated one; the Marsh study was based upon research undertaken by Oxford Metrica, which focused on reputational risk, in 2001.[2] Both of these studies reported similar findings.

Real-life case studies can also be used to reinforce the point here.

Apollo 13 lunar mission (1970)

NASA's Apollo 13 mission to the moon in 1970 might seem like a strange place to start, but anyone who has seen the Hollywood blockbuster of the same name is likely to know why this example is referenced here.

FIGURE 6.1   Results of a Marsh/Cranfield University study of the effects of recent corporate crises on share performance

Cumulative abnormal returns

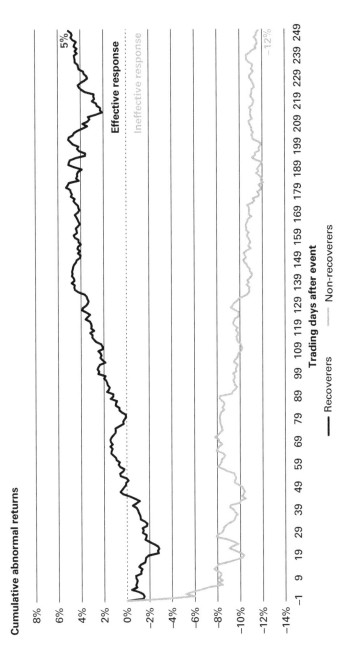

The Apollo 13 mission was abandoned before the lunar module could reach its target after a ruptured oxygen tank put the crew in mortal danger. What followed was a race against the clock to find an engineering solution to the immediate threats faced by the crew and to implement a rescue plan to get them safely back to Earth. Despite the original mission ultimately failing, NASA itself refers to Apollo 13 as a 'successful failure'.[3] This is because the organization learned a great deal from the crisis and was able to build this into doctrine that improved the safety of future missions. New procedures had to be written in days, when ordinarily they would have taken many months to build, and a large team of experts had to work together to resolve the problems that were facing the crew.

For Apollo 13, a good crisis response saved the lives of the three astronauts on board and gave NASA some valuable learnings it could apply to future missions. But what about a crisis case study that resilience practitioners would be more likely to experience personally?

It is actually quite challenging to find one example of an organization that has delivered a flawless crisis response. It is easier to spot a poor crisis response – the effects are usually much more public and widely reported. A good crisis response, on the other hand, can be a little more elusive since the outcome might be an organization's existing survival to continue business as usual – not exactly an exciting headline for the media to report. But look hard enough and there are some examples, both from larger crisis events impacting on multiple organizations simultaneously and the experiences of individual organizations, that can be used to demonstrate why a good response matters.

Japanese earthquake and tsunami (2011)

Chapter 2 explores in more detail the work that Nissan delivered to prepare teams and the business for a major disruption. These efforts seemed to pay dividends in the organization's ability to recover production processes more quickly and ultimately recoup the production time it lost as a result of the crisis. It can be argued that since Nissan had invested in preparation, they were able to deliver what appeared to be a more assured response when compared with industry peers.

Germanwings crash (2015)

Flight 4U 9525 was deliberately crashed by its co-pilot, Andreas Lubitz, into mountains in the French Alps after he locked the pilot out of the cockpit.[4] The crash killed everyone on board and appeared to be a deliberate act of suicide by the co-pilot – a truly tragic event that called into question the industry's approach to monitoring the mental wellbeing of pilots in command of aircraft. Germanwings was a subsidiary of Lufthansa and it was CEO Carston Spohr's immediate and compassionate response to the crisis that is worthy of mention here. His response showed he understood that the victims of the crash needed empathy and his customers would be looking for reassurance that their safety was his priority. His initial statement quoted him as saying that 'safety in aviation is not a given'[5] and set the tone for an industry-wide drive towards improving the health monitoring of pilots. Of course, no one wins from a crisis like this, but how leaders behave in the immediate aftermath can make a real difference to both the victims and the ultimate survival of the business.

KFC (UK) (2018)

In 2018 the UK arm of the fast food restaurant Kentucky Fried Chicken (KFC) temporarily ran out of chicken, resulting in outlets having to close. While not on the same scale as the other two case studies used here, a chicken restaurant running out of chicken presented a major problem for the business. The disruption was caused by glitches experienced during the transition to a new logistics supplier. However, the organization took a slightly different approach to handling their crisis. Instead of a rather dry press release, or a formal apology to customers from the CEO, the company took out a series of full-page adverts in British newspapers with the strapline 'FCK, we're sorry'.[6] The response was an instant hit on social media platforms and became a story in itself in the media. The organization had successfully turned their crisis into a public relations success story.

Reflecting on these case studies, a good crisis response can enhance company value, as measured by share performance, save lives, as illustrated by Apollo 13, help to limit the cost of disruption, as in the case of Nissan, help rebuild trust, as per the Lufthansa example, and strengthen an organization's reputation, as per the KFC example.

Yet despite the compelling evidence suggesting that a good crisis response matters, many organizations do not put sufficient effort into preparing for one.

What does good look like?

A good response does not happen by accident; it takes effort. All of the examples set out above relied upon some level of pre-crisis investment made by the organization, both in preparedness planning and the upskilling of staff so that they are able to make the best decisions possible in the interests of the organization and its stakeholders. So in judging what good looks like in a crisis response, it is first necessary to understand what happened before one occurs.

The five questions below can be used to provide an initial and very rapid health check of an organization's pre-crisis preparedness:

1 Has a crisis management plan been developed and do staff understand their role within it?

2 Has a crisis management command and control structure been defined to include response teams, clear response triggers, escalation, and information management and communications requirements?

3 Have key members of staff received training on their role in a crisis?

4 Have regular exercises been conducted to give teams the opportunity to practise their response to a crisis?

5 Have crisis procedures and any tools teams rely upon been regularly updated?

The answers to these questions are a good place to start in focusing attention on the key building blocks of good pre-crisis preparedness. However, they explore only half the story. As the Germanwings example above suggests, the public behaviours of individuals in the immediate aftermath of a crisis can either undermine the investments made in plans, or compensate for a lack of them. One of the best-known examples of an organization that has experienced the negative consequences of a challenging set of media interviews with its CEO following a crisis is BP.

The global oil company's 2010 Gulf of Mexico oil spill not only resulted in a tragic loss of life, it also caused huge damage to the natural marine environment and damaged the livelihoods of many coastal residents living in the southern states of the United States. Tony Hayward, the then CEO, had the unenviable task of being at the helm of a major organization at the time of what became an international crisis. During his many media interviews, not only did he seem to suggest that the volume of oil being leaked into the Gulf was tiny in relation to the total volume of water in the sea, but he was also famously quoted as saying there is 'no one that wants this over more than I do. I want my life back.'[7] Hayward would have been under enormous strain, working very long hours and dealing with a hostile media as well as a substantial amount of political interference. His words were completely understandable in that context. However, it came to define BP's image as uncaring and unsympathetic to the marine environment and the people whose lives had been affected.[8]

So a good crisis response is as much about people and how they react under stress and unusual situations as it is about plans. Returning to the Apollo 13 case study, like many other examples of teams working in high-risk, life-or-death situations – and looking beyond the engineering genius that secured a safe outcome – the NASA experience appeared to be grounded on:

- knowing your own personal role and the roles of those around you to allow rapid decision-making and an assured response;
- having robust and well-rehearsed procedures along with the ability to deviate from these when the circumstances of a crisis do not quite fit what was envisaged by planners;

- a pragmatic and evidence-driven approach to problem-solving, facilitated by having people with the right skills and experience on hand to help;
- having confidence and the authority to act when it is needed, or to flag issues to higher levels of management when required;
- strong leadership and a collaborative culture built around a common purpose, which, in the case of Apollo 13, was getting the astronauts back home safely.

All of these characteristics relate to people and not plans. Ultimately a true crisis will be a highly unusual, possibly never to be repeated again, set of events with a potential impact exceeding what normal business processes will be capable of coping with. Responding to these highly complex situations will require pragmatism and a strategic level of problem-solving that is capable of seeing beyond the most proximate issues. A crisis plan will certainly help in providing the structure needed to make consistent decisions, but it will never be capable of providing an exact blueprint for how an organization should or will respond. There are too many variables at play for a crisis response to be scripted in such a way.

This is where practice plays a crucial role. While practising a pre-scripted crisis plan may not make an organization's response perfect, it will help to increase the confidence of the teams involved and ultimately increase the speed, efficiency and effectiveness of the crisis decision-making process.

The building blocks for a good crisis response

The combination of people and plans will provide the bulk of an organization's crisis capability. So what are the core components of each that will help to improve the chances of delivering a more effective crisis response?

Teams

Crisis response teams should be made up of individuals who have both the right sort of expertise and the decision-making authority to commit the organization to action. In smaller organizations there may be one team, but larger entities will likely require a hierarchy of teams that are structured to provide command and control over the response.

The types of teams typically include:

- A **strategic-level decision-making authority,** often referred to as the crisis management team – this team sets the strategic direction and makes decisions that fall outside the remit of lower-order teams. This could include decisions about responding to staff injuries or deaths, committing the organization to significant expenditure, and coordinating response activities across a group, particularly where prioritization will be needed between business units or the allocation of company resources to resolve the crisis.

- A **tactical-level decision-making authority,** often referred to as an incident response team – this group helps to coordinate the operational response to the event, working with a range of disciplines and business functions to ensure that issues are being identified and addressed. The team will also be likely to have responsibility for ensuring information and decision requirements are communicated to the strategic team. It is also possible that this team will operate without oversight from a strategic team; this can happen when an incident has not breached the threshold that would require a strategic level of decision-making.

- **Operational response teams,** which deliver the response to the incident – there may be multiple operational response teams covering specific disciplines or areas of the business. For example, an IT response team and a security team might operate in parallel, each focusing on the issues that sit within their area of specialism and authority. These teams can operate without a tactical or strategic-level team if the incident has not reached the thresholds requiring a higher level of decision-making authority.

For all of these teams to be effective, they will need strong leaders who are able to facilitate effective discussions, can cut through complexity to understand the issues that need to be addressed and who can motivate and empower their colleagues to deliver. Strong leadership is a critical enabler of effective crisis management and will also play an important role in building confidence in consumers, regulators and other external stakeholders that the situation is under control and being well managed.

However, authority to make decisions should not rest with one individual. For all teams it is important to ensure that decisions are taken at the most appropriate level. This means taking decisions where there is sufficient knowledge of the issue to make informed choices, where resources are available to do something about the issue and involving individuals with the appropriate level of delegated decision-making authority. The consequences of getting this wrong include:

- burdening higher decision-making authorities with issues that would be better managed by operational teams, thereby reducing the amount of time available to cover more strategic concerns;
- decisions that are taken without a full understanding of their consequences or without a full view of the problem facing the organization. There is a risk of this occurring at any level of the decision-making hierarchy, but it will be particularly problematic when strategic decisions are made by operational teams who have limited knowledge of the wider and sometimes unintended consequences of the actions they are taking.

In geographically dispersed organizations that are working from multiple locations and different countries, there is often a need for multiple tactical-level teams to provide coordination of incidents and crises impacting on one particular geographical location or region. This approach encourages the use of more local expertise as a means to improve decision-making, and at the same time allowing central teams to focus on broader enterprise-wide issues that will require coordination. Such a model is also a helpful way of spreading the burden of tactical-level coordination activities when a crisis impacts across multiple jurisdictions.

Where 24/7 cover is required from crisis response teams, it may also be necessary to implement a 'follow-the-sun' model, where multiple crisis teams operating in different time zones take over from teams at the end of their working day, providing a constant level of coverage and vigilance. These structures are most common in organizations where a disruption could result in a loss of service to customers globally, or where the impacts of a disruption will be felt immediately. This model is often used by global technology companies and financial institutions.

Choosing the right team members

Team membership requirements will be influenced by a mix of the expected crisis impacts that need to be managed, the type of industrial sector the organization is operating in and the sort of decisions that will need to be made. Some of the characteristics needed of the individuals represented on the various crisis and incident response teams have already been discussed above. However, what about the specific type of expertise that may be needed?

In highly operational settings, such as a manufacturing plant, the operational and tactical response teams will include engineers, supply chain and logistics managers, operations leads and sometimes union representation. In professional services firms, or white-collar industries such as banking and aspects of the public sector that rely upon a heavy degree of office-based working, participation will look a little different. There will typically be an increased presence from technology teams, business service lines and corporate functions such as HR and finance. At the lower level there will be some overlap with the operational group of organizations in so far as there will be representatives from property teams and security functions.

At the strategic level the differences will be less noticeable. This is because many of the strategic-level issues that will need to be managed are broadly the same at this level in any sector. Decisions about external communications, reporting requirements for shareholders and other stakeholders, committing financial resources to manage the crisis and determining the impacts on the organization's strategy and business plan will be on the agenda of any strategic-level crisis team.

The crisis scenario will also play a role in defining team membership. While each team should have a core membership, additional individuals will likely be needed based upon the expected impacts arising from different scenarios.

Here are some examples:

- Crises involving a supplier failure or a contract issue will rely more heavily on legal professionals and supply chain teams.
- Events that lead to significant damage to reputation, but perhaps with no physical damage to the organization (for example a major fraud or alleged incidence of bribery) would place a heavier reliance on communications and compliance teams.
- Crises that disproportionally impact upon people will naturally lead to a greater involvement from human resources specialists.
- Events that result in environmental pollution will involve engineering teams, legal and perhaps compliance and regulatory relationship teams (depending upon the sector).

Some further examples are included below:

- **Strategic:** strategic-level decision-makers, usually executive level with some professional support services such as the legal counsel:
  - chief executive
  - chief operating officer
  - chief risk officer
  - chief finance officer
  - director of communications
  - director of HR
  - legal counsel
- **Tactical:** tactical-level decision-makers, usually the heads of customer or functional departments:

- ○ business unit (e.g. customer-facing teams)
- ○ functional departments (e.g. HR, finance, property, IT)
- ○ [additional members based upon the nature of the crisis]
- **Operational:** operational practitioners tasked with implementing the response:
  - ○ property
  - ○ information technology
  - ○ engineering
  - ○ operations
  - ○ [additional members based upon the nature of the crisis]

Tools and facilities

Response structure, check; team members, check. Now how and where should they meet? The answer to this question for many organizations pre-Covid would have been a dedicated incident or crisis response control room complete with all the communications infrastructure a team will need, access to critical data, maps and a place to grab refreshments. These control rooms can be expensive to build and maintain, particularly if they are not used for any other purpose than dealing with an incident.

To a certain degree Covid has changed our reliance upon one single physical location. Throughout the pandemic many response teams were forced to operate remotely, using voice- and video-conferencing facilities. However, for some command-room settings, a virtual environment is unlikely to be as effective as staff working together in one location. Police, fire or ambulance control rooms are good examples here. The fast-paced and dynamic nature of the events these control rooms deal with on a daily basis make face-to-face collaboration much more effective. Being able to collaborate in quick time, perhaps all poring over the same maps and other sources of information, cannot be perfectly replicated on any online platforms available today.

Virtual crisis meetings will be better suited to the more strategic levels of command. In fact, since many of the members of these committees will hold very senior roles, the likelihood of them all being in one place at the same time is very low. This likelihood is even smaller for global businesses, where the executive team might work from different locations. Since these more strategic meetings should not be discussing highly operational details or be asked to make important 'life or death' decisions (these should be delegated if there are any to be made), their discussions can easily take place over a phone or a secure video call. If a crisis room is necessary, they rarely need to provide anything more complex than a good phone line, video conferencing and a computer projector. Anything more substantial than this might suggest either that too much money is being spent, or the team is focusing too much of its time on operational details. When deciding what equipment might be needed and how much to invest, think of a crisis management team being an executive committee on steroids. Ultimately a table and a few chairs would deliver most of the team's equipment needs.

The UK Cabinet Office Briefing Room (or COBR, as the media portrays it) sits in a sub-basement of 70 Whitehall. The suite of rooms that make up COBR are the centre of UK Government decision-making during a time of a major national crisis. Terrorist attacks, severe weather events, infectious disease outbreaks and war have all been discussed here. The main room where the prime minister, or one of their ministers, makes the key decisions is an enormous anti-climax for first-time visitors. Anyone that has seen a Hollywood disaster movie will be significantly underwhelmed. The visitor is greeted by a nice large table, some comfortable chairs, a large video screen and various communications equipment. No big flashing red buttons, no klaxons, no men in white coats tending to whirring machinery. Just a room where decisions are made. Of course, the information and computer systems in the adjacent rooms are a little more secure than what would be found in most other organizations. But the point here is that it is not the infrastructure and whizzy equipment that makes a strategic-level crisis management team like COBR a success. What makes these teams successful are the structures that support them and the expertise and authority of the individuals present in the room. And of course the quality and timeliness of the information available to decision-makers.

In the case of COBR, that small room in the sub-basement of 70 Whitehall has at its disposal the entire machinery of the British Government. The analysis, number crunching, policy formulation and options analysis all generally take place outside this room. When the prime minister chairs a COBR meeting, they will be presented with information that has been reviewed, synthesized, analysed and processed by specialists from across government so that decision options are clear. The purpose of that room is to allow senior decision-makers to make choices, sometimes difficult choices, and this does not need a control room akin to NASA's mission control.

Control rooms that place a greater reliance on more advanced infrastructure, like the emergency services examples given above, tend to have a more operational focus. These teams, because they are monitoring events as they unfold and directing an immediate response, will generally need to be supported by more up-to-date information and will need more advanced control room infrastructure at their disposal. The control rooms of railway companies provide a great example. They need to provide constant monitoring of the railway network under their control, the ability to spot issues and fix them before they cause a disruption or disaster. This means knowing where the trains are at any given moment, the health of electrical circuits, signals and railway crossings, and monitoring for events near the railway such as line-side fires or vehicles striking railway bridges. It means being able to immediately communicate with train drivers, signal staff and other railway employees, and it could potentially mean shutting down the network to avoid a disaster. Thankfully such events are rare, but when they do happen, control room staff might have only a few moments to take action. For this they need good-quality, instantaneous information feeds and communication systems, making their control rooms look a little more advanced than the UK prime minister's polished oak veneer table. Similar set-ups are used by air traffic controllers, control rooms for major oil and gas facilities, nuclear power stations and motorway traffic control rooms.

The point that is being made here is that the infrastructure in a control room should be proportionate to the type of decisions being made there. If a crisis management team will not be making rapid decisions about diverting a runaway train, it is unlikely it will need the large display board showing the railway network with each signal, station and train represented by flashing LEDs. It may look good and appeal to the Bruce Willis in some crisis managers, but it is ultimately a complete waste of money.

There is, however, some equipment that is common to all control rooms and must be readily on hand:

- **Communications equipment** allowing team members to talk to other teams – this could be a basic phone line (which will be perfectly adequate for most control room settings) or something more advanced, like what will be found in military and government installations.

- **Logging** of key decisions and actions taken, either in an electronic form or hard copy – this is critical for all control rooms and any individuals that may be involved in responding to a crisis. Being able to refer back to decisions made either later on in a crisis as part of a handover process, or to justify actions made to an inquiry or even a criminal prosecution, is crucial.

- **Information management tools** to synthesize data so that it can be used to inform decision-making – the tools should be capable of providing a 'single version of the truth' that all key decisions can be based upon. This could be as simple as a whiteboard, or an electronic equivalent, or a more bespoke online incident response tool designed to build a common picture of events. Whatever means is chosen, information should come from trusted sources and be readily accessible to decision-makers.

- **Plans and supporting information** in either electronic or paper form – for more strategic teams, this may be limited to the crisis management team plan and access to key contact information. For teams making more operational decisions, these sources of information will be more detailed, such as electrical network or IT infrastructure diagrams.

- **Refreshments** and an area where staff can recuperate after a particularly difficult meeting or long shift – individuals who are not used to managing a crisis will be operating on adrenalin and may forget to drink and eat. Encouraging staff to take breaks and providing refreshments will help with this.

- **Access to the control room** will need to be carefully controlled so that only authorized decision-makers are permitted entry. This will be more of a concern for control rooms that have access to highly sensitive information, or where the actions of operators could cause a major disaster.

Information management

Access to, and the flow of, trusted information is a critical enabler of a good crisis response. Without it decisions will be taken 'blind', which could lead to poor outcomes and unintended consequences.

However, most crises are highly dynamic situations, meaning the availability of information is likely to be limited, at least in the early stages of the event. Decisions will still need to be made but sometimes with a bare minimum of facts to support them. The Covid-19 pandemic is a good example here. In the early stages of the pandemic little was known about the virus – how it was transmitted, what the symptoms were, if there were any long-term health effects, whether it could live on certain surfaces and infect others, and what treatment options would work. But this lack of information did not mean nothing was done. People were getting ill and dying, and so action by governments, citizens and businesses had to be taken. With hindsight it is certain that some of these actions will be considered not as effective as first thought, but sometimes no action is more harmful than taking an initial step, even if that step is not quite in the right direction. For the pandemic, and many other crises that will impact upon an organization, it is not always possible to wait until all the facts are known before taking that first step.

This means that during a crisis the validity of information must be carefully scrutinized before basing major decisions upon it. This is not to say that it should be discarded; instead, a crisis management team should be acutely aware of any limitations of the data they may be asked to base decisions upon. If limitations are known, these must be communicated; decision-makers should not be told or allowed to assume the information is fact.

A five-point checklist can be used to help determine how information should be treated. These questions are an equally valid way to identify so-called 'fake news':

1 Has the information come from a trusted source?

2 Has the information come from multiple trusted sources?

3 Is the information verifiable in some way?

4 Have you selected this information because it conforms to your own biases, i.e. are there other sources that contradict what is being said?

5 To what extent will this information be used to underpin major decisions?

What information is needed?

The type of information required to support a crisis response will of course depend upon the scenario being managed. However, the characteristics of information will often be consistent between different types of crisis event and so can be a useful point of reference when determining information needs.

Information characteristics include:

- **Relevance:** the extent to which the information will provide useful insights to support the decision-making process. Information that is not directly relevant to the issues faced by the organization or the decisions the team is required to make will slow down the process and could cause decision-makers to concentrate on lower-priority concerns.

- **Timeliness:** whether the information is relevant at the point in time that it is needed. Basing a decision to move staff between locations upon occupancy levels for a recovery site that has not been updated for many years could lead to problems. Efforts should be made to make sure that information underpinning critical decisions is up to date. If that is not possible, decision-makers must be made aware of its limitations.

- **Clear and unambiguous:** does the information provide clarity to the situation, or further confuse the issues at hand? In a crisis situation the latter may often be the case. If so, further work may be needed to collate more information, perhaps from additional sources, before it can be used to inform key decisions.

- **Avoid bias:** the extent to which the information presents an unbiased view of the evidence. Bias in decision-making is hard to completely eliminate, but awareness of one's own individual biases can help remove some of the risk. Information should be presented in the most objective way possible, avoiding conjecture and sticking to known facts. Recommended actions should be presented with additional options for decision-makers to consider.

- **Access and availability:** is the information available to all those who need access to it? During a crisis decisions will be taken at all levels of the incident response structure. Consciously or unconsciously holding back information needed by these teams could result in poorly informed decision-making. The converse is also true for information that will need to remain confidential; an extreme example would be negotiations with a group that has kidnapped an employee.

These characteristics can be a useful way of checking that the information available to the crisis team is appropriate for them to be basing their decisions upon. As outlined above, the exact type of information needed will be determined by the crisis scenario itself.

The following five questions can be used to further determine whether the right information is being collected and shared:

1 Is there **enough evidence** available for decision-makers to commit to a certain course of action?

2 Are there any **gaps in knowledge** that would stop decisions from being taken now, or slow down the process?

3 Have **all available sources** of information been considered (internal and external, to include what third parties such as legal, accountancy and insurance firms are advising)?

4 Can any **more information be easily collected** to improve the quality of what is shared?

5 **Does the information have any flaws** that will need to be communicated to decision-makers?

Sharing information: how much, how often and how shared

How much information is needed, how often it should be updated and the means through which it should be shared with response teams will all be highly personal to each organization.

However, there are some key principles that will help to inform the rhythm and mechanisms used for information management:

- **The frequency** at which information is shared should be relative to the complexity of the crisis situation and the number and frequency of planned crisis meetings.

- Crises involving highly complex or technical issues will by default require a more significant degree of information-sharing. Similarly, fast-paced crises that warrant frequent crisis management team meetings will create a greater demand for information.

- **Enough information** should be shared to allow staff to make the decisions that they are empowered to take.

- For most crises the majority of information can be readily shared. However, there are some exceptions, including when handling highly sensitive personal or commercial information or when operating under legal privilege (defined here as when discussions between a legal professional and client are to be held confidential).[9] For legal privilege to apply, there must be a communication between a legal professional and a client – information will not be covered just because the author has labelled a document as 'legal privilege'.

- It is also important not to overburden staff with information that will be irrelevant for their role. Before sharing any information, staff should be encouraged to ask:
  - ○ Does the individual need this information to help make a decision, or to contextualize the situation?
  - ○ Is there anything that might stop this information from being freely shared?

- The information upon which significant decisions are to be made should be **recorded, providing an audit trail to justify actions taken.**

- Not all decisions can wait for a complete set of information before they need to be made. However, all decisions should be able to be justified in the future, either as part of an internal lessons learned process, or to support an independent investigation or audit. Delaying a key decision because of a lack of information may be appropriate in some circumstances and entirely inappropriate in others.

- A simple impact analysis can be used to help determine a 'go or no-go' decision:
  - ○ What will the effects be if the decision is deferred? Will the situation become intolerably worse and the problem much bigger?
  - ○ What impact would a wrong decision have? Could it be worse than delaying a decision and could the situation be recovered if evidence later pointed to a better course of action?
  - ○ Are other actions highly dependent upon this decision? Would delaying these dependent actions result in an intolerable impact?
  - ○ When is more information likely to become known? Is this too late to prevent an intolerable impact or the problem getting substantially worse?

○ Is it possible that staff will be held to account by external authorities? Could a poor decision, or a decision based upon flawed or incomplete information, result in regulatory and criminal sanctions?

- **Information should be shared** using means that are appropriate and readily accessible to the staff who need access to it.

- For teams working in remote settings, perhaps in highly operational roles at the scene of an incident, radios and telephone will be more appropriate than email. Similarly for a strategic-level crisis team, the methods of sharing will likely more heavily rely upon email, formal committee papers and verbal briefings. Some organizations will also favour a dedicated incident or crisis management software tool designed to provide a central repository of information and associated decisions.

- Many of these tools can be accessed anywhere in the world and provide a highly flexible means through which to build and share a common version of the truth. However, unless these systems are to be used on a daily basis for other issues, they must be highly intuitive for users who may only access them on a very infrequent basis. Sometimes, because of their ubiquitous nature in most organizations, email, PowerPoint, Word and Excel are the best tools to use.

- When sharing any information, it will be important to ensure it is achieved using correct data protection markings and via methods appropriate to its sensitivity.

Decision-making cycle

This chapter has set out some of the foundations needed for effective crisis management decision-making. But what about the decisions themselves? What process should decision-makers follow when determining the best course of action?

The following five-step approach, which can trace its roots back to the 'plan, do, check, act' decision cycle set out in ISO 22301 (and many other management system standards), is a useful place to start:

1 **Situation:** Establish what is currently known about the situation and the impacts it has, or will have, on the organization. Stick to facts as much as possible, and where they are not available, ensure that limitations of the information being used are widely understood. If possible, address any gaps in knowledge prior to decisions being taken.

2 **Prioritize:** Determine what the organization's immediate and longer-term priorities should be. Prioritize outcomes that will drive the greatest benefit, either in reducing risk, preventing further damage, recovering the most significant parts of the organization or maintaining and rebuilding reputation.

3 **Action:** Determine and then implement actions that will deliver the agreed priorities, ensuring that they are allocated to individuals with the knowledge, expertise and authority to deliver them.

4 **Communicate:** Identify who needs to be informed of decisions made and actions taken. Determine the most appropriate channel of communication with each stakeholder group and set a regular schedule for communications.

5 **Monitor:** Track progress made against agreed actions and priorities, remain vigilant to changes to the situation that may warrant a change of course and monitor the impact of communication efforts on key stakeholders. The outputs from monitoring processes should be fed back into the decision-making cycle.

Just like the process of writing a business continuity or crisis management plan, the preparation phase of determining the best course of action is critical. Jumping too early to a possible solution could result in decisions being taken without knowing the full facts of the situation, or making a poor decision that takes significant effort to recover from. The discussions and ultimate decisions taken by a good crisis management team should be well structured and properly thought through. Of course, the decision-making process will need to run more quickly than members of the team might be used to; however, the quality of preparation and decision-making must not be allowed to suffer.

Communicating in a crisis

The evidence from the case studies discussed earlier in this chapter demonstrates the importance of good, transparent and timely communication during a crisis. How an organization is perceived by its stakeholders will greatly influence its reputation. The way an organization behaves publicly following a crisis may be the only means through which stakeholders are able to form an opinion of how well the response is going.

In the absence of any positive behaviour being shown and communicated by an organization's leaders, any void left will be filled by commentators, perhaps even peer organizations looking to speculate and pass judgement. In the past it would have been possible for an organization to more closely control the media agenda in the aftermath of a crisis. With the emergence of citizen journalism, social media and 24/7 news channels, the age of 'no comment' is long gone. News is instant – whether that is a social media post shared at the scene of the event or the smartphone footage shown close to live on news channels, organizations are expected to be readily available to respond to media scrutiny much more quickly than in the past.

Media scrutiny will not be new to most organizations. Most leaders want a positive relationship with the media as a means to position their products and services in a good light and build trust with consumers. However, in a crisis, the type of media scrutiny is significantly different from what is normally experienced. Whereas under normal circumstances the media scrutiny might come from industry press or professional bodies, during a crisis the journalists facing leaders will be seasoned reporters who are used to tearing apart an unprepared interviewee. While leaders might be comfortable dealing with some elements of the media, they will not be used to being interviewed in circumstances where people are looking for someone to blame.

The type and cause of the crisis will play a major part in influencing whether the media scrutiny will be positive or negative. Crises that have been caused by an organization, perhaps leading to injuries or deaths or harming the environment, will be scrutinized more closely, with poor performance judged much more harshly. Think of Tony Hayward's experience as the CEO of BP after their Gulf of Mexico crisis. For crises where organizations are the victims of events, such as a natural disaster like flooding, reporting will be generally more supportive of the organization.

Prior to a crisis, some effort is needed to ensure an organization is able to perform well in front of the media. This will mean:

- Train a group of suitably senior spokespeople to be the faces of the organization during a crisis. The training should be specific to handling the media during a crisis and prepare individuals for interviews for print media, radio and television.

- Prepare some pre-agreed messages that can be tailored following a crisis and used to deliver a proactive response to the media following a crisis event. It is essential that these messages are tailored to the exact requirements of the crisis at hand before being issued.

- Implement a rapid process through which media messages will be drafted, approved and issued. This will help to deliver a consistent approach to media handling.

- Issue a policy applicable to all staff on the expectations placed upon them about speaking with the media or commenting on social media during crisis. Typically staff will be prevented from commenting and asked to pass any press queries to the relevant team. However, staff may need some training on how to handle unexpected media questions, for example at the gates of their place of work, or via an unsolicited telephone call or message on social media.

- Following an actual crisis, a media strategy should be considered early in the response process to help drive a consistent, considered and proactive approach to issuing external messages.

Speaking with the media and the issue of formal statements will require careful planning. A poorly delivered message, an off-the-cuff remark or a fumbled response to an important question could wreck the organization's external image.

Messaging should:

- Seek to be as **transparent** as possible, sharing useful insights but without giving away confidential information or other highly sensitive data.
- Be **honest**; do not be tempted to lie. False messages will eventually be discovered and reputations tarnished.
- Show **empathy** where individuals or the environment have been harmed, being careful not to accept liability unless that is part of the strategy.
- Demonstrate **leadership**, setting out clear priorities for the response and a path to recovery. This will help to build a perception the organization is in control of the situation and the crisis is being well managed.

Communications issued to staff can be just as critical as those delivered to external media organizations. Without the goodwill of staff to work that little bit harder and that bit longer, the recovery from the crisis will be more drawn out and costly. How communications with staff are handled in the aftermath of a crisis can play a substantial role in the level of goodwill received. Leadership teams that fail to prioritize high-quality internal communications to staff could cause substantial damage to the organization's culture and its image as a good employer.

The process of preparing and issuing internal communications is broadly similar to making statements to the media – the big difference being that the delivery can be more easily controlled by leadership but the feedback (good or bad) can at times be much more rapid. In any crisis it is helpful to assume that whatever message is being shared with staff may eventually find its way into the public domain. Therefore internal communications that run counter to the external messages issued to the media could become a negative story in their own right. Messaging needs to be consistent.

At predefined intervals, particularly following a major external news story featuring the organization, it will be important to take stock and measure the effectiveness of the organization's media response. Brand index monitoring and customer sentiment analysis can be used to determine whether there have been any immediate negative or positive changes in the way the organization is being perceived. The results of these analyses can then be used to make adjustments to further improve the communications strategy. Similar principles can be used to improve internal communications. Staff focus groups, line manager feedback and formal staff surveys are all useful tools to help capture immediate reactions from staff and to check how they are feeling.

Debrief, reviews and lessons learned

Each crisis presents a unique opportunity to learn. Yet many organizations fail to deliver any adequate lessons learned process after a crisis has passed.

The business continuity planning cycle set out in ISO 22301 of 'plan, do, check, act' requires organizations to constantly monitor the performance of their business continuity management system and associated recovery and crisis management capabilities. Up until the point a disruption or crisis occurs, performance monitoring arrangements will never be able to categorically confirm that an organization's resilience arrangements will work. But a crisis affords us that opportunity, by providing a real-life test of plans, processes, teams and response tools. Of course, no one wants a crisis, but if one does occur an organization may as well make the most of the experience.

The lessons learned process starts the moment a crisis occurs. This does not mean the crisis team should dedicate too much time to reflect on their performance so far; they will be too busy managing the event. Instead, it relies upon making a clear and authoritative set of notes on the key decisions made and actions taken along with their rationale. This record will provide a valuable source of intelligence to support a more formal debrief in the future.

A debrief should be differentiated from a formal review:

- **Debrief:** an opportunity for individuals involved in a crisis response to provide feedback on the process, identify lessons learned and areas for improvement. This is usually conducted in a 'no-blame' environment designed to obtain honest feedback.

- **Review:** a more formal process involving a comprehensive analysis of evidence to develop recommendations for further improvements to the organization's crisis management arrangements. These reviews can be delivered in-house or by involving specialist third parties who are able to provide a more objective assessment of the response.

Four example debrief and review methods are set out below:

1 **Immediate 'hot debrief':** performed immediately after a crisis has been resolved, or at key points throughout the response process (particularly useful for events that last a long time). This debrief should be short and provide an opportunity for team members to raise any immediate issues and areas for improvement.

2 **Post-incident debrief:** delivered in the days after the crisis has been resolved to provide a more reflective assessment of how the organization responded. These reviews should capture input from all key members of staff who were involved in the response. Delivery is often achieved via a mix of workshops and questionnaires to capture lessons, and may also include an element of document review and root-cause analysis to help establish how future crises could be prevented or their impacts reduced.

3 **Post-incident review:** differentiated from a post-incident debrief by the depth of the analysis that will be undertaken. These reviews tend to place more focus on assessing response documentation, making comparisons between the response and the predefined response plans and exploring the root causes of the event.

4 **Forensic deep-dive review:** provides a comprehensive level of detail on how the organization responded. The process will involve a highly detailed analysis of key decisions taken, options that may have been discounted by response teams and an analysis of the root causes of the event. Such reviews can involve a substantial investment and so are usually only used following a major crisis, or in situations that could have escalated into something much

more significant. They are also widely employed by organizations operating in high-risk industries and environments where there is substantial interest from regulators.

Who should perform the review?

A debrief process can be facilitated by any individual with good stakeholder management skills.

However, it is important to be aware of the self-review threat, an issue explored in more detail in Chapter 14. If a debrief is led by an individual that has had a significant role in preparing the response plans, or delivering the response itself, it will be harder for the review to remain totally objective. This is not likely to be an issue for most crisis events, where participation from a wide group of stakeholders involved in the response and debrief itself will help to balance any unconscious biases expressed by the facilitator.

However, for a more formal review, additional independence may be beneficial. This is particularly true if the conclusions of a review will be widely publicized or relied upon by regulators and other important stakeholders. In these circumstances the process may be delivered by another unaffected business unit to provide a peer review, an in-house internal audit team or a third-party specialist supplier.

Review follow-up

The whole purpose of holding a debrief or review is to identify lessons and drive improvements. All debriefs and reviews will need to be followed up to ensure that any recommendations made are actually delivered. A failure to do this will mean the organization is likely to make similar mistakes during the next crisis.

The follow-up after a debrief or review should include:

- the issue of a formal report setting out any observations and recommendations;
- assignment of improvement actions to individuals;

- the identification of dates for actions to be completed by;
- performance measures to assess whether actions have been delivered and were successful in delivering the improvement needed;
- a mechanism for the outcomes of the review to be reported to senior management.

'Normal' crises vs. cyber

Of course there is no such thing as a normal crisis, but some will warrant a slightly different approach to decision-making. The decision of whether to pay or not to pay a ransom following a cyber-attack is a good example of when existing crisis structures may need to be adjusted.

In these events usually a crisis team would make a recommendation to the board to either pay or not to pay. But the process is fraught with risk, including legal, reputational and personal liabilities for directors of the organization. For these reasons the decision-making would usually follow a slightly different approach. And crucially, the whole decision process should be made taking legal privilege, putting the General Counsel (or external Counsel) at the heart of the decision-making process.

Deciding whether to pay

The decision to make a ransom payment is likely to fall outside the delegated authority of the executive team, meaning the board would need to opine on any final decision. This is partly driven by the personal liabilities of the organization's directors, who will want some say in what is being done in their name and the significant risks of getting such a decision wrong. For many larger organizations this will be one of a very small number of crisis-related decisions that can ultimately only be taken by the board. This means the executive crisis team would need a mechanism to rapidly convene a group of company directors who, on advice from management and specialist advisers, decide whether making a payment is the most appropriate path to take.

But deciding on whether to make a payment is highly situation dependent and fraught with danger. The team responsible for taking a recommendation to the board will need to step through a series of considerations:

1 **What do we know about the threat actor?** Knowing who might be behind the attack may give clues as to their motives. Are they motivated by profit, in which case they may be only interested in receiving a payment, or are they using the attack as a means to cause embarrassment, draw attention to an issue or support the political interests of a nation state? It may also be possible to tell whether the threat actor has a track record of unlocking systems and decrypting data once a payment has been made. Ultimately, for attackers that are driven by profit it would be bad for business if organizations had no trust in their ability to get their data back once a payment has been made.

2 **What are the business impacts?** The considerations here are wider than the cost of paying the ransom versus the costs of recovering the business. In most cases the cost of the recovery will far outweigh the payment demand. Most attackers will have done their homework – they will know how much damage they are likely to cause and what might be affordable to the business in terms of a ransom, using this to make a demand that maximizes the likelihood they will get paid. Other considerations here include:

   a Potential reputational damage of paying a ransom to what is a criminal enterprise.

   b Any safety impacts of systems and data being compromised. This is particularly important where the disruption to operational technology could result in harm to staff, customers or communities living near an industrial plant.

   c Environmental impacts arising from the disruption. For example, a disruption to a large, mechanized dairy farm may mean that milk may be unable to be processed, but cattle would still need to be milked each day, leading to a need to dispose of large quantities of raw milk (an environmental contaminant).

3 **What are the legal and regulatory risks?** These range from the obvious (can we pay a known criminal entity, or make a payment to an entity that is subject to sanctions?) to the less obvious (using the example above, would the legal risks associated with polluting the environment outweigh the risks of being found in breach of sanctions or terrorism financing regulations?).

The decision to pay will come down to a difficult judgement call of what constitutes the least worst option. But any decision should be based upon the best possible advice from legal advisers and cyber response experts, some of which will be available to organizations through any cyber insurance coverage they may have.

It may also be possible to negotiate with the threat actor in order to bring the cost of the ransom down. Such a strategy would require specialist third-party support – most crisis teams would be ill prepared to enter into a negotiation themselves.

Making the payment

An agreed process will be needed to secure a sufficient amount of currency (as determined by the ransom demand) and then physically make the payment. Often these payments are requested by the attackers in some form of cryptocurrency, which is not something that most organizations will have lots of experience with – but there are plenty of third-party specialist providers that do.

Prior to making the payment it would be sensible to obtain a 'proof of life' from the threat actor. Can they prove that they actually hold your data, can they demonstrate that they can decrypt it and will the decryption keys work when deployed on the network? The board will need to be given assurance on these questions prior to any payment being processed.

The process does not stop when the ransom has been paid. It will take time to screen the decryption keys to ensure that they have the best chance of working and do not introduce more problems into the network.

Adjustments to the crisis team

The special circumstances presented by a ransom attack will warrant some adjustments to normal crisis management arrangements:

1 **The board will have a more prolific role.** As a means to speed up decision-making and limit the impact of any personal liability risks on individual directors, a special sub-group of the board should be stood up.

2 **Decision escalation.** The executive team, who are likely to act for other crises as the main decision-making authority, would need to escalate a decision about the payment of a ransom to the highest governance authority, in most cases a board of directors.

3 **Legal privilege.** The decision-making process should be covered by legal privilege to reduce the risk of legal issues later on and potential disclosure.

4 **Documentation.** The decision to pay or not pay a ransom should not be written down in a policy document or plan. Organizations should assume that threat actors will have access to their entire IT network and will find this document, meaning they will have the upper hand in any negotiation.

TABLE 6.1   Chapter checklist

Pre-crisis	
☐	Implement a crisis response team structure appropriate to the organization (reflecting on size, geographical locations, nature of risks faced by the organization).
☐	Identify team members with the appropriate knowledge and decision-making authority.
☐	Provide training to all staff who are expected to be involved in a response to a crisis.
☐	Repeat training on a regular basis to ensure staff knowledge is kept up to date.
☐	Identify and source equipment needed for crisis response teams.

TABLE 6.1   *continued*

Pre-crisis	
☐	Set up video and telephone conference lines for use by crisis teams.
☐	Develop a crisis communications procedure, including the identification of spokespeople, template messages and mechanisms to sign off messages for communication internally and externally.
☐	Ensure spokespeople receive specialist crisis communications training.
☐	Ensure crisis procedures are documented in a plan that is shared with response team staff and is kept up to date.
During a crisis	
☐	Use the crisis management decision-making cycle to inform discussions.
☐	Identify information requirements to support decision-makers.
☐	Implement a regular routine to manage and share information.
☐	Set a crisis communications strategy tailored to the crisis scenario.
☐	Record all key decisions and actions for future reference.
Post-crisis	
☐	Undertake an immediate debrief followed by a more comprehensive post-incident debrief.
☐	Consider the need for a more formal deep-dive review, and whether that review should be delivered by a third-party specialist.
Ransomware	
☐	Identify the governance arrangements needed to support the 'pay or no pay' decision, paying attention to where these may diverge from existing crisis management procedures.
☐	Ensure that the process for the 'pay or no pay' decision can be covered by legal privilege.
☐	Identify specialist third parties to provide advice to the board (e.g. legal counsel, IT forensics, ransom negotiation and crypto payments). **Note:** organizations that hold a cyber-insurance policy may have access to these third parties through their insurer.
☐	Identify the circumstances that might influence the decision to pay a ransom (e.g. financial loss, reputational damage, legal and safety and environmental concerns).
☐	Walk the board through the decision-making process so they are as prepared as they can be for a cyber-attack that involves a ransom demand.

Notes

1 Crask, J and Stark, D (2019) To survive or thrive: how crises impact company value, November 2018 https://www.marsh.com/content/dam/marsh/Documents/PDF/UK-en/Exploring%20the%20Effects%20of%20Organisational%20Crises.pdf (archived at https://perma.cc/N725-HD6D)

2 Knight, RF and Pretty, DJ (2001) Reputation and value: the case of corporate catastrophes, www.oxfordmetrica.com/public/CMS/Files/488/01RepComAIG.pdf (archived at https://perma.cc/RA95-7379)

3 NASA (2009) Apollo 13, 8 July, www.nasa.gov/mission_pages/apollo/missions/apollo13.html (archived at https://perma.cc/6VC2-WJBC)

4 Der Spiegel (2015) The death wish of a Germanwings co-pilot, 27 March, www.spiegel.de/international/europe/the-germanwings-crash-and-the-pilot-who-caused-it-a-1025914.html (archived at https://perma.cc/S4HL-VXDJ)

5 Wings (2015) 'Safety in aviation is not a given': Lufthansa CEO, 26 March, www.wingsmagazine.com/safety-in-aviation-is-not-a-given-lufthansa-ceo-11778/ (archived at https://perma.cc/EN3V-HAHF)

6 Hickman, A (2018) The crisis comms lesson behind KFC's 'FCK bucket', 8 November, www.prweek.com/article/1498405/crisis-comms-lesson-behind-kfcs-fck-bucket (archived at https://perma.cc/6JTZ-HZGW)

7 Reuters (2010) BP CEO apologizes for 'thoughtless' oil spill comment, 2 June, www.reuters.com/article/us-oil-spill-bp-apology/bp-ceo-apologizes-for-thoughtless-oil-spill-comment-idUSTRE6515NQ20100602 (archived at https://perma.cc/N8ZH-P6BP)

8 Usborne, D (2010) Tony Hayward's latest PR gaffe is pilloried in US, 21 June, www.independent.co.uk/news/world/americas/tony-haywards-latest-pr-gaffe-is-pilloried-in-us-2006090.html (archived at https://perma.cc/VC6L-ZNDZ)

9 Wananbwa, A (2020) Legal professional privilege – a guide, 5 May, communities.lawsociety.org.uk/civil-litigation-features-and-comment/the-long-read-legal-professional-privilege-a-guide/6000999.article (archived at https://perma.cc/4522-F86A)

07

Lessons from the *Permacrisis*

Since the year 1500 there have been over 50 conflicts between what were considered at the time as the *Great Powers*, with three of these taking place since 1900 (the First and Second World Wars and the Korean War). One could argue that since the end of the Second World War in 1945 most of the world has experienced a long period of relative stability and growth. During that time the size of the global economy has grown from $9.8 trillion to over $100 trillion.

Most governments, citizens and businesses, in the West at least, have grown used to operating in a relatively benign risk environment where investment decisions could be made with greater confidence when compared with earlier generations. The beginning of the 2020s seemed to shatter that expectation and following a string of global crisis events and disruptions to the global economy many commentators described our experience as living through one permanent crisis, or *permacrisis*.

So what impact did this permanent state of crisis have on our organizations? This chapter will explore our experiences with global crisis events (the Covid-19 pandemic and the wars in Ukraine and the Middle East) and draw lessons for business continuity and resilience from them.

Covid-19 – lessons for resilience

At the beginning of 2020 few people had heard of Wuhan, a city in central China. But by July of the same year it had become as familiar a name as New York, London and Beijing.

It was not its culture or hi-tech industry that most people became familiar with. Instead, Wuhan became the centre of the initial outbreak of a novel form of coronavirus that developed into a global pandemic, changing the lives of millions across the world.

From 'somebody else's problem' to 'battle stations'

For many individuals, businesses and governments west of China, the early stages of the pandemic were business as usual. The outbreak was seen as someone else's problem.

This was the first big mistake, as many countries and organizations lost valuable preparation time. By the end of 2020, four phases of response activity had become clear.

The first ran between January and late February, and was characterized by either complete inaction from organizations (other than those directly affected in China and wider Asia) or a rapid scramble to review and secure supply chains that had a dependency on the region. For many, though, particularly businesses in Europe and the Americas, the risk and associated impacts of the virus spreading was not quite yet on their boards' agendas.

Life mostly carried on as normal, except for the occasional disruption to travel.

TIMELINE OF THE EARLY STAGES OF THE 2020 OUTBREAK

- **10 January:** Technical guidelines are published by the World Health Organization (WHO) covering detection, testing and management of Covid-19.

- **13 January:** First official confirmed case outside China in Thailand.

- **22 January:** WHO suggests there is evidence of human-to-human transmission.

- **30 January:** WHO declares the outbreak as a Public Health Emergency of International Concern (PHEIC).

- **11 March:** Covid-19 declared a pandemic by WHO.

However, for those organizations directly affected, with operations in Wuhan, wider China and the rest of Asia, the impact was very real. According to a report in the UK's *Telegraph* newspaper, 300 of the world's 500 largest companies had a presence in the city,[1] and the province as a whole created a GDP similar to that of London. The scale of the potential impact was clearly significant.

For other businesses the concern at this stage related to their supply chains. With many Chinese production facilities shuttered and transport networks disrupted, there were widespread reports of shipments of raw and processed materials being delayed, creating a knock-on impact on production, affecting automotive businesses, hi-tech manufacturers and even Easter gifts due for delivery to supermarkets.

The second phase was signalled by the increasing infection rates in Italy from February 2020 onwards. It was at this point that many businesses in Europe and further afield seemed to begin to understand the level of disruption that was looming. This is the period in which many businesses turned to their business continuity plans, invoked their crisis management teams, or if they did not have one, rapidly considered the strategies needed to protect staff and the organization.

It was in this second phase that many European countries initiated their own government-directed lockdowns. Approaches varied between governments, with little in the way of much visible early coordination from the European Union.[2] National governments determined their own policy approaches to containing the virus. Countries like Italy and Spain took a much more authoritarian approach to their lockdowns, effectively putting citizens under house arrest, while other governments took a more relaxed approach, such as Sweden, where much of normal daily life continued.

All of these countries, however, typically took five common measures:

1 **Hygiene:** encouraging citizens to increase their personal hygiene.

2 **Distance:** implementing 'social distancing' guidelines, effectively forcing people to stay between one and two metres away from each other to reduce the risk of the virus spreading.

3 Travel: encouraging less travel, including passing new laws to stop people from making unnecessary trips outside.

4 Closure: forcing or encouraging the closure of non-essential shops, public gatherings, bars and music venues in order to reduce contact between citizens.

5 Remote working: asking businesses to arrange for staff to work from home if they were able to do so.

A combination of these five measures changed how many organizations worked overnight. Some businesses were forced to close and lost revenue, particularly if they had no other means to continue trading in a world where physical contact with colleagues and customers was impossible. Others were forced to make drastic changes to the way they worked in order to continue operations. From adjustments to shift patterns and the layouts of production facilities, to the rapid mobilization of an entire population of staff to work from home, these changes were far-reaching and took significant effort to implement.

For many organizations, many of the decisions taken during this second phase of the pandemic were previously unscripted. Few had pandemic plans that were comprehensive enough to help the organization navigate through such a prolonged and widespread crisis. And it was during this phase that the importance and value of the resilience professional was finally realized.

Organizations with high-quality business continuity arrangements were in a better position to respond:

- They knew from the business impact analysis which roles were critical and therefore who needed to be prioritized for access to the technology equipment needed for homeworking.

- They understood the dependencies between departments, functions and processes, allowing the organization to more quickly address risks as they materialized.

- They managed the command-and-control structure used to respond to crises and so had a central role to play in making sure the right decision-makers were involved in the response.

- They had the networks, both internally and externally, to help make more informed and rapid decisions. Simply put, when an issue arose, their network helped to quickly solve the problem.

But of course many organizations would not have had a pre-existing business continuity plan. This group was starting from zero and had a much steeper hill to climb.

People and technology challenges

The challenges facing organizations in this second phase appeared to be centred on people and technology.

People

Knowing where staff were at any given point in time was a challenge for organizations, particularly those with a highly mobile workforce. With government travel advice changing rapidly, keeping track of where people were and where they had been was a constant challenge. This was compounded by challenges associated with communication. Communicating the risks to staff to allay any concerns and anxieties was problematic when government and scientific advice was changing almost on a daily basis. With a vast array of data and expert advice available, proliferated by 24-hour news media, it was hard for businesses to know which source of the truth to base their decisions and communications on.

Managing the welfare of more vulnerable staff was also difficult in an environment where so little was known about the virus. The definition of potential at-risk groups regularly changed in the early stages of the pandemic, meaning organizations had to be ready to respond quickly to government advice and staff anxieties as they evolved. In addition, with large numbers of staff working from home, concerns over mental health and wellbeing were also quick to emerge. Individuals working in unusual circumstances with less regular interaction with colleagues and line managers, combined with the general pressure created by lockdown arrangements, brought mental health to the fore. Numerous studies have shown a significant increase in the level of mental health and wellbeing issues[3] being experienced as a result of Covid-19.[4] In addition, many organizations were faced with the need to ensure employees' new places of work met their company's health and safety obligations.

Technology

There were early difficulties experienced in gaining access to the physical hardware needed to allow staff to work from home. Organizations that wanted to procure new supplies of desktop and laptop computers, screens, keyboards, mice and other peripherals found that their usual suppliers were under strain and certain products in short supply.

For many organizations, the pandemic necessitated a rapid expansion of online sales platforms. For businesses that had previously relied on face-to-face contact with customers to make sales, this was a major change to their business model. Under normal circumstances such a change could take years to implement successfully, but many managed the change in a couple of weeks. With the increased use of remote working, cloud-based services and electronic means of interacting with customers, cyber vulnerabilities became more of a concern. Organizations that moved to homeworking were forced to rapidly stress-test remote access tools, some of which had not been used at such scale before, and others that had implemented new e-commerce platforms were faced with myriad new risks relating to information security that they had not previously considered.

Organizations entered the third phase of response at different times, relative to local infection rates and the extent of any government lockdown rules that had been put in place. As the initial restrictions were lifted, this phase was for many characterized by the beginnings of an orderly return to the workplace.

The variability of the policy approaches taken by national and local governments, and the ever-changing advice given to citizens and businesses, provided a constant frustration to organizations that were hoping for a coordinated return to their workplace. This phase of the crisis presented new challenges that many had not previously had to tackle. These included:

- concerns of staff not wanting to return to their normal workplace as a result of anxieties caused by the virus, or seeking to keep some of the benefits of working from home;
- implementing sustainable health and safety controls in places of work, balanced against the need to create environments where collaboration and contact between staff could be allowed to happen;
- staff who continued to work remotely requiring additional health and wellbeing support – managing a split workforce with some working from their normal place of work and others from home presented challenges to line managers unused to the situation;
- what health screening (if any) should be implemented prior to staff returning to their place of work and each time they entered one of the organization's premises – temperature checking, Covid antigen and antibody testing were implemented by many organizations at great expense and sometimes to limited effect;
- the constant yo-yoing between lockdown (when infection rates soared) and a return to normal (when things improved) created administrative frictions and was a constant distraction for a workforce that was growing weary of the situation.

From a resilience perspective, putting aside the myriad people issues that needed to be managed, the impacts of this stage for most were relatively limited. By this point the changes that needed to be made to protect workers that remained in their normal place of work had already been implemented, and most of the technology issues experienced by homeworkers would have stabilized. However, there were still some lingering issues:

- a growing concern over the mental wellbeing of staff that had been operating for several months in unusual settings or isolated from their normal support network at work;

- concerns about productivity were beginning to surface, with staff having spent many months working with no face-to-face supervision from line managers;

- supply chain disruptions were still a cause for concern in some sectors, resulting in temporary shortages and significant cost increases and delivery delays.

The fourth phase of the pandemic covered here coincided with the winter influenza season in the northern hemisphere and was characterized by cycles between low and higher rates of infection and a slow return to normality. Many office-based organizations at least initially kept most of their workforces working remotely, while others that had to continue operating from a physical location continued to do so but with additional Covid controls in place. The issues during this phase were characterized by:

- uncertainty over how long the situation would last and the effectiveness of the vaccines;

- planning for potential staff shortages as a result of infection or individuals being told to self-isolate after coming into contact with an infected person – this was a particular issue in environments where staff had to be in the same location (such as a meat processing plant or distribution centre);

- concerns about how long an economic recovery would take, and if organizations and the wider economy would be able to survive in the medium term;

- increasing levels of social unrest from a population that was growing tired of both the uncertainty and the ongoing disruption caused to their daily lives;

- a polarization of opinion in workforces that had been working remotely between colleagues who were keen to return to a physical place of work, and those who wanted to keep some of the benefits of home working.

As the vaccinations had their desired effect, many of these issues began to fade; however, the return of staff to a physical place of work was slower. By mid-2023 offices in the United States were running on average at a 50 per cent occupancy rate[5] – much higher than during the depths of the pandemic but still well below pre-crisis norms. Many larger organizations began to mandate a return to the office, but often on a hybrid basis where colleagues could spend some time working from home and the rest in the office. The motivation behind this change was likely driven in part by the costs associated with maintaining expensive office buildings that were lying empty, but of course the main drivers related to productivity. We had learned that there are limits to our ability to innovate, learn and share knowledge if none of us ever physically meet. Collaboration requires some level of face-to-face interaction so a fully remote workforce was never going to be sustainable.

The lessons learned from Covid-19

The lessons learned from Covid-19 by organizations can be structured into six categories:

1 delays to taking action, resulting in a lost window of opportunity;

2 the scope of most business continuity and crisis plans being too narrowly defined and assumptions not adequately tested;

3 most plans not having been stress-tested as rigorously as they should have been;

4 not enough being known about supply chain vulnerabilities;

5 organizations not being prepared for a long-haul emergency and people risks not having been adequately addressed by most plans;

6 information management and data assimilation were weak.

Delays to action

The lack of an early response by many large global businesses is staggering in hindsight when considering that public officials in China were, as early as February 2020, busy setting up field hospitals[6] to treat the growing number of cases. Early data also suggested the virus was both highly contagious and deadly. However, it was not just businesses that seemed to be caught napping; the speed of response from many governments was also slow, or in places inadequate.

The UK Government in particular was heavily criticized for apparent delays in instigating an initial lockdown which many believed would have saved lives.[7] The government's justification for the delay appeared to rest in part on a concern over what it called 'behavioural fatigue': the concept that citizens would struggle to maintain discipline in a lengthy lockdown period. Yet according to the *British Medical Journal*,[8] the origins of this term are not well understood. This was the beginning of what became a recurring theme of criticism levelled at the government, who throughout the pandemic were accused of not following the science in their decision-making.

Further damage was done by the prime minister's senior strategic adviser Dominic Cummings, who allegedly broke lockdown rules by travelling 420 km from his primary residence to his parents' home, including a circa 80 km trip to a local beauty spot, which, in his defence, was to 'test his eyesight'.[9]

The response by US authorities was just as chaotic – from the president publicly suggesting that consuming disinfectant could act as a good treatment for Covid,[10] which resulted in a scramble by public authorities to ensure citizens did not take his advice too literally, to the lack of leadership and coordination throughout the pandemic[11] shown by the US administration. The slow and poorly coordinated response created a chaotic environment for citizens and organizations to work within. Bob Woodward, a well-respected US journalist well known for his role in exposing the Watergate scandal of the Nixon presidency, quoted the president as early as February 2020 as saying that his administration knew of the risks but actively chose to downplay them to avoid panic.[12] Crucial time was wasted when plans should have been in the process of being ramped up.

Leaders are elected to make difficult decisions and to take control in a crisis to protect lives and the economy. Government delays, particularly in the western hemisphere, to taking proactive policy steps to first contain the infection, ready the health sector for an increased caseload and encourage businesses to prepare, cost many lives and even more jobs. In the United States alone, 40 million citizens had been made redundant by May 2020[13] as well as 1.76 million in Japan.[14] Sectors that bore the brunt of the crisis were most impacted, with the hospitality sector, travel and leisure all experiencing significant job losses.

Of course it is worth remembering that the virus was new to science and so there was a great deal of uncertainty in what its long-term health impacts would be and how it might mutate. This did make it difficult for policymakers to plan. The scale of the challenges facing governments was immense, but that should not detract from the apparent lack of preparedness. The risk of a pandemic had been a top risk on the UK Government's public-facing National Risk Register since its first publication in 2010,[15] and warnings of a pandemic had featured in numerous World Economic Forum risk reports and World Health Organization publications. The world had even experienced an actual pandemic in the form of an influenza virus, H1N1, originating in Mexico in 2009, and an epidemic of Ebola in West Africa in 2014.

It is not as if an outbreak of a human infectious disease or the possibility of a pandemic had not been forecast. This was not a black swan risk; policymakers and planners simply chose not to prioritize their preparations for it.

The scope of business continuity plans and planning assumptions

Plans cannot be expected to cover everything; there have to be limits. From a purist point of view, the business continuity approach to this is to plan for managing impacts, rather than lots of individual scenarios. This is why plans focus on the recovery of resources like people, IT, premises and suppliers. It does not matter what has caused these resources to be disrupted – what matters is how the organization responds with workarounds and recovery solutions.

The very thing that gives business continuity plans their strength can also be their Achilles' heel. While a scenario-agnostic plan is a helpful way of covering a broad range of potential disruption types, its downfall is that the nuances of some specific scenarios can often bc missed. For Covid-19 this caused problems for some organizations and these issues were experienced again when faced with war in Ukraine in 2022 and then the Middle East in 2023.

For many practitioners, planning had become focused on implementing recovery solutions for property and technology. The more traditional solution to either of these resource types becoming disrupted, particularly property, would be to move staff to an alternative location where work could continue. The financial services sector had become a particular advocate of this approach, with large and very expensive, often third-party-managed recovery centres that replicated a full working environment for traders and other critical staff. The problem with a heavy reliance on these work area recovery locations was that they failed to take account of scenarios where staff needed to be kept apart in order to reduce the risk of infection. Financial institutions found that a 100-seat recovery centre would be limited to a fraction of that capacity due to social distancing rules.

Many plans also failed to appreciate the possibility of a disruption impacting the entire enterprise at the same time and over a sustained period. The global spread of the pandemic meant that recovery strategies that relied upon moving processes between different countries and regions to provide resilience were less effective. In addition, this also caused difficulties for organizations heavily reliant upon supply chain partners. Since most organizations' entire supply chains were being impacted in similar ways, the redundancies and alternatives that had been put in place for resilience delivered little in the way of a benefit. When primary suppliers were unable to meet their contractual obligations, back-up suppliers were also likely to be unable to help. This was compounded by the impacts felt across all industries. In circumstances when a disruption is limited to one organization, there are likely to be alternatives somewhere in the market. While these alternatives might be more expensive when the buyer is under stress, and while it might take a while to ramp up their supply, at least there is an alternative. During the pandemic this was not necessarily the case. An organization's suppliers would have been under pressure from their entire customer base; the demand side was as much a problem as the supply side.

These issues come down to two weaknesses in most plans:

1 a too narrowly defined scope that failed to appreciate the global impacts of a pandemic;

2 a lack of challenge of the assumptions built into plans – for example, assuming that a crisis is unlikely to impact on all geographical locations at once, or that there will always be some capacity in the market if key suppliers are unavailable.

Essentially the plans lacked imagination. Many planners had failed to consider some of the more high-impact disruption risks. It is also highly likely that planners came under pressure to keep costs to a minimum and were therefore pushed towards implementing recovery solutions that made best use of the organization's existing resources (such as alternative premises in the case of a building being inaccessible) without thinking more broadly about other recovery solutions. These alternative recovery solutions may have provided more resilience but also likely would have required investment (for example, IT systems that allowed an entire workforce to work from home). Perhaps some planners simply followed the path of least resistance, preferring to repeat a planning process that had been followed for many years without deviation or challenge.

The lesson for resilience practitioners here is to have more imagination about the disruption scenarios that need to be planned for, and to challenge the business harder for investment in recovery solutions that will provide resilience for these scenarios.

Stress testing

The validation of business continuity plans through exercises is an important step in the planning cycle. Without running exercises to stress-test a plan, it is hard to know whether it will work in the event of a disruption, or whether teams expected to follow it will understand what to do. Delivering high-quality exercises takes a significant degree of effort to prepare, deliver and follow up, and at times requires substantial investments of time from senior leaders. It is not surprising that securing sufficient management time to participate in exercises can be a real challenge for practitioners organizing them. Too often resilience professionals are obliged to make shortcuts in their approach to exercise delivery – perhaps by reducing the length of time spent discussing a scenario, or using a scenario that presents minimal challenge to decision-makers, or indeed limiting exercises to a basic table-top format rather than exploring more advanced forms of simulation.

The Covid-19 pandemic demonstrates why this can cause problems. Pandemic-based scenario exercises had gone out of fashion in the years before Covid. At one point many organizations had a pandemic plan and were actively exercising it – the interest in this type of planning coincided with the H1N1 influenza pandemic in 2009 and the SARS outbreak experienced in the Far East in 2003. Since then the focus seemed to move from crises centred on people to those affecting computers – the emergence of cyber as a threat to organizations became in vogue for planners. It is now known that the pandemic threat never went away, and as time went on organizations who had previously invested heavily in planning around the topic were losing the resilience they once had.

Three factors appeared to have contributed to this:

1 The emergence of a new, fashionable and what was considered a more proximate set of risks in cyber used up the management time that had previously been set aside to discuss a broader range of disruption scenarios.

2 Governments, professional bodies and the media stopped talking about pandemics as much as they had been – perhaps as a result of the H1N1 outbreak not being as severe as risk assessments had previously reported, or because we simply forgot about the potential consequences of a major pandemic, having not experienced any recent outbreaks. While the 2014 Ebola outbreak was certainly scary and hugely devastating for communities in West Africa, it was happening far away from where most developed economies were located – yet again it was someone else's problem.

3 The constant pressure on resilience professionals to limit the administrative burden they place upon the organizations they support makes more advanced forms of exercise the exception and not the rule. Had resilience planners lost their imagination for more challenging forms of exercise or scenario? This is unlikely, as the community's entire existence is all about thinking up worst-case scenarios and then planning for them. It is more likely that planners simply lacked a sufficient amount of time with executives to discuss more challenging disruption risks or deliver more advanced forms of exercise.

Resilience planners need to become much pushier. The Covid-19 pandemic will have highlighted to leaders that resilience is more than just IT and cyber. The door to the executive boardroom could now be finally opening for resilience practitioners. Now is the time to bash on that door and capitalize on the heightened interest that leaders will currently have in resilience.

Supply chain

For many organizations with no physical presence in the region of China where Covid-19 began, the effects of the pandemic were first felt through their supply chains; it showed that supply chain risks are systemic and often poorly understood. Put simply, organizations do not know enough about their supply chains and where their vulnerabilities might lie.

Supply chains have become highly complex systems, which has resulted in many disruption risks becoming invisible to buyers until they materialize. Parallels can be drawn with the earthquake and tsunami experienced in Japan in 2011. This disaster resulted in a rethink for car manufacturers in the way they managed their supply chains. The US mega-car manufacturers Ford, GM and Chrysler all discovered after the earthquake that they were supplied by the same single-source supplier for certain pigments of paint. The disruption resulted in Ford stopping the sale of certain red and black pigments. The problem was that the pigment, known as Xirallic, was not only produced by just one supplier – it was made in only one factory.[16] That factory was located close to the Fukushima-Daiichi nuclear power plant and was therefore evacuated after the explosion. Pigments were not the only concern. Airflow sensors manufactured by Hitachi were in short supply, causing GM, Peugeot and Citroen to temporarily slow their production processes,[17] and concerns were raised about micro-processers, certain industrial gases and silicon wafers used in electrical circuits.[18]

The experience in 2011 was a warning shot of what was to come with Covid-19. It highlighted the tension that exists in many organizations between balancing cost with resilience. Just-in-time manufacturing techniques provided enormous economic benefits, but usually at the expense of resilience in the face of high-impact, low-probability risk events. The Japan experience also showed us how little many organizations knew about their supply chains. Professor David Yoffie from Harvard Business School was quoted in the *New York Times* in March 2011 as saying, 'it's in the secondary layers of suppliers – things that are smaller, barely noticed – where the greater risk is.'[19] This was Ford's experience with its red paint.

Fast-forward to 2020 (and again in 2022 with the war in Ukraine) and organizations experienced similar issues, only the scale of the impact was much more widespread. The 2011 earthquake and tsunami led to changes being made by car manufacturers, who seemed to be disproportionately impacted when compared with other industries. The pandemic and our experience of the war in Ukraine have now pushed supply chain risks to the top of many other organizations' agendas.

The resilience practitioner has a critical role to play to ensure:

• supply chains are comprehensively mapped, with a more detailed analysis performed on the critical steps that make up an organization's value chain, including below the first tier of suppliers;

• a comprehensive analysis of supply chain vulnerabilities is performed for all supplies critical to an organization's most important processes and activities;

- there is an ability to undertake 'deep-dive' assessments on specific suppliers to look for vulnerabilities, including single points of failure or structural risk built into the supply chain;
- supply chain resilience activities are prioritized in areas of highest risk, or greatest vulnerability;
- a rolling programme of supply chain resilience reviews and supplier due diligence is undertaken to spot emerging vulnerabilities for treatment.

Protracted crisis and people risks

The Covid-19 pandemic was first and foremost a public health emergency which led to some very significant and protracted secondary impacts on business operations. Health risks were the immediate and enduring concern throughout the crisis; the health, feelings, perceptions and anxieties of staff became just as important to manage as the more physical aspects of an organization's resilience. Yet traditional business continuity plans had typically remained relatively quiet on the human aspects of a disruption or crisis, and many of the issues faced during the pandemic did not lend themselves to significant amounts of pre-planning.

During the pandemic organizational leaders found themselves having more direct contact with staff. Many arranged all-staff video conferences and town hall meetings where senior leadership briefed colleagues on the plans that were being put in place. These techniques provided a useful means through which to maintain staff engagement and directly receive feedback from colleagues on what their concerns were, which could then be taken into account in planning. However, this also exposed leadership to direct feedback from staff, whereas usually this would be filtered through many additional layers of governance. At times, leaders came face-to-face with staff who were anxious and looking for comfort. Few leaders would have been prepared for this increase in exposure and found that empathy towards the feelings of staff became an important tool in their approach to people management.

The length of the crisis also presented challenges. Recovery plans typically assume that a disruption or crisis will be resolved relatively quickly. This is evident in the targets set by recovery time objectives (RTOs), where recovery times greater than one week, or one month, are often covered in much less detail than the recovery of higher-priority processes and activities. This is completely understandable given that the specific longer-term impacts of a disruption may be difficult to pre-plan for and the costs involved in doing so would be significant. The sensible approach taken by most planners would be to review recovery strategies and solutions and crisis response arrangements when more is known about the scenario. The business continuity plan used in the early stages of a disruption will flex and change as more becomes known about the event, its impacts and how effective certain recovery options have been.

There are some hidden dangers with a 'wait and see' approach. Individuals involved in a response can easily become wrapped up in focusing on the issues at hand and be carried along by the adrenalin of the situation. This could result in less time being spent on medium- and longer-term planning and a step towards a more reactive, rather than proactive, approach to tackle the effects of the scenario as they become known.

Two issues compounded the challenges set out above:

1 Resilience practitioners, response teams and crisis decision structures are usually small in size with minimal redundancy available. For a long-burn crisis, the individuals involved can quickly become exhausted, a situation that could lead to poor decision-making. In addition, for such a complex crisis that affected every corner of an organization and its external relationships, the capacity of response teams and practitioners to manage the crisis would have been significantly constrained.

2 The broad range of possible futures arising from the pandemic were hard for many to predict. This was made worse by the lack of reliable data available upon which to make quality forecasts, particularly in the early stages of the crisis. These limitations would have meant many organizations were making decisions in

the dark and simply reacting to government policy and regulation as they emerged rather than taking a more proactive stance.

The people lessons arising from the pandemic suggest that resilience practitioners should be giving greater consideration in their planning to:

- additional redundancy being built into response structures through the training and exercising of more deputies to operate key roles – one unintended benefit from the pandemic is that most organizations now have a cadre of staff that have lived through a crisis and so have had the best possible training for the next one;

- how the opinions, feelings and anxieties of staff should be captured and responded to during a crisis – this implies a greater degree of input from internal communications teams and a more extensive use of staff surveys and other forms of collating feedback;

- a greater degree of emphasis during crisis exercises placed on the human aspects of an event, allowing leaders to experience and practise how they will show empathy to staff;

- longer-term 'what-if' scenario planning to walk through how the organization would respond to a protracted crisis event – such planning should give consideration to when a crisis response would become part of business as usual and for normal governance structures to be used for ongoing decision-making and oversight.

Information and data assimilation

The early stages of an outbreak of a novel form of human disease will always be characterized by uncertainty. Little will be known about the disease, how it spreads and what effects it will have on people's health. For Covid-19 this meant many decisions had to be taken with a minimal level of understanding of how the disease may evolve. There was no other option open to governments and organizations – decisions could not wait and action had to be taken based upon the best information available at the time.

Covid-19, and crises like it, relied upon a substantial amount of input from the scientific community. The challenge here for policy- and decision-makers is that the scientific process is an iterative one. This means it is extremely hard to rapidly arrive at one single author- itative conclusion, particularly for complex problems.

Instead, the scientific method involves a process of iteration covering:

1 making observations;

2 asking questions that help to form a testable hypothesis;

3 making predictions based upon the hypothesis;

4 testing the predictions;

5 using the outputs to make new hypotheses or predictions.

The process set out above may never be completed to the levels that policymakers and leaders would like in order to inform their decisions. They will be seeking clear and unambiguous advice from the scientific community, which they are very unlikely to be able to provide.

This is at the heart of the tensions seen between the scientific community and policymakers in respect to Covid-19. Multiple hypotheses and predictions will all be subject to testing by different scientific groups running in parallel. The heterogeneity of the scien- tific process, which leads to more diverse thinking and better scientific outcomes, also creates more ambiguity for decision-makers. It gives individuals the opportunity to pick and choose the studies that best suit their personal biases or political goals and to pass blame should a policy decision later turn out to be flawed.

The lesson here for resilience practitioners and organizational leaders is not to expect science to provide a definitive solution all of the time. Instead, planners should look for areas of scientific consensus and constantly challenge themselves and decision-makers to check their own biases are not adversely affecting the scientific studies chosen, or the way they are being interpreted.

While some of the challenges referenced above relating to data availability were unavoidable for Covid-19, the pandemic experience did highlight a weakness in many organizations' resilience preparations.

The collection, collation and analysis of data to inform crisis and recovery decision-making was typically poor. Resilience practitioners are not generally data scientists and are therefore unused to building and using models to help forecast the need for future decisions.

These limitations, combined with data availability and short-comings in data analytics capabilities, present four challenges to organizations and resilience practitioners:

1 It makes medium- and longer-term scenario-based planning much more difficult to achieve. The lack of readily available data and the skillsets needed to analyse it means forecast modelling either simply does not happen or is poorly executed.

2 Taking a proactive approach to planning for longer-term issues is harder to achieve. There are parallels here with climate change. The lack of proximity of climate risk impacts to individuals undertaking the planning makes climate change a problem for tomorrow, for someone in the future to worry about. Yet models suggesting severe weather will become more severe have been widely available for many years. It is the lack of understanding of data and how it should be used that means climate risks are always considered a problem for tomorrow.

3 It erodes an organization's ability to spot the need to quickly respond and pivot towards a new way of working to reduce the impact of the crisis and the length of time its effects will be experienced for. Without good-quality information, the ability to make informed and definitive decisions will become harder.

4 The time lost to building a sound information picture is time that could be spent preventing a disruption from occurring or limiting the effects of one should it occur.

The important lesson to learn here is that the resilience professional of the future will need to hold a good understanding of the importance of data and how to analyse it. While it is unlikely planners will need to personally become experts in actuarial science and risk quantification, they will need to understand the basic concepts and methods and the circumstances under which to deploy them.

War in Ukraine

Few commentators predicted that Russia would mount a full-scale invasion of Ukraine. But just like in the pandemic, governments and organizations were in February 2022 caught on the back foot, struggling to keep pace with what became a rapidly changing geopolitical outlook. The horror of another war in Europe, a continent that since 1945 had chiefly remained peaceful, challenged assumptions held by many that peace was a given.

The invasion challenged the last 25 years of investment decision-making which had assumed global conflict was highly unlikely and saw Russia as a trusted trading partner. These decisions needed to be rapidly revisited and many organizations found they had significant risk exposures that the night prior to the invasion had since the 1990s been firmly inside their risk appetite.

As with the pandemic, the immediate focus for many was on protecting staff and their families affected by the conflict, with the second-order effects relating to business disruption taking the back seat, at least initially. Over time, organizations with operations and supply chains in Ukraine and Russia were forced to think hard about longer-term impacts and how they could be managed.

For many organizations, the immediate impacts arising from Ukraine related to similar issues experienced during the pandemic:

1 The **safety and sustainability** of operations in Ukraine and Russia, which were called into question. Some organizations found that Ukraine was the source of a significant amount of their IT expertise, specifically software coding, which was not easy to relocate or find elsewhere. However, whilst the initial phases of the war resulted in significant migration there was also anecdotal evidence that some businesses saw an increase in productivity as a result of staff choosing to stay and 'do their bit'.

2 **Supply chain risks** specific to the geography of Ukraine and Russia and their effects on global trade. For example, Ukraine produce significant amounts of grain and sunflower oils and Russia is a significant exporter of fertilizer. The war triggered another round of price increases for certain commodities which, when combined with the continuing global shortage of computer chips, was beginning to bite.

3 **Proximity risks** for organizations that had operations close to the conflict zone and were worried about a possible escalation of the war into neighbouring countries.

4 **Reputation risks**, particularly for companies headquartered in countries that were backing Ukraine and had operations in Russia. Many large brands came under significant pressure to exit the Russian market at extensive cost.

Behind these impacts were the more systemic changes in the ways governments, citizens and organizations viewed geopolitical risk. Even organizations that were not immediately impacted by the war were left wondering, what if it happened here? Just like in the pandemic, the resilience practitioner was well positioned to help their organization address this question, which for many would have resulted in an acceleration of scenario planning for other 'what if' events, such as:

- What would happen if the war spread to other territories?
- What would the impacts be of China invading Taiwan?
- What if the conflict between India and Pakistan turned into a *hotter* war?
- What if countries previously considered relatively stable were to have their own 'Arab Spring' moment?

Stepping into the future

Prior to the pandemic and the war in Ukraine few resilience practitioners would have been able to engage decision-makers on what would have been considered highly unlikely. But if the *permacrisis* has taught us one thing, it is that the unlikely can (and probably will) happen.

Many organizations have emerged stronger from these recent experiences having adapted well to new ways of working and by responding promptly to the impacts of the wars in Ukraine and then Israel.

However, there are still many other global risks that are receiving the same degree of inaction as a pandemic risk was pre-2020. The effects of climate change, for example, will be felt by all. Many of the characteristics of the Covid and Ukraine experiences can be applied to climate change, and many of the lessons that need to be learned will also help organizations and governments to better prepare for the effects of a warming climate.

For practitioners, recent crises presented an opportunity to raise the profile of resilience at the executive and board levels and a chance to work in collaboration with parts of the organization that had previously been closed to them. As these crises dragged on and became the new normal, discussion has slowly turned from short-term resilience to longer-term sustainability and adaptation. For the first time, many resilience professionals have found themselves sitting at the same table as strategy teams, business planners and HR directors, having become a central part of organizations' adaptation efforts for Covid and Ukraine. These new connections and experiences will serve practitioners and the organizations they support well when the next crisis strikes.

This kind of improved collaboration is what will be needed to tackle the effects of climate change and other global catastrophes that are yet to firmly make it onto our radar screens.

TABLE 7.1   Chapter checklist

☐	Have the lessons from recent crises been identified and addressed?
☐	Consider whether resilience arrangements are scalable to a broad range of crisis events. Is the scope appropriate to the risks faced by the organization and have planning assumptions been challenged?

TABLE 7.1   *continued*

☐	Build a scenario stress-testing programme to provide a regular and rigorous validation exercise for plans and other capabilities. Keep asking 'what if'.
☐	Check whether the organization understands enough detail about its supply chain, where its vulnerabilities are, how to manage them and what would happen under a range of possible crisis scenarios.
☐	Consider whether sufficient attention has been paid to the needs of people during the response and recovery phases of a disruption or crisis.
☐	Check there is sufficient redundancy in response teams to manage a prolonged crisis event. Have deputies been identified, trained and involved in exercises?
☐	Build mechanisms to ensure the right information is collected, analysed and used in response to a disruption or crisis.
☐	Be prepared to constantly challenge personal biases and group think to prevent a blinkered view of risks and response options from being considered.
☐	Build a more integrated approach to the management of resilience risks, involving a broader range of experts and functions in the process.

Notes

1 Foy, S and Chowdhury, H (2020) Wuhan: a burgeoning technology and automobile hub at the centre of the coronavirus, 29 January, www.telegraph.co.uk/business/2020/01/29/multinationals-suspend-business-china-fallout-coronavirus-deepens/ (archived at https://perma.cc/BZ2W-45UR)

2 Herzenhorn, DM and Wheaton, S (2020) How Europe failed the coronavirus test, 4 June, www.politico.eu/article/coronavirus-europe-failed-the-test/ (archived at https://perma.cc/U7TC-ZYCD)

3 Public Health England (2020) COVID-19: Mental health and wellbeing surveillance report, 8 September, www.gov.uk/government/publications/covid-19-mental-health-and-wellbeing-surveillance-report (archived at https://perma.cc/6VG6-BTYL)

4 Pierce, M, Hope, H, Ford, T, et al (2020) Mental health before and during the COVID-19 pandemic: a longitudinal probability sample survey of the UK population, *The Lancet, Psychiatry* 7 (10), pp 883–92

5 Christian, A (2023) CEOs drawing a hard line on return to office policies. https://www.bbc.com/worklife/article/20230905-workers-now-face-a-hard-line-on-return-to-office-policies (archived at https://perma.cc/PBH3-EKPH)

6 Miller, H (2020) China is building two hospitals in less than two weeks to combat coronavirus, 3 February, https://www.cnbc.com/2020/01/31/pictures-china-builds-two-hospitals-in-days-to-combat-coronavirus.html (archived at https://perma.cc/DRS7-KFHS)

7 BBC (2020) Coronavirus: Lockdown delay 'cost a lot of lives', says science adviser, 7 June, www.bbc.co.uk/news/uk-politics-52955034 (archived at https://perma.cc/B5CG-DT25)

8 BMJ (2020) Covid-19: Was the decision to delay the UK's lockdown over fears of 'behavioural fatigue' based on evidence?, 7 August, www.bmj.com/content/370/bmj.m3166#ref-6 (archived at https://perma.cc/QE6V-XUPQ)

9 Dodd, V (2020) Dominic Cummings potentially broke lockdown rules, say Durham police, 28 May www.theguardian.com/politics/2020/may/28/dominic-cummings-potentially-broke-lockdown-rules-say-durham-police (archived at https://perma.cc/6F9A-Y6V8)

10 Rogers, K, et al (2020) Trump's suggestion that disinfectants could be used to treat coronavirus prompts aggressive pushback, 24 April, www.nytimes.com/2020/04/24/us/politics/trump-inject-disinfectant-bleach-coronavirus.html (archived at https://perma.cc/659M-NJZN)

11 Lipton, E, et al (2020) He could have seen what was coming: Behind Trump's failure on the virus, 11 April, www.nytimes.com/2020/04/11/us/politics/coronavirus-trump-response.html (archived at https://perma.cc/B88P-FKQU)

12 Woodward, B (2020) *Rage*, Simon & Schuster, London

13 Aratani, L (2020) US job losses pass 40m as coronavirus crisis sees claims rise 2.1m in a week, 28 May, www.theguardian.com/business/2020/may/28/us-job-losses-unemployment-coronavirus (archived at https://perma.cc/P6LS-T8K7)

14 Kretchmer, H (2020) How coronavirus has hit employment in G7 economies, 13 May, www.weforum.org/agenda/2020/05/coronavirus-unemployment-jobs-work-impact-g7-pandemic/ (archived at https://perma.cc/P34H-7UGL)

15 UK Government (2010) National Risk Register for Civil Emergencies – 2010 edition, 19 March, www.gov.uk/government/publications/national-risk-register-for-civil-emergencies-2010-edition (archived at https://perma.cc/Q68D-B9GH)

16 Seetharaman, D (2011) Automakers face paint shortage after Japan quake, 11 March, https://www.reuters.com/article/us-japan-pigment/automakers-face-paint-shortage-after-japan-quake-idUSTRE72P04B20110326/ (archived at https://perma.cc/T5S3-8XUE)

17 Boudette, NE and Bennett, J (2011) Pigment shortage hits auto makers, 26 March, www.wsj.com/articles/SB10001424052748703696704576222990521120106 (archived at https://perma.cc/Z3XK-J4SH)

18 Lohr, S (2011) Stress test for the global supply chain, 19 March, www.nytimes.com/2011/03/20/business/20supply.html (archived at https://perma.cc/ZCN8-G4BR)

19 Lohr, S (2011) Stress test for the global supply chain, 19 March, www.nytimes.com/2011/03/20/business/20supply.html (archived at https://perma.cc/ZCN8-G4BR)

PART TWO

Guidance on delivering an effective business continuity capability

08

Gaining and maintaining the attention of the board

Without senior management support, a business continuity programme will struggle to deliver its intended objectives. Resources needed for delivery will be difficult to secure, and much-needed investments to support the development of recovery solutions will be out of reach.

ISO 22301 requires a significant amount of what it calls 'top management' input into the business continuity management system, without which it implies that a business continuity capability will be unable to succeed. However, even without these requirements, any change management programme or project, whatever its focus, that will require resource commitment and investment will need sustained senior management support.

In addition to directing planning activities, senior management also plays a more fundamental role in leading an organization through a crisis event. An effective response requires preparation, training and practice, none of which can be achieved without support from the board and executive.

Recent high-profile corporate crises, global events, supply chain disruptions, the growth of cyber-risk, the Covid-19 pandemic, and the wars in Ukraine and the Middle East have put business continuity and resilience firmly on to the board agenda. It has never been easier to gain senior management attention, yet many practitioners struggle to secure and then maintain their interest.

Taking the first step

Imagine you have started a new role as a business continuity manager for an organization that has no current structured resilience capability. Within the first month of the job you are asked by the executive to present a paper outlining the importance of resilience and the steps needed to enhance the organization's preparedness. Your paper must also set out the investments that will be needed to make this happen.

Confidence and brevity in the delivery and a focus on the business imperatives for change are important ingredients of a successful engagement with an executive team or board. This means being clear on what is being asked for, the reasons for the request and the benefits it will deliver to the organization.

First impressions matter. A poor first performance at this early stage can be highly damaging to the success of a business continuity programme. It is also harder to rebuild trust once it has been damaged, so getting it right first time is important.

Practitioners who have had limited previous experience of interacting with senior executives should seek opportunities to practise. This might mean speaking and presenting papers at other senior management committees, or asking a colleague to peer-review papers before submitting them. The executive sponsor for the business continuity programme can also be helpful here. They have a vested interest in making sure the discussions go well so should be happy to invest some time to provide coaching to individuals who are due to present at an executive or board committee.

How do the board's needs differ from the executive?

Often the roles of the board and executive can become conflated. The danger of not fully understanding the nuances between their roles can be extremely damaging to achieving the objectives of the business continuity programme.

The Institute of Directors defines the role of the board as being 'to ensure the company's prosperity by collectively directing the company's affairs, while meeting the appropriate interests of its shareholders and relevant stakeholders'.[1] In essence, a board is involved in providing strategic direction and making decisions for the benefit of shareholders, customers, regulators and staff. The board should therefore be less involved in day-to-day decision-making. In order to successfully discharge its duties, a board must simultaneously know enough about the inner workings of the business to direct its activity, while at the same time standing back from the day-to-day management of the organization. It is a difficult balance to get right – a common complaint of an executive is that their board members are too involved in operational delivery activities. The board achieves this balance by setting the organization's vision, strategy and structure and then discharging delivery to management.

For business continuity, the role of the board includes signing off on the requirements for recovery and resilience – setting what the organization's tolerance might be to business disruption and holding management to account for delivering response and recovery arrangements that support this requirement. The board is not there to get into the detail of planning activities – that should be reserved for management. It is also possible that for certain crisis events individual board members may hold personal liabilities, especially if an investigation later finds that a board has managed a particular risk exposure poorly. These tend to be risks that are subject to some form of regulation that may be industry specific (e.g. in the banking sector), or universal (e.g. fraud, corruption, corporate manslaughter). Generally speaking though, members of the board (in a well-run organization) will be well protected against some of these risks, but knowledge of these issues is useful when engaging senior decision-makers, particularly during crisis exercises where some of their impacts may be tested.

Management then has a responsibility for ensuring plans are effective in meeting the board's needs. In the context of business continuity and resilience, the roles of the board and executive can be summarized as:

- **The board** will be looking for assurance that recovery and resilience arrangements are in place, are effective and meet their requirements in managing the risks to delivery and the achievement of the organization's strategic objectives.

- **The executive** will be more concentrated on the 'how'. They will expect to be making decisions on how to implement a resilience capability that meets the board's needs. This means signing off on programme design, policy documentation and other key business continuity outputs.

It is worth remembering that some organizations do not have a formal board of directors. This could be because of their size or ownership structure (e.g. companies that are owned privately or public entities that have elected members acting as their highest decision-making authority). However, most organizations will have levels of governance involving managers overseeing delivery (a bit like an executive team as described above) and a decision-making body (akin to a board of directors). Whatever the structure employed, it is important for practitioners to hold a good grasp of the governance structures in place within their organization and, crucially, understand their decision-making authority (and its limits).

Key executive-level stakeholders

The majority of a business continuity or resilience professional's time dealing with senior stakeholders will be spent interacting with the executive, rather than the board. The make-up of an executive team and the interests and needs of different senior-level stakeholders must be properly understood before taking the first step to engage them.

The size and construct of an executive team can vary significantly. Some organizations have very small teams; others much larger ones. However, regardless of size, knowing the requirements and the personal objectives of the individuals sitting on the executive will help improve the quality of any interactions with them.

In addition to the chief executive, there are other important executive members with a role or interest in business continuity and resilience.

Chief finance officer (CFO)

The CFO is the 'numbers person'. Often the perception is the CFO will say no to any requests for investment in the interests of saving money. A good CFO will be much more objective in balancing investment decisions against the value that will be realized from their implementation. For resilience, this means presenting clear justifications for any investment requirements and setting out how they are intended to reduce the organization's risk exposure. Some organizations, particularly private entities, will make provisions on their balance sheets for certain risks should they materialize. This will be capital that is locked away from being available for other purposes, and so if it is possible to link resilience investments back to capital provisioning and show how this could be eased with better resilience, it will be easier to convince the CFO and wider executives of the need for investment.

Chief operations officer (COO)

The 'organizer', the COO has an image of being the no-nonsense delivery person as they are often focused on outcomes and results. An initiative that does not make their life, and the life of their teams easier, more efficient and ultimately better is unlikely to get their support.

Chief technology officer (CTO)

The 'techy', the chief technology officer is a relatively new addition to many executive teams, sometimes referred to as the IT director. Their role can be quite broad – ranging from overseeing research and development into new forms of technology innovation that will radically transform the business, to overseeing the latest Windows upgrade. Our dependence on information technology makes the CTO a key stakeholder for any resilience programme; their teams will be critical in supporting the implementation of IT resilience arrangements.

General counsel (GC) and company secretary

The 'enforcer' – sometimes not full members of an executive team, these individuals bring the legal and governance expertise to the table. They ensure that the executive has access to relevant and timely legal advice and are operating in compliance with governance standards. They are often an underutilized resource for business continuity and resilience. They can play an important role in helping set up the right governance for the programme, both for overseeing plan development and for responding to a crisis. They can also be highly influential in helping to persuade other executive-level stakeholders of the importance of resilience.

Supply chain director

The 'head of the Q branch of the business' – like the CTO, the supply chain director can play a highly important role in a business, particularly those managing significant supply chains like those found in manufacturing organizations. The supply chain director has a difficult role to play – they ensure that the organization's current supply chain is not only strong enough to support today's operations, but is also flexible enough to respond to shocks and agile enough to evolve to meet future strategy requirements of the board. The supply chain director operates in a world of contract negotiations, supplier performance appraisals and managing cost pressures. They can be both a strong advocate of better supply chain resilience and a blocker, particularly if cost is the major focus of supply chain discussions.

Chief risk officer (CRO)

The 'threats and opportunities person', the chief risk officer is not a common role on most executive teams outside the financial services industry. But where they do exist they play an important role in acting as the conscience of the team by giving the executive insights into the organization's key risk exposures and the health of the controls that support them. Their interests are often aligned to those of the CFO

– they will be keen to understand how risk exposures manifest themselves in costs to the business (financial and less quantifiable impacts) and whether they take the business outside its risk appetite. They will therefore be interested in specific details, evidence and numbers to back up any argument justifying requests for investments in resilience. In situations where resilience arrangements are poor, the CRO can play an important role in persuading other executive colleagues of the need to improve by highlighting the risk exposures the organization is facing.

Engagement can vary by industry

In addition to understanding the detailed needs of the stakeholders sitting around the executive or board table, the organization's industry, the products and services it delivers, its interactions with customers and the role regulators play in supervising its activities can all have a significant impact on the level of engagement and support for resilience. Being aware of how these characteristics influence the way an organization thinks about resilience will help with executive- or board-level interactions.

So, what are the characteristics?

Heavily regulated

Heavily regulated industries where regulators take a close interest in the health of an organization's resilience arrangements are likely to include resilience as a regular item on board and executive agendas. The financial services industry is a good example. Here regulators are keen to ensure that banks and other financial institutions are delivering activities in a way that protects consumers and limits any systemic risks on the wider markets. Their interest has grown significantly since the 2008 financial crisis and the myriad IT failures experienced by banks such as Royal Bank of Scotland, TSB and Lloyds.

Customer-focused

Organizations that are in regular and direct contact with their customers, and where customer demands can have a significant and immediate impact on an organization's revenue and market presence, are more likely to be interested in resilience measures that improve reliability and service quality. Such characteristics can have a profound impact on the way business continuity and resilience benefits are positioned with an executive or board team, with a greater focus on the outcomes that customers will see as a result of improved recovery planning.

IT-dependent

All businesses are dependent upon IT in some form, but some are more dependent than others. For example, there are many consumer businesses that operate solely through internet sites and online applications or process such vast amounts of data that alternative workarounds that avoid the use of technology are simply no longer possible. The business models of these organizations have become almost entirely dependent upon technology that works. For these organizations, the role of the IT director or CTO is crucial and they will likely have significant influence over where investments in resilience are to be made.

Safety-critical

It would be reasonable to expect that businesses operating in high-risk, safety-critical environments, such as oil and gas companies, mining and nuclear industries, would pay significant attention to business continuity and resilience given they face many risks that could result in major disruption or a crisis on a daily basis. However, that may not always be the case. In these industries, while significant effort is quite rightly expended to prevent incidents, disruptions and crises from occurring in the first place, investments in business continuity can sometimes become deprioritized.

These industries can be the hardest of all in which to obtain support and ongoing buy-in from senior management for resilience. This is because the concept of resilience has become synonymous with pre-vention and emergency response planning, which tend to be quite mature in these organizations. Executives for these organizations will need to be briefed on how business continuity differs from other forms of resilience the organization currently maintains, and why extra effort is needed to manage the potential disruption consequences of some of the risks they face.

Preparing and making the pitch

A common mistake is to assume that senior management is interested in knowing the detailed principles and processes behind business continuity. Most will be indifferent about the details, or will consider the subject a distraction from other key decisions they need to take. Agenda time will always be limited and so it is important to make it count.

Papers presented to an executive or board committee should be crisply written using minimal jargon, remembering that the audience is unlikely to be experts in business continuity. That means avoiding too many references to business continuity processes, or international standards such as ISO 22301. While standards and processes are important for practitioners, very few executives will have an interest in these details. Instead, time should be spent focusing discussion on the issue that needs to be managed and the recommendation or decision that the committee needs to discuss.

In preparing the pitch, the following five questions can be used as a guide:

1 What is the issue that needs the immediate attention of the executive or board? This should be expressed in as few words as possible.

2 What action (recommendations) should the executive or board be taking, and have any alternatives been considered and already

discounted? Make sure these are realistic and achievable.

3 Why do they need to make this decision now? Management committees are presented with myriad decisions; business continuity and resilience is competing with a wide range of other issues.

4 What benefits will be delivered to the organization and wider stakeholders? These need to be specific and ideally measurable so that future reports to senior management can show whether the benefits of the investment have been achieved.

5 How will it be delivered? What are the resource needs, timeline and expected disruption to the business (if any)? Be clear and realistic about the resources and effort needed to implement the recommendations made. An unrealistic plan will undermine the confidence of management.

BE CLEAR ON WHAT YOU ARE ASKING

Don't make the executive or board work for it. They need to understand the issue and the recommendation being made within the first 30 seconds of the briefing.

Making the business case stand out

An executive or board committee receives hundreds of papers and pieces of information and is expected to make big decisions, sometimes with limited background knowledge. The practitioner's role is to arm senior management with just enough information to make informed and accurate decisions, without taking up too much of their time.

This means having a laser focus on the benefits of business continuity and resilience. Many, however, make the mistake of assuming that generic statements suggesting a more efficient or faster response to a disruption can be achieved with the investment being requested. This rarely works as it provides few tangible details.

Instead, benefits need to be easily understood and quantifiable, using real practical examples wherever that is possible. The role of the practitioner is to show how business continuity and resilience can influence the overall cost of risk to the business. In this case, money talks.

This means being clear on the key disruption risks the organization is currently exposed to and using statistics to frame the discussion. The analysis does not have to be hugely scientific – the trick is to provide just enough to convince senior management that action should be taken.

Often much of the data needed to develop a paper is readily available from other teams. For example:

- **Maximum and estimated loss** data is likely to be held by the insurance team and is a useful means to understand the value and potential business disruption impacts of key assets and premises.

- **Revenue figures** held by finance and **customer retention/sales** data held by marketing will be helpful in showing a link between critical assets and financial impacts.

- **Capital risk provisioning** data can be helpful in showing how business continuity and resilience controls can have a significant impact on the amount of capital a business needs to hold to provision for its key risks.

These data sources will help the business continuity or resilience manager to speak the committee's language and make it easier to get their attention and support for the investments needed.

A data-driven approach can also have benefits in improved integration between business continuity and risk transfer solutions, such as insurance. For example:

- Factory A's outputs support $20 million of revenue per month for an organization.

- The organization's business continuity plan is capable of moving 65 per cent of the factory's normal output to two other locations.

- This leaves a net risk exposure of $7 million a month.

In this basic example, management may then decide that the coverage provided by their business interruption insurance policy could be reduced to the 35 per cent of revenue that is left unmitigated. This would make their insurance spend cheaper and, crucially for the resilience practitioner, position the business continuity plan as an important management tool to manage risk exposures and financial risk. The more that resilience practitioners can collaborate with other teams like insurance and risk management, the more effective their discussions at the senior level will become.

Sustaining their interest

Getting senior management attention is the first step. Maintaining it in the face of many conflicting and seemingly more important issues surfacing can be a real challenge.

Maintaining a board or executive team's support and interest relies upon five enablers:

1 a credible, professional and competent business continuity and resilience manager;

2 good-quality, relevant and timely management information;

3 benchmarking against peers and competitors;

4 proof (through objective and measurable evidence) of benefits being realized;

5 a senior management sponsor.

Earlier chapters cover some of the characteristics of what makes a good business continuity and resilience manager, so this section will start at point 2 on the list.

Good-quality, relevant and timely management information

There is a big difference between management information that concentrates on tracking programme delivery milestones or compliance, and more insightful reporting that provides management with an indication of whether the benefits of business continuity and resilience are being realized.

In general, good management information will provide a bit of both, but too often many examples focus on reporting on what is easier to measure, rather than on what should be measured. Generally speaking it is easier to measure the completion of processes or compliance with a standard or a guideline than it is to measure benefits or outcomes. So if your management information concentrates on reporting the number of business continuity plans completed, or exercises delivered, it is likely it is not providing the data that executive teams and boards really want to see, or need, in order to make key decisions.

Examples of good management information would include:

- the current level of disruption risk that the business is exposed to – if possible, expressed in tangible terms such as revenue at risk;
- measures of how effective a response or recovery was following a real incident – for example, whether recovery time objectives were met.

Benchmarking

HOW DO I COMPARE WITH MY PEERS?

It is a common question raised by senior management when presenting a new idea, or investment request. Benchmarking is much more than a gimmick of the management consultant. Delivered correctly, it helps an organization to implement best practice as demonstrated by its peers and competitors. It can be a useful tool for the business continuity and resilience professional to employ, as a means to justify an approach that is being taken or to persuade decision-makers the organization is falling behind others.

Benchmarking gives management an opportunity to understand whether the decisions they are being asked to take will bring them in line with other organizations, or push them out in front. For some, being a trailblazer is not a key motivation – they just do not want to be left behind. For others, they want to lead, and benchmarking affords them an opportunity to test whether they actually are.

Choosing the right organizations to benchmark against is important. Financial services organizations are likely to be only interested in understanding what other banking organizations are doing. They would be less interested in how a manufacturing business tackles resilience.

The types of organization that will be appropriate to benchmark against will vary for a variety of reasons:

- based on industry, as in the financial institutions example used above;

- as a result of fierce competition, where one organization is keen not to fall behind another rival;

- as a result of a senior manager's personal interests and relationships – they might have a preferred list of organizations they like to be benchmarked against.

The circumstances in which benchmarking can be a useful tool include:

- when an investment is needed, as a means to check if other organizations have delivered anything similar;

- during a crisis response, to quickly establish how other organizations are planning to respond or are responding;

- to help build an argument to change a regulation or regulatory rule – a group of organizations making a case for change will likely be more effective than a single voice.

Proof that benefits are being realized

Evidence of benefits realization will only really be needed in papers providing an update on the progress being made to implement enhanced resilience. Objective facts providing evidence of benefits being realized will be essential. They will need to be accurate, relevant and reliable if they are to provide any meaningful evidence of progress.

Proof should fall into two categories:

1 **Milestones:** evidence that key deliverables have been implemented. Information presented could include a summary of the business continuity programme plan showing the milestones completed and those that are outstanding, or statistics on the number of plans that have been implemented since the last update and how many teams and individuals have been trained. An executive will be unlikely to spend a significant amount of time scrutinizing this element of the report unless delivery has been delayed, in which case they may be interested in understanding why.

2 **Capability:** evidence that resilience has increased. These metrics are much harder to define and are subject to further analysis in Chapter 14. As a summary, evidence could include the outputs from recent crisis exercises or a quantification exercise to determine the organization's actual current exposure to disruption risk (defined in terms of revenue at risk or reputation).

Senior management sponsor

This chapter started with a suggestion that without senior management buy-in to business continuity and resilience, the programme would likely fail. Part of obtaining that buy-in requires having a strong advocate who can sponsor the programme at an executive and, if necessary, board level.

The sponsor performs a crucial role:

- They give legitimacy to the programme.
- They sponsor agenda and committee papers to give the programme sufficient management time.
- They champion the programme by encouraging senior management peers to take it seriously and provide staff to perform the role that is expected of them in the policy.

Most business continuity and resilience practitioners do not have a choice as to who their sponsor is. However, building a good relationship with this individual is critical. Ultimately, any one of the executive team can be a very effective sponsor. This author has seen a wide range of individuals in the role, from company secretaries to COOs, CTOs, CFOs and CROs. The better sponsors are those with a detailed understanding of how the business works, the risks it faces, and who have the trust of staff and their executive colleagues. In other words, they can get things done.

Dealing with difficult senior stakeholders

No amount of preparation will completely remove the risk of being confronted by a difficult stakeholder in an executive or board meeting.

Being asked a difficult question or receiving criticism in an open forum like an executive committee or board can create enormous anxiety. The first step to dealing with this is to accept it will happen at some point in the process of implementing business continuity. Once the inevitable has been accepted, attention can be spent working out strategies for either preventing these situations from occurring every time, or dealing with them in a professional way when they do.

On the preparation side, the guidance about understanding stakeholders set out above will help. Spending time understanding the needs and interests of different stakeholders and planning the pitch is the best means of preventing a difficult confrontation. Having a supportive executive or board sponsor will also help to deflect difficult questions and even defend the project if needed.

But let's assume all this preparation amounts to nothing. The pitch has been delivered, and it is immediately clear an individual is not happy. What is the best way of responding to the challenge?

First, it is important to avoid becoming defensive; even if the individual has been rude, it is better to remain calm and professional in responding. A challenging situation like this can easily escalate, and without fully understanding the motivations behind the intervention, it is possible that their criticism is a valid one.

A good coping strategy is to recognize that the criticism, if there has been one, is unlikely to be a personal attack. Rather, there will be another reason – perhaps the individual has had a previous poor experience with business continuity, or this is their usual style in meetings, or they have had a bad meeting. The point is, it is dangerous at this stage to try to second-guess the reasons for their challenge – there are too many variables.

This leads us to the second step. Listen. By actively listening to their intervention and by welcoming it as an opportunity to learn and improve, it is possible to pacify the challenge by demonstrating that their point has been heard and is being considered. However, unless there is an obvious solution, it is important not to rush to agree a solution to the issue that has been raised. Most individuals are unlikely to make rational and informed decisions in such a pressured, potentially highly emotional environment, particularly if it is their first experience of presenting at this level.

Third, throughout the conversation a balance should be struck between showing humility in responding to valid criticism on the one hand and providing robust challenge on the other. This is a difficult balance to strike in some situations, but the use of questions directed back to the challenger can be a useful strategy to employ here. Asked in the right way, questions can be used to focus the challenger's energy towards helping to find a solution. The benefit of doing this is that when the individual actively helps to identify the solution to the issue they themselves originally raised, it becomes much harder for them to continue their criticism (particularly if that solution still falls short of their original demands).

Questions could include:

- Do you have any views on how we might be able to address that issue?

- Do you have any advice on how we could overcome that problem?

- Can you help me to understand how to achieve that?

Finally, be prepared to come back to the committee to make a further presentation if the issue could not be addressed in the meeting.

This should not be seen as a sign of failure. While it is not an ideal outcome, a worse result would be to rush into agreeing a solution that later transpires as being inappropriate or unworkable. Taking time to develop the solution is best for everyone; it maintains the professional reputation of the person delivering the message and ensures the organization gets the best outcome that can be achieved. In taking this approach, it is often useful to gather feedback from other members of the committee and views on the solution that will be presented at their next meeting. This step will help ensure the solution is a best fit for all stakeholders around the table and it also builds support for the next meeting.

TABLE 8.1   Chapter checklist

☐	Identify the different needs of executive- and board-level stakeholders.
☐	Determine how the organization's context and environment might influence the focus of senior management.
☐	Prepare a compelling business case that meets the requirements of all senior stakeholders.
☐	Secure the support of an executive sponsor.
☐	Use the sponsor to 'road test' executive and board papers to ensure they hit the mark.
☐	Be prepared to deal with difficult senior stakeholders.
☐	Get feedback after each executive or board interaction.

Note

1 IOD (2018) Factsheets: what is the role of the board? 25 September, https://www.iod.com/services/information-and-advice/resources-and-factsheets/details/What-is-the-role-of-the-board (archived at https://perma.cc/3HTL-KPNX)

09

Developing the governance and implementing resources

Good governance matters. Without a system to direct and control the delivery of activities, our organizations would be run by an unruly rabble with each of us driving towards our own personal objectives and subsequently pulling in different directions. There would be limited coordination or collaboration to achieve a common purpose.

While such a dystopian vision might be a little over the top, the point here is that to sustain a high-quality business continuity management capability, strong governance is absolutely essential. Without good governance, it might still be possible to deliver a business impact analysis, write a plan or run an exercise, but it would be hard to make the capability 'stick'. Once key milestones have been delivered, the focus would invariably turn to the next priority, plans would lay unread and teams would be poorly prepared.

Governance is defined in the British Standard BS 13500 (Governance) as 'the system by which the whole organization is directed, controlled and held accountable to achieve its core purpose over the long term'.[1]

When applied to business continuity, this means building a programme of activities that are supported by:

1 leadership and management commitment to drive delivery of business continuity;

2 policy documentation that sets the requirements for business continuity;

3 a defined set of roles and responsibilities to achieve the programme's objcctives.

These components of a healthy governance regime will need to be supported by management committees to provide oversight and challenge for delivery and a performance management regime to monitor the health of the overall system. In addition, good governance goes hand in hand with the resources needed for implementation. A combination of strong and effective governance and competent resources to oversee delivery will be needed together to deliver an effective resilience capability.

The exact nature of an organization's governance regime and resource needs will vary, but they share many common characteristics. This chapter sets out some of the common components that will make a strong governance regime, along with considerations for how to secure and maintain the right mix of competent resources needed for delivery.

What does good governance look like?

Before addressing this question it is important to differentiate between management and governance:

- **Management** can be defined as getting the job done.
- **Governance** is about making sure the job is done right.

So governance is about direction control and continuous improvement. This simple differentiation means there should be a clear difference between the individuals who are tasked with setting direction and those who are delivering. In very small organizations the differentiation can be hard to achieve, but larger organizations typically use what is known as a 'three lines of defence' model as a means to set out a clear delineation of responsibilities for the management of risk, in this case disruption risk.

The three lines of defence can be summarized as shown in Figure 9.1.

FIGURE 9.1   Summary of the three lines of defence model

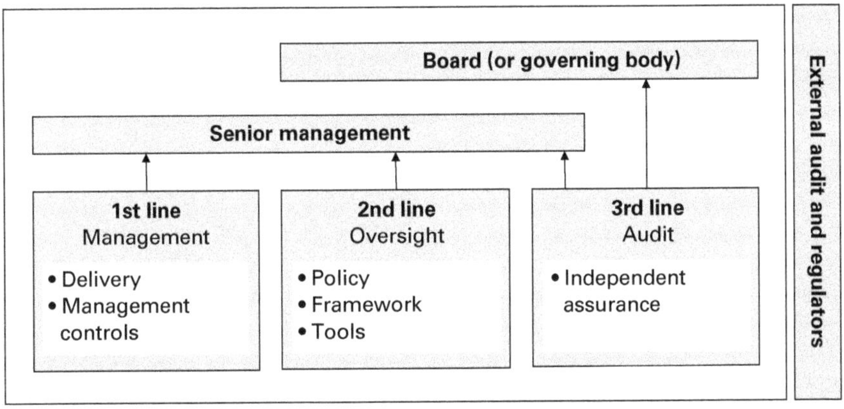

SOURCE Adapted from ICAS[2]

In the context of business continuity, the three lines of defence model can be expressed as shown in Table 9.1.

TABLE 9.1   Three lines of defence model

	Summary of role	Business continuity activities
First line: Management	**Delivery:** Maintain management control over local operational risks.	• Undertake the business impact analysis. • Prepare recovery plans. • Ensure teams are trained and exercises have taken place. • Ensure recovery arrangements are kept up to date and reflect the needs of the business. • Identify, assess and report any disruption risks of concern. • Deliver the operational response to a disruption.
Second line: Oversight	**Direction:** Set direction and requirements and monitor for compliance.	• Set the policy for business continuity. • Prepare a framework for business continuity to set methods to follow and to provide guidance to delivery teams. • Monitor compliance of first-line teams against policy requirements. • Implement tools, including plan templates, to help improve the quality, efficiency and consistency of delivery.

TABLE 9.1   *continued*

	Summary of role	Business continuity activities
		• Ensure the policy and framework are aligned with the latest good practice.
		• Support the consolidation of the business impact analysis data to help inform any enterprise-wide recovery strategy and options development needed.
		• Ensure that disruption risks reported from the first line, or where an aggregated exposure exists, are appropriately reported.
Third line: Audit	**Assurance:** Provide independent assurance over the effectiveness of internal systems of control.	• Deliver periodic independent audits of the organization's business continuity management controls. • Conduct a mix of business unit, site and enterprise-wide audits. • Report any findings to the board, or audit committee. • Ensure that any improvement actions agreed are tracked through to delivery.

While the three lines of defence model is a good way of differentiating between the responsibilities of different teams, it does not specify the exact structures that will be needed to ensure delivery. These will need to be tailored for each organization, and to a certain degree will need to fit in with already established governance regimes.

The following four principles can be used to help determine what and how much governance will be needed:

1 **A senior management authority or committee** in the second line should provide oversight of business continuity performance and for any disruption risks material to the enterprise as a whole.

Committees could be dedicated in their focus to business continuity, or the responsibility might fall to another existing governance structure (for example a risk management committee). It is common to find dedicated steering committees in organizations that are in the early stages of implementing business continuity; in these examples, a dedicated programme or project committee is a useful means to drive progress. In organizations with more mature business continuity arrangements, or with already mature risk management governance structures, the topic may form part of an existing committee's terms of reference.

The more business continuity can be integrated into an organization's broader approach to managing enterprise risk, the better the outcome is likely to be. A committee structure that covers both business continuity and other operational and strategic risk issues will provide a useful mechanism to explore the relationships between risks and the controls in place to manage them. The ultimate benefit here is the possibility of achieving an improved and more informed balance between the investments made on risk prevention versus recovery.

2 **The management of disruption risks** should be delegated to a level where sufficient knowledge is held about their causes and impacts, and the appropriate resources are in place to manage them.

The size and complexity of the business will determine how much resource might be needed to undertake this activity. In larger organizations it is common to find business continuity coordinators sitting in the first line of defence who are tasked with ensuring planning takes place within their department, function or the site they are responsible for. In smaller organizations this role is unlikely to exist and the task is likely to form part of someone's wider role.

3 **An individual or team** sitting in the second line should be made responsible for preparing the policy, framework documentation and developing tools needed by first-line teams to deliver business continuity arrangements.

The size of this team will be dictated by the complexity and scale of the organization; it could be a part-time role for a single individual, or a substantial team staffed with dedicated specialists. And in smaller organizations this might not be needed, relying instead on accessing templates and tools that can be sourced externally. It will be important to ensure that this team maintains some level of independence from the staff responsible for delivery in the first line. For a seasoned business continuity expert who has been used to rolling up their sleeves and getting involved in planning, this can be hard to achieve. However, if a true three lines of defence model is to be used, it will be important for this not to happen as management need to be encouraged to own and address the disruption risks in their areas themselves.

4 **Proportionately speaking, more time should be spent delivering rather than checking.**

Providing oversight and the delivery of reviews and audits are important components of a healthy governance regime. However, the focus of activity should always be skewed towards delivery. First-line delivery teams that are bombarded with requests for progress reports to second-line teams, or that are the subject of multiple audits, will become overburdened. The danger here is that these governance processes and compliance activities, however well intentioned, could become the focus of the programme and resilience will suffer. There is a distinction to be made here between actively managing disruption risk and managing the process of risk management.

Challenges to implementing a three lines of defence model

The three lines of defence model is not without its critics. Some say it overly simplifies what is a highly complex system of overlapping risk management responsibilities and has led to a lack of clarity over exactly who is accountable for the management of certain types of risk. This confusion can lead to a half-hearted attempt at implementing the model, where the principles may be followed and the physical governance structures implemented, but the actual management of risk takes place outside the boundaries of the system. Staff essentially play along with the idea that the structure is being used, making the right noises to senior management and dutifully filling in their reports even if they have no belief in their contents.

It is hard to argue against some of these criticisms, especially when considering how organizations have changed since the model first gained traction. With the expansion of a multiplicity of specialist risk management roles covering a range of specialisms such as IT, finance, people and supply chain, the picture has become murkier.

So what are the signs that the model may not be working (see Table 9.2)?

TABLE 9.2   Warning signs of weaknesses in the three lines of defence

Traits	Visible symptoms
1 **Lack of clarity over who does what**	• Teams and individuals are not clear on their responsibilities and how these differ from their colleagues. • Evidence of overlapping roles, especially where management have created their own oversight functions in the first line, repeating what should be done, or is already in place, in the second line.
2 **Disconnect between policy, guidance and actual action**	• The activities that staff deliver do not reflect what is set out in the organization's policies and guidance. • Role and job descriptions do not include any (or limited) references to responsibilities defined by the three lines of defence model.
3 **Lack of alignment on how risks are managed across the organization**	• There is limited interaction between specialist risk management disciplines resulting in overlaps and gaps in how risks are being managed. • Competing risk management policies, and even risk appetite statements, are evident throughout the organization. • There is a general reluctance of specialist risk management teams to consider change or new, more collaborative ways of working.
4 **Repeated failures are experienced and there is evidence of gaps being left unaddressed**	• Multiple audits find similar issues in the way risk is being managed, but limited coordinated action is taken to address them. • There is a lack of sharing of knowledge and learning following near-misses and actual events. • Where action is taken, second-line teams deliver the bulk of the heavy lifting on behalf of first-line teams.

Overcoming governance challenges with the business impact analysis

Business continuity provides some helpful tools that will help address some of the challenges referenced above. The most significant of these is the business impact analysis itself.

By identifying critical processes and activities along an organization's value chain, including the resources they are dependent upon for delivery, the business impact analysis can be used to build a blueprint for where disruption risks are likely to materialize and who should be ultimately responsible for addressing them.

Processes, activities and corporate resources will all have an ultimate owner. By working through a business impact analysis it is possible to clearly and quickly identify who these owners are and begin to build a response to the following three questions:

- What is their role and how does it relate to the organization's broader objectives and purpose?

- What would the impacts be to the business if the processes and activities they are responsible for were disrupted?

- What risks could materialize that would result in a business disruption?

The answers to these questions can help to clarify where first-line responsibilities for business continuity activity should rest.

The same questions can be used with the owners of corporate resources such as finance and HR to help establish where the line is drawn between first- and second-line activities. The only difference with these corporate resources is that many of their activities will be delivering services to other first-line teams, for example property, procurement or technology teams. If confusion persists in the breakdown of responsibilities between first- and second-line teams, it is likely to be most acutely felt in the teams that look after these resources, particularly in medium and smaller-sized organizations where individuals might be performing multiple roles.

In these smaller organizations it is possible to find a team delivering a corporate resource dependency involving both second-line and first-line responsibilities. For example, a property team might be responsible for a second-line policy covering physical security, at the same time as implementing it at the organization's premises. Technically speaking, this mixing of first- and second-line roles should not happen for purists of the three lines of defence model. However, in some settings, perhaps where staff resources are constrained, it cannot be avoided. The business impact analysis can be useful here too. The identification of critical processes and activities and an assessment of their impact on the organization should they be disrupted will help to weed out less immediately important activities. Returning to the property team example again, the analysis should differentiate the team's critical first-line responsibilities (in this case, maintaining security) from its less time-critical second-line activities (policy writing).

If doubt remains about where first- and second-line responsibilities rest, the following test can be helpful. A yes to any of the questions below might point to a first-line team responsibility:

1 Does the team manage the staff responsible for delivering the critical process?

2 Does the team manage the budget that funds the salaries and other associated costs related to the delivery of the process?

3 Does this team have the necessary knowledge and authority to prevent disruption risks before they materialize?

4 If a disruption risk were to materialize, would this team be the one that is first to know and/or respond to it?

Differences between project and business-as-usual governance

The governance arrangements needed to support the initial implementation of business continuity and resilience arrangements will look slightly different from the enduring structures that will be needed to manage business as usual.

During the implementation phase, a project-based approach to governance can be helpful, involving a project working group and a project steering group (see Table 9.3).

TABLE 9.3   Delivery governance structures

	Summary of role	Expected membership
Working group	• Oversee the preparation of project deliverables. • Report project progress, risks and issues associated with delivery to the steering group. • Track benefits realization.	Staff actively engaged in delivery of project outcomes. Usually chaired by the business continuity manager.
Steering group	• Approve project planning and resource budgets. • Coordinate project delivery activities. • Approve key milestones, including business continuity deliverables. • Resolve risks and issues reported to the steering group.	Senior project sponsor and ultimate accountable owners of business continuity deliverables. Usually chaired by the project sponsor.

Once the initial project has delivered its objectives and business continuity moves into business as usual, the working group and steering group will be disbanded and replaced with either existing forms of governance, or something bespoke to business continuity and resilience. This could include a dedicated permanent committee focused on business continuity risks, or form part of an existing governance committee focused on the management of other forms of operational risk.

How a crisis affects organizational governance

During a crisis strange things happen to an organization's governance structures. In normal periods of operation, decisions to secure budgets, adjust a strategy or alter the course of a business plan might take many months, sometimes even years, to agree. But during a crisis the decision cycle rapidly speeds up. The need for this is clear in that rapid but effective decision-making is needed to contain a crisis and begin to recover from it. Any delays will likely mean more damage, additional costs and a bigger reputational issue to fix in the longer term.

One reason why it is possible for the decision-making cycle to speed up is down to what happens to an organization's normal governance structures in a crisis. In a crisis, layers of governance seemingly evaporate and the gap between strategic decision-makers and operational staff narrows. This allows information and issues to flow more quickly between operational, tactical and strategic response teams, allowing more rapid decisions to be made. Under normal circumstances a decision to implement a new type of technology could be subject to business cases, departmental reviews and sign-offs, change management boards, investment committees, reviews from risk management teams, perhaps even an independent audit, before reaching the executive committee for approval. In a crisis, however, and if the requirement is strong enough, a similar decision could be escalated from operational technology teams to the crisis management team in a single day.

This rapidity of decision-making during a crisis has clear benefits, but it also presents some risks too. Most governance structures exist to help organizations make better decisions. Stripping away the checks and balances these governance arrangements provide during normal operating conditions in a crisis could lead to the potential for poor decisions being made.

These risks are driven by:

- limitations in the availability of quality information to underpin the decision process in a crisis;
- the limited degree of challenge and diversity of input provided prior to the decision being made;
- the pressure to make rapid decisions and the stresses that individuals will be under.

There are some steps that can be taken to help minimize these risks:

- Plans and procedures should clearly set out the decision hierarchy.
- Delegations of authority, especially where these may deviate from normal arrangements, should be pre-agreed and documented.
- Response team members should hold the appropriate competencies for their role.

- Additional input should be called upon if issues arise that fall outsided the response team's expertise.

- Avoid making decisions that are not core to the organization's response to the crisis. For example, investments in building a new data centre or headquarters location, while spurred on by the crisis, should be subject to normal governance oversight and control.

- All decisions and actions should be recorded along with a clear rationale for why they were made.

- Seek to return to normal governance arrangements as soon as possible once the acute impacts from a crisis or disruption have been managed.

Some of the effects a crisis has on an organization's governance will be beneficial in the long term and may even help to improve the organization's future speed of decision-making. It will therefore be important for any debrief to capture the opportunities to continue doing things in a different way that may benefit the organization in the longer term. Such changes will need a substantial amount of input from company secretaries and internal audit teams who can advise on any unintended governance and risk consequences of the improvements being proposed.

Components of an effective governance regime

As set out earlier in this chapter, ISO 22301 describes three main components of a good governance regime for business continuity:

1 **leadership and management commitment** to drive delivery of business continuity;

2 **policy** documentation that sets the requirements for business continuity;

3 **defined set of roles and responsibilities** to achieve the programme's objectives.

We will take each of these components in turn.

Leadership and management commitment

Good governance starts with strong and positive leadership and a commitment from management that drives delivery. Without this, a business continuity and resilience programme will stall.

In practice this means leaders should:

- endorse a policy for business continuity and actively champion its implementation;
- make time at key senior management meetings to discuss resilience risks and business continuity deliverables;
- provide challenge when performance dips below expectations, and support to teams in addressing any underlying issues;
- make sure there is sufficient investment behind the recruitment of suitably competent resources to deliver the programme;
- actively participate in training and exercises to help validate plans;
- support communication initiatives to reinforce the importance of business continuity and resilience;
- create an environment where continual improvement is encouraged.

Leaders will be ultimately accountable to their shareholders, trustees (in a charity) or elected officials (in public sector organizations). This accountability is enforced by the organization's governing body, usually a board of directors, who will have a keen interest in protecting the long-term interests of the organization's stakeholders. The governing body should encourage the behaviours it expects to see from staff in the pursuit of the organization's stakeholder interests. This is where direction on resilience will originate from and so it is important for practitioners to understand how this will influence the organization's approach to resilience. Any substantial problems exhibited in the behaviours of the organization's leaders or its governing body will be difficult, if not impossible, for a business continuity practitioner to remedy themselves.

Leaders also have a role to play in making sure the organization does not underinvest in its approach to business continuity. It is common for business continuity to be considered by some as an unnecessary distraction from daily business and to pass key roles to staff who may be too junior or lack sufficient knowledge of the business to drive the process. This can be particularly apparent in first-line teams where the role of maintaining a business continuity plan can often be passed to a junior member of the team who receives little by way of support from local management.

The result can be a plan and a recovery capability that is unlikely to work, either because it has been prepared without a full understanding of the team or because staff are simply not engaged, to the extent that they are not aware of what their roles would be in a disruption. In these situations, leaders should put a stop to this behaviour and make local management more accountable for the quality of resilience arrangements in their areas of the organization.

Policy

Policies provide a means through which an organization's leaders can set requirements for the way things are done. A strong policy will set direction and drive consistency in the approach to delivery – both critically important for business continuity. However, a policy will only be as good as the strength of an organization's culture for accountability. Put simply, where staff fail to assume accountability and responsibility for their actions, no policy, however well drafted, will lead to positive change.

As practitioners it can be frustrating having worked with leaders to define and then implement a policy to find that nothing changes, staff carry on as they were before and the document has no material impact on the way things are done. If this happens, it could be a sign of one of two things:

1 The policy could be poorly worded, creating ambiguity and a lack of clarity over what expectations are being set – an issue that is relatively easy to address.

2 There is a more significant governance issue at play caused by poor leadership, resulting in a lack of a culture of accountability or clarity of differentiation between roles – an issue that is much harder to fix.

TABLE 9.4   Characteristics of a good policy

Format	• It should be short and to the point, making it a quick read and easy to understand. • It should be readily accessible by all staff that need access to it. • It should be translated into local languages where an organization has operations overseas.
Contents	• Its contents should be mutually exclusive and collectively exhaustive. • Define management's top-level intent and direction for business continuity. • Define the scope of business continuity, specifically referencing any areas of the organization that are deemed out of scope. • Identify the authorities responsible for implementing the policy requirements, and assign any delegations as necessary. • Set measurable objectives for business continuity and any principles that should be followed in delivering recovery arrangements. • Set out processes that must be followed to deliver a business continuity capability, including committing to a requirement of continual improvement. • Reference relevant standards, regulations, laws or other existing organizational policies that apply to the organization. • Provide document and version-control mechanisms.

Focusing on the first cause, as this is within the power of a practitioner to address, what constitutes a good policy?

The answer can be split between policy contents and format (see Table 9.4).

Following its completion, the policy will need to be communicated to staff, paying particular attention to colleagues who play a crucial role in implementing business continuity. The physical act of communicating the policy will be easy to achieve, perhaps involving an announcement from the senior sponsor, an update on a staff intranet page or a posting to a physical display board. However, communicating the policy does not mean staff will necessarily understand it, or know what to do with it. Therefore, some level of awareness-raising will be needed so that staff with a role in implementing aspects of the policy are trained in the requirements it places upon them. Further details about training can be found in Chapter 12.

Defined set of roles and responsibilities

Roles and responsibilities will need to be defined throughout the organization to ensure business continuity and resilience arrangements are implemented, monitored and maintained. The number of roles required will be dependent upon the size of the organization, with larger organizations likely to have a dedicated business continuity or resilience manager and a substantial team supporting them. In smaller organizations these dedicated specialist roles are less common as a result of cost constraints and because the scale of the organization does not warrant them.

The requirements for business continuity and resilience roles should be set by leadership. This should include clearly defined delegations of authority covering both the planning process in preparation for a disruption and the respose to a disruptive event should one occur.

Roles should differentiate between the staff who are:

- setting the requirements for business continuity and resilience, through a policy;
- raising awareness of business continuity and providing training to staff to allow them to deliver their roles;
- monitoring compliance against the organization's policy and any external regulation or guidance of relevance;
- implementing and maintaining business continuity procedures;
- monitoring the performance of business continuity arrangements against the organization's policy and any external regulation or guidance of relevance;
- supporting the response to and recovery from a disruptive incident following the invocation of the organization's business continuity plans.

Some individuals will hold multiple roles from the list above, for example a business continuity manager, while others will be limited to delivering a narrower set of responsibilities. Roles should be carefully distributed to avoid any possibility of the blurring of responsibilities between the three lines of defence.

Tables 9.5–9.9 provide a summary of roles, exploring both the pre-event planning and post-event recovery responsibilities for each.

TABLE 9.5   Leadership

Pre-event planning	Post-event response
• Set the expectations for business continuity and the behaviours expected from staff. • Provide direction and oversight for delivery activities. • Ensure that business continuity deliverables keep the organization within its accepted tolerance levels for disruption risk.	• Take a leadership role in coordinating the response to a disruption or crisis. • Act as the voice of the organization when speaking with staff, external stakeholders and the media.

TABLE 9.6   Business continuity manager

Pre-event planning	Post-event response
• Be responsible for business continuity. • Lead the business continuity programme and coordinate activities across the organization. • Prepare policy and framework documentation and ensure appropriate tools are available to staff to implement business continuity. • Provide regular reports to leadership on progress, current exposure levels of disruption risks and areas that need further improvement. • Support the preparation of business cases for investment to improve the organization's resilience. • Build and manage a network of competent individuals to support the delivery of business continuity.	Some organizations may choose for the business continuity manager to play an active role in facilitating a response to a disruption or crisis; in others they may play a more supportive role. The role could therefore cover: • provision of advice and support to management as they respond to the disruption or crisis; • active facilitation of response teams and response discussions to ensure the effective recovery of the organization; • delivery of a post-incident review and the collation of lessons learned.

TABLE 9.7   Business continuity team

Pre-event planning	Post-event response
• Implementation of business continuity arrangements across the organization.	• Support to response teams.

TABLE 9.8   Functional or departmental management

Pre-event planning	Post-event response
• Undertake or participate in the business impact analysis.	• Execute the business continuity plan.
• Maintain business continuity plans covering their areas of responsibility.	• Perform an assessment of the impacts of a disruption or crisis on their area of the organization.
• Provide regular reports to the business continuity manager and leadership on the performance of arrangements in their areas.	• Trigger recovery solutions. • Report response and recovery progress to the business continuity manager and/ or leadership.
• Ensure that recovery strategies and solutions for all critical resource dependencies are in place and are working effectively.	• Provide input into any post-incident debriefs and reviews.
• Ensure that staff in their areas are fully trained and actively participate in exercises to validate the team's plans.	
• Respond to management reviews, audits and the outputs from exercises and live incidents to improve business continuity.	
• Keep business continuity plans and their associated recovery solutions up to date.	

TABLE 9.9   Other risk management disciplines (enterprise risk, cyber-risk, supply chain risk)

Pre-event planning	Post-event response
• Participate in the business continuity planning process to deliver recovery arrangements for the critical processes and activities managed by their function. • Take outputs from the business impact analysis where risks have been identified that relate to their area of responsibility. • Provide specialist risk advice to the business continuity team when developing specific scenario-driven response plans and exercises.	• Provide expert input and advice to response teams as required.

Maintaining competent resources

Some business continuity and resilience roles require a greater degree of competence and expertise than others to perform. Staff who would be expected to work from home following a disruption and delivering their normal duties are likely not to require a significant degree of knowledge about business continuity when compared with the business continuity manager and team itself.

Competence requirements are relative to the role the individual is performing. Structured mechanisms to ensure competent resources are in charge of key business continuity roles will be needed. This should be supported by a training programme to maintain the knowledge and skills necessary for delivery. The design and delivery of a training needs analysis as a tool to inform an organization's training needs is covered in Chapter 12.

Competency in the context of business continuity management and resilience is captured by three themes:

1 mastery of the process;

2 understanding of the business;

3 capability to respond.

Mastery of the process

Individuals with a sound knowledge of business continuity will be needed to perform the roles involved in directing the programme. Ideally these individuals will bring:

- practical implementation experience from similar organizations or industries;
- a level of knowledge and experience relative to the seniority of the role and complexity of the organization;
- a broader understanding of business management processes, modern corporate governance and risk management regimes.

Understanding of the business

Staff tasked with implementing business continuity plans and procedures will need to hold a good understanding of the business. These individuals will require:

- knowledge of the organization's purpose, objectives and current business plan and longer-term goals;
- a detailed understanding of processes, activities and resource dependencies required to support business-as-usual delivery activities and how these contribute to the organization's objectives;
- an understanding of the organization's key external stakeholders and their interest in resilience;
- knowledge of the main disruption risks the organization, or their component of it, is exposed to.

Capability to respond

Individuals who support an organization's response to a disruption or crisis will need an appropriate level of competency to carry out their role. These roles will need:

- A suitable level of delegated authority to deliver their role during a disruption – this may mean decision-making authority to commit organizational resources or funding, or indeed to make an operational decision on behalf of leadership (e.g. a building evacuation).

- Direct experience of the risks and issues that are likely to materialize during a disruption and that they will be expected to resolve – this does not mean they must have experience of every possible disruption scenario; instead they should have broad expertise that can be drawn upon to facilitate the response. For example, certain members of the crisis management team will need expertise in handling the media and operational staff may need to know how to isolate gas supplies into a building.

- Detailed knowledge of the business processes, activities, resources and stakeholders that support their area of the organization – this will help to facilitate more rapid and accurate assessments of the impacts of a disruption on business as usual, and will provide the knowledge needed to lead a response and recovery.

In some cases an individual's competency for their role can be quite transient in nature. Without regular practice or a proactive effort to update knowledge so that it continues to reflect the latest best practice, an individual's competency will start to wane. For roles that experience regular practice through their daily activities, the requirement for frequent training will be less. However, every individual will have elements of their role that are delivered on a less frequent basis. In the context of business continuity, it will be response and recovery roles that are more likely to fall into this category. Given the importance of these roles, regular training and practice through exercising will be necessary. The relationship between how often skills are likely to be needed versus the criticality of those skills to support a crisis response and therefore the frequency of training needed is explored in more detail in Chapter 12.

TABLE 9.10   Chapter checklist

☐	Is business continuity being delivered as a new project? This may suggest the need for a project working group and steering group to oversee its delivery.
☐	Identify the extent of any existing governance arrangements already in place. Can these be utilized for business continuity?
☐	Determine whether the three lines of defence model is appropriate for the organization/the business continuity programme, or is indeed already in use.
☐	Identify roles for: • leadership; • business continuity manager (if needed); • business continuity team (if needed); • departmental/functional heads; • heads of other risk management disciplines.
☐	Prepare a policy for business continuity.
☐	Widely communicate the business continuity policy with staff and other stakeholders who need to see it.
☐	Implement mechanisms to build and maintain the competence of staff involved in planning and response.
☐	Ensure that competency requirements are aligned to training programmes.

Notes

1 BSI (2012) BS 13500 Code of practice for delivering effective governance of organizations, British Standards Institute, London
2 Bruce, S (2017) Internal audit: three lines of defence model explained, 6 November, www.icas.com/professional-resources/audit-and-assurance/internal-audit/internal-audit-three-lines-of-defence-model-explained (archived at https://perma.cc/3S6J-EPYK)

10

Delivering the BIA and determining recovery strategies

The business impact analysis (BIA) is defined by ISO 22301 as 'the process of analysing the impact over time of a disruption on the organization'.[1] The BIA provides a structured analysis of an organization's critical activities, their impact on the organization should they become disrupted, along with the resources that are needed to deliver these activities. The BIA is a crucial step towards building effective business continuity plans. Mistakes or shortcuts at this stage will have a significant impact on the quality of the plans developed at a later stage.

The process is used to set recovery time objectives (RTOs) and to define the maximum tolerable period for disruption (MTPD) for critical activities and their resource dependencies. These will then be used to support the development of recovery strategies and solutions and to underpin the development of the recovery plans themselves. The RTOs are an expression of the time by which a critical activity would need to be resumed following a disruption. The MTPD is an expression of the point in time at which the disruption would become unacceptable to the business. The RTO will therefore be a lower number than the MTPD.

In practice, and for the development of the plans themselves, it is the RTO that is the most important number. While the MTPD is a useful point of reference to ensure that recovery strategies and solutions are built to resume operations within an acceptable timeframe, they tend to have less influence on what is actually written into the plans. After all, an organization would not want to wait until the impacts of a disruption had become intolerable before recovering from them.

WORKED EXAMPLE – SHARE TRADING

The activity of making share trades will be of critical importance to an investment bank, which may set a recovery time (RTO) of one hour for the process to be resumed following a disruption.

The MTPD may be 24 hours, which would be the time at which the disruption would cause intolerable impacts on the business.

During the analysis, the bank will also identify the resources it needs to execute this trade, namely an appropriately skilled and licensed trader, trading platforms and other IT systems and physical infrastructure, and information sources needed to inform the transaction.

In this example, all of these resources would need to be available to deliver the activity within one hour of the disruption.

The BIA is of critical importance to the process of developing plans and enhancing an organization's resilience. While it may be tempting to cut this step from the business continuity management process in order to advance on to the development of the recovery plans themselves, the lack of any underpinning analysis will likely render those plans ineffective. Errors made at this stage of the process can damage the organization's overall recovery capability, and so it is critical to ensure the BIA is designed and delivered effectively.

When faced with the significance of the BIA process to the overall programme, the temptation can be to deliver a highly detailed and comprehensive analysis, running multiple data collection interviews and compiling myriad data. Much of this effort can be wasted and in itself harmful to the success of the programme, by either taking too long to deliver, costing too much or disengaging staff from the overall process. The delivery of the BIA needs to balance the need for high-quality, insightful data to inform business continuity plans against the cost and effort required to collect it.

This chapter will explore the basic concepts associated with designing and delivering a BIA. It will also explore the common challenges to delivering a good-quality analysis along with some common pitfalls and how to avoid them.

The BIA process

Top-down or bottom-up?

The first choice facing many practitioners about how to embark upon delivery of the BIA is whether to start at the top of the organization to capture a strategic view of its recovery requirements first, or take a bottom-up approach, where the analysis starts within business departments, functions or sites. This is summarized in Figure 10.1.

Each approach has its own benefits and disadvantages, as described in Table 10.1.

TABLE 10.1   BIA Delivery methods – benefits and disadvantages

	Benefits	Disadvantages
Top–down	✓ Gains rapid buy-in from the executive ✓ Opportunity to explore organization-wide recovery requirements, dependencies and recovery strategies that may not be visible at an operational level ✓ Sets clear parameters for further analysis and planning	✗ Could miss a critical activity or single point of failure that would undermine the effectiveness of plans ✗ Could result in executives assuming a more detailed analysis is not needed and stop the project prematurely
Bottom–up	✓ Provides a comprehensive analysis of recovery requirements ✓ Gives ownership of the analysis and output to the business ✓ Engages the business early in the process, potentially making it easier to implement plans at a later date	✗ Can take too long ✗ Can collect too much superfluous information not needed for planning purposes ✗ Can result in a loss of interest in business continuity from the business ✗ Can miss strategic-level recovery options only visible, or available, at an executive or group level

FIGURE 10.1   A summary of the top-down and bottom-up approach to the BIA

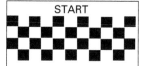

Top–down

START

1. Map the value chain.

2. Meet executives to identify the most critical processes along the value chain.

3. Agree strategic-level recovery options.

4. Identify critical areas of the business requiring a deeper BIA analysis.

Outcomes:

Strategic recovery requirements are identified setting parameters for detailed analysis and planning.

Executive fully engaged in the process.

Bottom–up

Outcomes:

Comprehensive analysis providing a detailed view of recovery needs and strategy options.

5. Communicate the result to aid local-level planning.

4. Seek endorsement for BIA outputs, including recovery strategies.

3. Consolidate data and prepare recovery strategy options.

2. Run questionnaires and interviews across the business.

1. Develop disruption impact scorecard for a consistent analysis.

START

Neither approach is right or perfect. The reality is that a combination of both approaches will be needed in most organizations.

The exact method deployed will be directed by three main factors:

- The **level of buy-in and support** already available from the executive – there may be circumstances where a lack of initial buy-in from leadership would mean a top-down approach would be more beneficial, at least initially, in order to obtain support for the BIA and wider programme.

- The **complexity and size of the business** – less complex businesses with minimal operations and a smaller number of locations and departments would mean a bottom-up approach is likely to be quicker to achieve.

- A **recent internal audit (or similar)** report has been issued setting out clear recommendations on how to address gaps in the organization's resilience arrangements. This may provide enough of the direction and top-level support needed to jump into addressing the issues identified, assuming that the report and associated management actions have already been agreed by leadership.

Prerequisites

Regardless of the approach taken, there are a number of prerequisites that will be needed before a BIA can be delivered successfully.

A senior sponsor and a clear mandate

A senior sponsor will give authority to the process. The senior sponsor should be an individual with sufficient influence at executive level and hold the authority and capability to broker agreements between different departments and teams should any conflict or blockages arise.

The mandate itself could be in the form of a documented executive decision, or an approved project, or business continuity policy that commits the organization to undertaking the process. On occasion the mandate is derived from an external source such as from a regulator placing requirements upon the organization. Ultimately, the BIA process is likely to struggle without a suitable sponsor and mandate.

Capable resources to implement the process

This means an individual or team with a combination of sound business continuity knowledge and a deep understanding of the organization's business operations. The more the resources leading the business continuity process understand the business, the easier the task of implementation will be.

Resource requirements are not limited to the individuals directing the process. Support and input will also be needed from individual departments and teams to complete the analysis. This is because much of the detailed knowledge of the business will be held at an operational level, and the success of the BIA, and the plans that follow, will be influenced by the degree to which the business supports, buys into and owns the process.

A sound methodology

The method used should deliver a comprehensive, systematic and consistent analysis, which ensures sufficient attention is concentrated on the most critical parts of the business. The components of the methodology are discussed in more detail below and summarized in Figure 10.2.

At a summary level the method should provide an assessment of the impacts over time of a disruption to business-critical activities and their resource dependencies. The method used should also provide for a repeatable process that will deliver consistent results wherever it is used across the organization. The rigour, consistency and repeatability of the method will make it much easier to compare recovery needs across the organization and to deliver a more consistent prioritization process.

The importance of consistency in the way the BIA is delivered cannot be overstated. If multiple methods to define criticality and to identify recovery solutions are being used across the organization, there is a greater risk that business continuity plans will deliver a poorly coordinated response. This risk is particularly acute where IT teams conduct their own assessment of the criticality of technology systems in the absence of any input from business users, or in parallel with a wider BIA being undertaken across the organization by another team. A technology-focused BIA run by IT professionals is not wrong and is often preferable, but it is important to make sure that outputs align with what the business considers to be critical. The resulting technology resilience and disaster recovery arrangements could fall short of what the business actually needs, or on the other hand introduce unnecessary cost where a lower level of resilience could have been tolerated by system users.

A governance mechanism

Outputs from the BIA will need to be reported to a governance authority who will act in a decision-making role to approve the results and direct the next phase of planning. For some organizations this will be an existing risk management committee, the executive or senior management team itself, or a dedicated business continuity committee.

Governance arrangements for business continuity are discussed in more detail in Chapter 9. For the BIA the most important measure of an appropriate governance regime will be its ability to provide senior-level endorsement of its outputs and agree upon next steps.

FIGURE 10.2   Summary of the BIA process

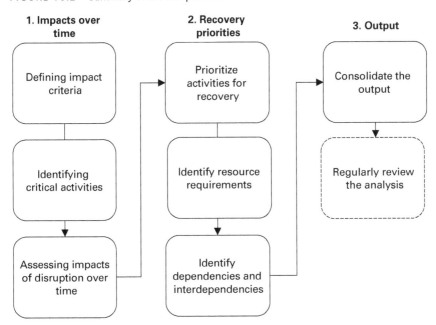

Defining impact criteria

At the heart of BIA is an assessment of the business impacts that would be experienced over time if a critical process or activity is disrupted. To ensure consistency in the analysis and to act as a guide to the business in conducting the assessment, a single business impact scorecard will be needed.

Scorecards can range in style between organizations. The impact categories chosen and the criteria and the thresholds used will be influenced by an organization's context and risk landscape. For example, the criteria used to establish the criticality of activities that support dialysis treatment services in a hospital will look very different when compared with bottling processes at a food manufacturing organization.

Since the BIA impact criteria are an expression of an organization's appetite for disruption risk, the first place to begin the process of designing the scorecard will be to undertake a review of risk registers and hold discussions with the risk team (if there is one). The more the business continuity process feeds from and aligns to the risk impact categories used to inform enterprise-wide risk assessment processes, the easier it will be to encourage the business to perform the assessment. This will also help to ensure recovery plans are comprehensive in their coverage for the sort of impacts of concern to the organization.

Typical impact criteria types include:

- **financial** impacts, such as revenue, sales, operating costs and cash flow, to provide a cost driver to determine recovery priorities;
- **customer delivery** impacts measuring the degradation to, or loss of, services or outcomes to key customers;
- **regulatory** impacts that could result in fines or other forms of legal and regulatory enforcement action;
- **reputation** impacts that seek to measure a potential erosion of trust in the business or brand damage.

An example of an impact criteria matrix is provided below for a fictitious business (Tables 10.2 and 10.3).

TABLE 10.2   Step 1: Defining impact criteria

	Impact criteria			
	Mission-critical	**Major**	**Minor**	**Insignificant**
Financial	$10,000,000 loss of revenue $5,000,000 increase in operating costs	$5,000,000 loss of revenue $1,000,000 increase in operating costs	$250,000 loss of revenue $150,000 increase in operating costs	<$200,000 loss of revenue <$100,000 increase in operating costs
Customer delivery	Customer disruption is catastrophic, resulting in customer attrition and significant liability and reputation issues for the business	Customer disruption is widespread but recoverable with significant effort, or is very significant for a small number of critical customers	Very little impact on customers with a minor degree of effort needed to manage customer dissatisfaction	No noticeable impact on customers
Regulatory	Organization's regulatory licence to operate is threatened	Highly damaging regulatory enforcement against the business	Regulatory enforcement that has a minor impact on the business	Not of concern to regulators
Reputation	Sustained, catastrophic and irrecoverable damage to reputation	Major damage to reputation requiring sustained effort to rebuild trust	Some damage to reputation, perhaps involving exposure in trade media or with a small number of stakeholders	No reputational damage

Listing the critical activities and plotting the impacts of their disruption to the business over time (using the scorecard from Table 10.2) will help to determine the recovery time objective and the maximum tolerable periods of disruption.

In the example in Table 10.3, the recovery time objectives are likely to be three days for Activity 1, one week for Activity 2 and one hour for Activity 3. For this example a recovery is needed before impacts become 'major'.

TABLE 10.3   Step 2: Determining impacts over time

	Impacts over time					
	1 hour	**4 hours**	**1 day**	**3 days**	**1 week**	**1 month**
Activity 1:	Insignificant	Insignificant	Minor	Major	Mission-critical	Mission-critical
Activity 2:	Minor	Minor	Minor	Minor	Major	Major
Activity 3:	Major	Major	Mission-critical	Mission-critical	Mission-critical	Mission-critical

The maximum tolerable period of disruption is likely to be set at the point that impacts become 'mission-critical'. However, the exact threshold set for where to plot the RTO and MTPD will come down to how much appetite the organization may have for a disruption.

There is also a third number that will be needed to support the planning process, particularly by the technology teams who will be implementing disaster recovery arrangements. The recovery point objective (RPO) represents the maximum amount of data that the organization could tolerate losing in the event of a disruption of technology services. This number is important as it will help to set the organization's strategy for technology resilience. In most disruption events some data will be lost owing to the way data back-ups are taken and aggressive RPOs could result in a significant amount of additional cost in implementing technology resilience arrangements. The RPO is measured from the point at which the last back-up was taken, to the time of the incident occurring.

As an example, an RPO of 48 hours would suggest the organization is able to tolerate up to 48 hours of lost data in the event of a disruption. This might mean data back-ups are taken every 48 hours. However, should the RPO requirement be set at one hour, and in order to reduce the risk of data loss, the frequency of data back-ups would need to increase. The RPO must also be considered in the context of any wider technology resilience arrangements, for example in the use of mirrored data centres or cloud-based services that copy data in real time to increase the redundancy available to the organization.

Identifying critical activities

But what is a critical activity? Critical will mean something slightly different for everyone consulted during a BIA process. There is a danger here that the BIA analysis, in the absence of a sufficient degree of robust challenge of its outputs, results in a very long list of activities that would make planning and the actual recovery process difficult to achieve.

The answer to this is in executing a well-thought-through prioritization process. Business continuity plans are rarely used when an organization is operating normally. Instead, plans are designed for use during a disruption to help an organization prioritize those areas of the organization that are essential to protect value. This means that not every activity will need to be recovered urgently, as there will be many activities that, while important to the organization, will not be immediately critical to protect value. Only those activities that are fundamental to the successful operation of the business, a lengthy disruption to which would have intolerable consequences for the organization and its stakeholders, are likely to be needed to be recovered in the first instance.

Part of the prioritization process comes from the analysis of disruption impacts over time set out above. This process will help to deliver an initial sift of what is urgently needed for a recovery and allow practitioners to overlook some of the less critical activities in the first instance. However, a further step is often needed to provide an enterprise-wide view of recovery time objectives that will deliver a final 'truing up' of the analysis. This step is particularly helpful where the analysis has been purely a bottom-up approach.

The reason this is sometimes needed comes down to human behaviour. Teams that are providing input into the analysis might over-assess their own criticality, perhaps because they think this will help strengthen a business case for more resources, for fear of being seen

as less important and therefore vulnerable to possible future efficiency savings. Other reasons can be less Machiavellian in their
motivation – for some they may be so close to their own delivery
activities that they are unable to make an informed judgement of the
criticality of their area when compared with other departments or the
organization as a whole.

This is why a consolidated enterprise-level output from the BIA is
a helpful means not only to obtain an endorsement for the analysis
from senior management but also as an opportunity for them to challenge the assessments made by the operational teams.

Consolidating the outputs

Without undertaking a consolidation of the BIA outputs to put the
data in one place where the information can be compared and more
easily analysed, the efforts made to collect it may be wasted.

By consolidating the BIA data in one place, we can ensure assessments of criticality have been performed in a uniform way between
teams, better identify gaps in our understanding of dependencies
between processes, and highlight points of failure and concentration
risk that are harder to spot at a team or department level. Consolidating
the data also provides an opportunity to spot recovery strategies and
solutions that may be impossible to see at a local level, or impossible
to implement without enterprise-wide investment.

One method of consolidation includes building a simple temple
model of the business to show the organization's departments as
pillars and the value chain that ties them together. By plotting critical
activities on this model, it is easier to visualize where the priority for
recovery planning might lie, where there are key dependencies that
should be focused on, and if departments or teams have over- or
underestimated their criticality when compared with other parts of
the business.

The example in Figure 10.3 is a highly simplified version of a
temple model approach to consolidating the BIA for a news agency.
For the purposes of the example, critical resource dependencies are
not shown.

FIGURE 10.3   An example consolidated BIA output for a news agency

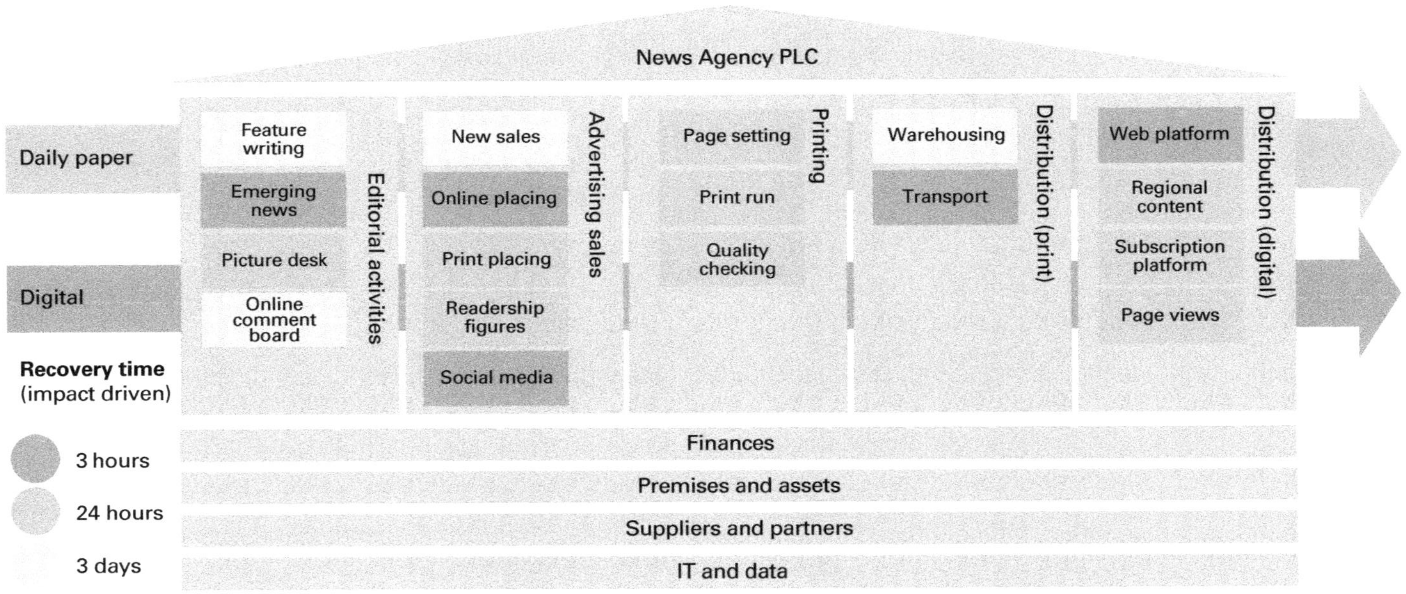

News Agency PLC

Distribution (digital)
- Web platform
- Regional content
- Subscription platform
- Page views

Distribution (print)
- Warehousing
- Transport

Printing
- Page setting
- Print run
- Quality checking

Advertising sales
- New sales
- Online placing
- Print placing
- Readership figures
- Social media

Editorial activities
- Feature writing
- Emerging news
- Picture desk
- Online comment board

- Daily paper
- Digital

- Finances
- Premises and assets
- Suppliers and partners
- IT and data

Recovery time (impact driven)
- 3 hours
- 24 hours
- 3 days

This example shows two main components to the value chain – traditional print media and a digital channel. It shows the activities linked to driving advertising revenues, news reporting on emerging and breaking news, and the ability to push content online are of greatest criticality to the organization.

Therefore, it could be concluded having conducted this process that recovery planning should be prioritized in the following areas:

- news gathering;
- mechanisms of placing adverts;
- platforms to maintain an online presence.

Delivery methods

Much of the success of the BIA will be down to the skill and competency of the person facilitating it. Knowing what data collection methods to use with each audience and when to flex the approach and style to fit different personalities and cultures is critical. Some of the most underrated skills of the business continuity and resilience practitioner are those of good stakeholder management, strong communication and a highly tuned ability to facilitate complex discussions. These are particularly important when delivering the BIA.

There is no single delivery method for a successful BIA. Instead, the practitioner must draw upon their wider toolset to flex their approach to each interaction with their colleagues.

Table 10.4 provides a summary of the different types of data collection methods and considers their benefits and potential drawbacks.

The reality for many organizations will be a hybrid approach involving elements of all three of the techniques set out in Table 10.4. This may mean starting with a basic online questionnaire, followed by a series of workshops and then a smaller number of interviews to fill gaps in knowledge.

TABLE 10.4   Different types of data collection method

	Best used when...	Limitations
The workshop	✓ Rapid results are needed with little time available to run interviews ✓ Provides a quicker way to explore dependencies between teams as consensus is faster to reach ✓ The group setting allows the testing of assumptions and recovery strategy to reach conclusions more quickly	✗ Could miss some of the detail needed for the analysis ✗ Not suitable for very large groups as the discussion will take too long, and some individuals may not get a chance to speak ✗ Mistakes made in a workshop in front of a larger audience could potentially undermine the entire programme
The interview	✓ More detail is needed, or if conclusions from a workshop need to be clarified ✓ Time is available for a systematic review ✓ If there are stakeholders that in a workshop setting would dominate the discussion at the expense of others being heard	✗ Can result in the collection of too much data, slowing down the process and increasing costs ✗ Could mean dependencies between teams are missed, or overemphasized
The questionnaire	✓ Data is needed from a large number of individuals ✓ To provide some basic source data for an important workshop or set of interviews ✓ To make some rapid comparisons of recovery needs at an operational level	✗ Can be difficult to gain buy-in to a lengthy questionnaire ✗ Requires a strong questionnaire design – a poorly worded question can give erroneous results ✗ The time taken to analyse the outputs can take longer than expected

For many staff not involved in the process regularly, business continuity can be a major distraction to their normal duties. When delivering the BIA, and in fact any part of the business continuity process, it is important to use a method that delivers just enough output to enable the development of high-quality recovery plans, without having an undue impact on normal business activities. This will mean coming well prepared to BIA interviews and workshops with some of the data already in hand, if it is available. A most common complaint from individuals on the receiving end of the process is that they are repeating answers already provided to another programme or stored elsewhere.

Before embarking on delivering the BIA, it will be important to check for sources of existing information that can be used to speed up the process and reduce the amount of time staff need to spend supporting the analysis.

Such sources could include:

- **business planning documentation**, particularly for details of current business objectives, processes and value chain information;
- analyses from other **risk management programmes and management systems**, such as information security or quality management systems, particularly for risk information and to support detailed process mapping;
- outputs from recent **organizational restructures**, particularly information relating to the organization's value chain and overall structure;
- **audit reports** or results from regulatory investigations.

Risk assessment

Business continuity is another form of risk management, and the BIA is a form of conducting a risk assessment. The main difference is that analysis is weighted towards an assessment of impacts, with the likelihood of these impacts occurring of secondary importance.

ISO 22301 requires an organization to conduct a formal risk assessment as part of the BIA process. The intent of such a process is to ensure disruption risks that can be treated prior to a disruptive event materializing are properly identified and mitigated. This does not mean the business continuity plan becomes redundant, as the whole premise of the process is to assume that disruption will occur and to build plans that are agnostic to the scenario causing the disruption. However, as discussed earlier in this chapter, the BIA affords an opportunity to collect a wide range of data on an organization's vulnerabilities and exposure to disruption risks. It would be a failure to not act upon this data to prevent disruption risks from materializing if it is possible to do so, or to reduce the overall impact of a disruption.

The risk assessment process conducted as part of the BIA is therefore critical. Disruption risks identified through the BIA process should, wherever possible, be recorded using existing enterprise risk management (ERM) methodologies, including borrowing the ERM approach to describing risks and scoring them.

An example is shown in Table 10.5.

TABLE 10.5   Example risk register

Risk title	Description	Owner	Controls	Rating
Should be clear and precise	*Statement that covers risk and impact, being as specific as possible*	*Senior-level owner accountable for managing risk*	*Precise listing of controls in place or available to mitigate risk*	*Split into gross (pre-controls applied) and net (showing effect of controls)*
Server room flood risk	There is a risk that the location of Server Room A could result in critical IT equipment being damaged by a flood in the sub-basement area, resulting in a loss of IT systems controlling the customer call centre	AN Other, IT Director	Server room upgrade programme Utility maintenance programme IT disaster recovery Insurance programme	Gross: **RED** Net: **AMBER**

The risk assessment should be conducted periodically to identify any new and emerging risks that have not been previously discussed. The process used to identify these newer risks should encourage broader and more diverse thinking, involving colleagues from across the organization to provide different perspectives than what would be achieved normally. This might mean involving colleagues from strategy teams and marketing teams who can provide a broader external perspective of risks that are just over the horizon.

The emerging risk process should be capable of capturing:

· risks that emerge from within the organization;
· risks that are emerging from the external environment.

The process should also differentiate between strategic (for example market deterioration, industry disruptions and political changes) and bottom-up risks (for example asset price deflation and natural hazards impacting on individual sites). The outputs from the emerging risk analysis can be used to determine whether existing business continuity and resilience arrangements are strong enough, and whether any additional scenario-specific response procedures might be needed.

Results from the risk assessment processes should be shared with the enterprise risk management team, if one exists, or the relevant management committee that would be ultimately accountable for its mitigation. This is to ensure that the treatment of these risks is tracked as part of existing risk management processes.

Recovery strategies and solutions

Once the BIA is completed, the next step is to prepare the recovery strategies and the recovery solutions that will allow the strategies to be implemented. The differentiation between strategies and solutions is a subtle one, but was a key improvement to the 2019 revision of ISO 22301.

A strategy is by definition not implementable without a solution or a plan. The use of the terms 'strategy' and 'solution' allow greater differentiation and clarity between the intent of an organization (the recovery strategy) and its practical implementation (the solution).

Using an example, a viable recovery strategy should access to premises be denied might be to allow employees to work from home. The solutions that support this strategy would include a secure means of accessing the organization's IT systems and data remotely and the availability of IT hardware for employees working from home. This nomenclature allows business continuity practitioners to identify all of the detailed and practical processes, assets and systems that are needed to realize a strategy. By exploring in more detail the solutions that will be needed, it becomes easier to build the business case for any investment that might be required for implementation.

Identifying strategies and solutions

Some solutions will be entirely obvious, like the working from home example outlined above, while others may be more nuanced or require a significant investment to implement and maintain.

Strategies should be carefully chosen based on their ability to:

1 recover prioritized activities to an agreed capacity and by the time set by the RTO;

2 reduce the likelihood of, or shorten the period of, a disruption;

3 limit the overall impact of a disruption;

4 ensure adequate resources are available to continue or resume activities.

A non-exhaustive summary of potential recovery strategies and their associated solutions is included in Table 10.6.

TABLE 10.6   Example recovery strategies and their supporting solutions

Strategy	Example solutions
Moving staff to an alternative premises	• Third-party work area recovery location • Designated internally sourced alternative location • Reciprocal agreement with another organization for use of their premises
Moving activities to an alternative location	• Cross-training of teams so activities can be transferred • Temporary outsourcing of an activity to a third party
Ensure critical members of staff are able to work from home	• Implement remote access technology to key staff • Issue specialist IT hardware to staff that need it • Install improved broadband connection at the homes of staff with large data processing needs
Have an alternative to replace a critical asset (eg a machine critical to a manufacturing process)	• Implement an enhanced maintenance regime and keep a stockpile of critical spares • Agree call-off contracts with suppliers that can source replacement(s) • Temporarily outsource the process to a third party with a similar machine
Hold contingency stocks for critical supplies	• Build an inventory of extra stock that will be needed for critical activities • Agree call-off contracts with additional suppliers

Selection of strategies and solutions

The final selection of strategies and solutions will be based on their ability to recover activities within the timeframes set, the extent to which they ensure the business stays within its appetite for disruption risk and the cost of implementing them.

Of the three criteria, cost can be the hardest to quantify. However, assuming the BIA has been delivered to a sufficient depth, the answer is already halfway to being complete. In arriving at the RTO and MTPD, the impacts of each activity will have been calculated. This should have included the financial impact of the activity becoming disrupted. Once this figure is understood, it can be compared against the cost of implementing and then maintaining the recovery solution itself.

It is also worth exploring other existing sources of information that might be available to help with the calculation. An organization that purchases business interruption insurance is likely to have undertaken some kind of quantification exercise to understand the extent of the organization's exposure to disruption risks. These business interruption figures are used to ensure sufficient insurance is being purchased.

These business interruption figures, if they are available, should be used in coordination with the impact assessment arising from the BIA. This is because relying purely on an insurance data set may introduce a wider margin of error than might be acceptable. Business interruption figures will be very unlikely to provide an assessment of all non-insurable risks and may not have been conducted to the level of detail needed for business continuity.

An example model of how these numbers can be used is set out in Figure 10.4.

The role of insurance

Insurance plays a critical role in providing protection in the form of capital to organizations should they suffer a loss. In many jurisdictions, without the purchase of certain statutory insurance products, an organization is unable to trade.

In organizations that are not fully convinced about the benefits of implementing business continuity, insurance is often used as the reason why recovery plans are not needed. However, while insurance policies may provide some capital relief, many of the impacts caused by a disruption are unlikely to be fully covered. It can also take a long time for the money to be paid. Organizations are often left with a degree of risk that is not mitigated by insurance and, even if money is paid, work to recover the business to normal operations will still be required.

For insurance to pay out, an organization will need to have experienced a loss. A loss can come in different forms and be covered by different types of insurance, some more relevant to business continuity than others:

FIGURE 10.4   The relationship between recovery solutions costs, disruption exposures and the likelihood of an investment being approved

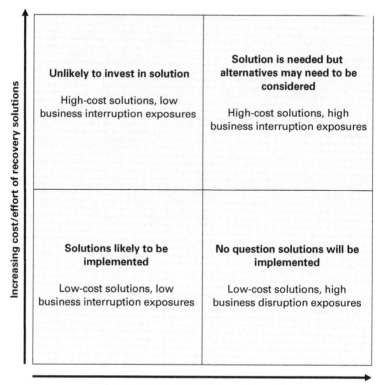

- A fire that destroys a building or a fixed asset may be covered by property insurance, which may pay for the cost of rebuilding, repairing or buying new equipment.
- The commercial failure of a large customer before a contract is paid may be covered by some form of credit insurance.
- The interruption to business caused by severe weather might be covered by business interruption insurance.
- An attack on the organization's IT systems could be covered by a specific cyber-related insurance policy.

While business continuity and resilience practitioners do not need to be experts in the field of insurance, they should seek to understand what cover the organization has in place. This is for two reasons:

1 It helps to hold a general understanding of coverage and the circumstances under which it would be triggered. This is useful to support planning processes and to inform discussions during a response to a disruption.

2 Understanding the risk exposures being borne by insurers can be used as a useful tool to help justify investments in resilience controls.

The following example brings the second point to life:

Factory A is located in a flood plain and is at high risk of flooding. The factory would cost $100 million to rebuild and contributes to annual revenues of $500 million to the organization. A property and business interruption insurance policy is in place providing a combined cover limit of $300 million for a fictitious annual premium of $2 million.

What does this mean for resilience?

1 Solely relying on the insurance policies could leave the organization exposed to a $200 million loss in the first year of interruption (under circumstances where the entire site is lost).

2 A business continuity plan could be used to help mitigate some of the loss by relocating factory operations to another location.

3 Flood defences could be installed to further reduce the risk of the site being flooded, reducing potential losses further.

In this example, it would be possible for a business continuity or resilience professional to make a strong case to invest in increased resilience for this factory. The exposure numbers available from the organization's internal insurance team, broker or insurance company can be used to help frame any business cases needed for investment. It is also possible to use these numbers to negotiate what the insurance industry calls 'bursaries', which are made available to their clients to pay for certain risk remediation activities. For example, a case could be made that for a small bursary (perhaps to pay for the development of a business continuity plan), the insurer's overall risk exposure under the policy would be substantially reduced. In other words, paying for the plan up front will reduce the amount of money the insurer has to pay when a claim is made. These bursaries are not guaranteed, however, so it will be necessary to conduct some homework on what might be possible.

Turning strategies into solutions

For each of the recovery solutions chosen, the organization will need to ensure sufficient resources are in place to implement them effectively.

The resources typically fall into seven categories:

1 people, with the right skills needed to implement the solution;
2 IT systems, information and data;
3 physical infrastructure, including buildings, workplaces and utilities;
4 third parties, including suppliers and joint venture partners;
5 equipment and any consumable items that may be required;
6 transport and logistics resources;
7 finances needed to operate the solution (as separate to what may be needed to implement the solution in the first place).

Using the delivery of the monthly payroll run as an example critical activity and some example recovery solutions from Table 10.6, the resource requirements can be plotted as shown in Table 10.7.

Implementing solutions

Once the solutions have been defined and their resource requirements mapped, work can commence on implementing them. This step of the process for many solutions will be very simple, for example ensuring a spare bank payment card is available at the alternative location where the activity it supports will be recovered to. Others will require significant effort, such as a major IT implementation project to deliver remote working or to install networked computers in a separate location set aside as a recovery site.

TABLE 10.7 Identifying resource needs for each recovery solution

Solution	People	IT & data	Infrastructure	Third parties	Equipment	Transport & logistics	Finances
Cross-training teams so activities can be transferred to an alternative location	2x payroll technicians 1x approver	Access to payroll system Latest HR payroll data	None	Payroll processing partner	Payment cards	None	None
Temporary outsourcing of an activity to a third party	1x finance lead to issue data	Payroll data in a secure form for transmission	None	Payroll provider	None	None	Contract payment to third party

It is critical at this stage to check that recovery strategies and their solutions have indeed been put in place. Mistakes are easy to make at this stage, leaving a recovery plan unusable when disruption strikes.

TABLE 10.8   Chapter checklist

☐	Ensure there is an appropriately senior sponsor for the BIA process.
☐	Train the resources that will implement the BIA to ensure the process is conducted correctly.
☐	Check that the BIA methodology chosen is appropriate for the business; run a pilot if not sure.
☐	Ensure the method of scoring the impact of a disruption is appropriate to the business and builds upon any existing risk-based scoring mechanisms, if there are any.
☐	Ensure that all critical activities and their resource dependencies are captured by the BIA process.
☐	Check that disruption risks identified during the BIA process are recorded and shared with the relevant team for treatment.
☐	Ensure that recovery strategies and solutions are defined for each prioritized activity.
☐	Build a sound business case for any investments needed to implement proposed recovery solutions.
☐	Identify the resources needed to implement and operate each recovery solution.
☐	Complete a final check to be sure that recovery solutions have actually been implemented as planned.

Note

1 ISO 22301 (2019) *International Standard Business Continuity Management*, British Standards Institute, London

11

Writing plans and procedures

A good plan should be easy to read and quick for someone to implement.

The acid test of a good plan is whether it actually tells the reader what specifically needs to be achieved in order to help recover an organization from a disruption. Imagine standing outside your place of work; it is 3 am and there has been a large fire damaging the premises. Thankfully no one has been injured, but the building will be unusable for some time. You open your recovery plan and turn to page one looking for guidance. Does it give you your first immediate instruction without having to read through pages of introductory materials about business continuity? If it fails in this task, the plan is unlikely to be a useful tool in the midst of the disruption.

The adage that it is harder to write informatively and concisely is true here. Often plans are too long, include superfluous information that would be better stored in a company policy or framework document, or simply fail to actually set out the tasks that need to be delivered to recover the business.

So a good plan should be concisely written, informative and easy to access for individuals who may not have had a huge amount of training in business continuity and will certainly be under pressure to make the right decisions. A benchmark of showing what is achievable in the art of writing easy-to-follow, concise and simple plans is in the seat pocket of every passenger airline seat. Regardless of the reader's language or reading skills, the emergency instructions contained in that short pamphlet are clear and easy for anyone to follow. Of course such brevity is unlikely to be repeatable for many business continuity plans, but it does at least show what could be possible with some smart design and clever formatting.

A good plan should:

- be concise and to the point;
- offer practical, action-oriented guidance to the reader;
- be able to be picked up by a reader with limited business continuity and crisis management knowledge and provide enough information to help them respond, or at least know who to call.

This chapter explores the different types of plans and procedures that may be required by an organization, what they should seek to achieve, common formats to use and tips on how to put them together.

Plan types

There are broadly five types of plan or procedure available to the business continuity and resilience practitioner:

1 **Incident response plans** are usually highly operational in their focus and designed to help with the immediate response tasks needed to stabilize an emergency situation. For this reason they tend to give highly precise instructions for staff to follow in the immediate aftermath of an event. These plans can cover a broad range of incidents, from the restoration and recovery of disrupted information technology assets to the procedures to follow in response to a suspected gas leak.

2 **Crisis management plans** are designed to support an organization in managing the strategic issues arising from a crisis event. For this reason they tend to be aimed at more senior members of staff and focus on the governance structures, tools and decision-making authorities needed to support a response.

3 **Business recovery plans** provide the step-by-step tasks that are needed to recover an organization's critical activities and resource

dependencies that have been identified through the BIA process. These documents are what most people consider to be business continuity plans.

4 **IT disaster recovery plans** set out the technical steps needed to recover critical IT systems and data within agreed RTOs and RPOs. These documents are usually maintained by technology teams and are highly practical in their focus on providing a step-by-step guide to recovery.

5 **Scenario-based plans** are specific to individual scenarios. These could be highly operational in their nature, akin to an incident response plan, or designed to deal with more strategic issues. Examples could be a cyber-incident, physical security concern or a pandemic. These plans tend to be highly prescriptive in setting out the actions that need to be taken in the event of the chosen scenario.

In some cases, particularly for smaller organizations, all four of the plan components above can often be found in one single document. For larger organizations, though, they are likely to be separate plans.

What should plans contain?

A good method of starting the process of building a plan is to seek answers to the following eight questions:

1 How do we find out what has just happened?

2 Who should we tell, why and when?

3 Who is responsible for taking the lead and delivering the response?

4 What should our first actions be?

5 How should we work together as a team?

6 What are our options for recovery?

7 Which stakeholders do we need to engage, and who should speak with them?

8 What do we communicate internally and externally?

1. How do we find out what has just happened?

Receiving a timely notification of an event will ensure the right people are made aware of an issue quickly. The plan should ensure notification routes, and the individuals who will receive this notification are clearly identified.

2. Who should we tell, why and when?

Once the initial notification has been received, it is important to ensure that a rapid triage of the event is undertaken so that it can be escalated to the appropriate individual or team for further management. The circumstances under which a formal response to the notification of an event is triggered must be clearly defined and leave no ambiguity so as to avoid any confusion at what is a crucial stage of a response. Delays during the triggering and escalation process could significantly damage an organization's ability to respond effectively. Individuals or teams that need to be notified at this stage should be documented, along with any contact information needed to make the call.

3. Who is responsible for taking the lead and delivering the response?

Plans need people to make the decisions, direct the response and deliver the tasks needed to recover. The roles of staff involved in a response to a disruption should be clearly defined and assigned and should include an unambiguous set of tasks for individuals to deliver. It is critical to ensure that when assigning roles they do not overlap with other individuals, or conflict with the tasks or decisions that are being asked of others. This will prevent any conflicts arising during the response.

Decision-making authorities should also be clearly defined, including who will be accountable for final decision-making, who will act as the chair of incident management, crisis management or business recovery teams, and who will take the lead on important tasks such as communicating with customers and regulators. The limits of an individual's decision-making authority should also be clearly defined so no confusion is left as to the point at which certain decisions will need to be escalated to a higher level of authority.

4. What should our first actions be?

Now that the notification of an event has been received, and the right people have been made aware, staff need to know what to do. For most people a response to a business disruption or crisis will be a rare event in their careers, so it is important not to assume any knowledge of what they should do. The first actions need to be comprehensive and written clearly so that they are easy to follow. However, there must also be a sufficient degree of flexibility to allow the plan to be tailored to the specific circumstances of each disruption or crisis event.

As staff involved in a response become more familiar with working in a crisis environment, their reliance on detailed action lists will likely wane. However, for certain roles and in certain plans, it is essential for the action plans to deliver a full end-to-end response to the event. This is particularly true for incident management plans where there is a life safety element to the response.

The first actions to be taken should establish:

- the nature of what has happened, or what may be about to happen – information and facts about the event will need to be collated;
- the extent of any impacts on the organization, staff and other stakeholders, or anticipated impacts, including whether the situation may get worse;
- whether any staff, visitors or other stakeholders have been injured;
- the type and extent of any damage to facilities, infrastructure and other assets;
- immediate control over the response, with tasks designed to limit damage and contain the event as far as it is possible or safe to do so;
- whether the event warrants a wider response, including the escalation to a higher decision-making authority.

5. How should we work together as a team?

Now we are getting into the mechanics of an organization's response architecture. The plan will need to set out a command-and-control structure that can be scaled to a range of event types, from small, localized situations to very large enterprise-wide or global events. This structure should provide for a focus on different types of decision-making needs:

- **Strategic,** sometimes referred to as gold: usually a team of senior decision-makers, often with the highest levels of authority. This team will concentrate on the big strategic issues that will need to be addressed, and will therefore be less engaged in operational decision-making associated with the immediate response.
- **Tactical,** sometimes referred to as silver: often middle management grades tasked with coordinating a response across multiple locations, departments or business lines. This team will not be delivering the operational tasks but they are likely to be directing them, ensuring the response is being well coordinated.
- **Operational,** sometimes referred to as bronze: usually involving highly technical teams or staff involved in service delivery. These individuals will be engaged in delivering the physical tasks needed to effect a response and recovery.

Ensuring teams can work effectively together will require the provision of some basic tools and infrastructure, including:

- a room or rooms if meetings are due to be held face to face;
- secure and reliable telephony and video-conferencing facilities to aid remote working, thankfully more of a norm in a post-Covid-19 world;
- information management tools, which could include manual and paper-based systems, or electronic in the form of logging software and online messaging systems;
- staff mass alerting systems, or manual call cascades to ensure important messages can be communicated quickly;

- mapping software, and sometimes even aerial survey capabilities to visualize an impacted area – such capabilities are particularly useful in organizations that are managing large sites in remote locations.

6. What are our options for recovery?

To a certain extent recovery options will be dependent upon the nature of what has just happened and the impacts the event has generated. However, this is also where the outputs from the BIA process will help. The recovery strategies and solutions developed from the outputs from the BIA process will need to be actioned in order to allow the continuation or resumption of the prioritized activities they support.

As an example, the invocation of a work area recovery location could be as shown in Table 11.1.

TABLE 11.1   Example recovery tasks

Task	Responsible	Deadline
Contact the work area recovery (WAR) provider and request the site to be opened	Head of facilities	First 10 minutes
Issue WAR invocation alert to critical staff	Head of business continuity management	First 10 minutes
Invoke emergency travel provider plan to transport staff to WAR	Head of business continuity management	First 15 minutes
[...]	[...]	[...]

7. Which stakeholders do we need to engage, and who should speak with them?

Interested parties will want to know what has happened and will be seeking assurance that management are on top of whatever the event is. Stakeholders, and what their interests are likely to be following a crisis or business disruption, should be identified prior to a disruption or crisis occurring. Their needs should be clearly identified and individuals assigned to act as a point of contact for each of them.

It is also important to ensure that any communications issued to stakeholders, whether formal or informal, should be subject to the same clearance process as messages intended for external general release. This is particularly important for highly interested stakeholders such as significant customers, regulators, shareholders and even government. Managing the contact and communications with these important groups will be necessary to help safeguard the organization's reputation post-event.

8. What do we communicate internally and externally?

The speed at which information travels internally or externally is faster than ever. We know from the research of Knight and Pretty (2001)[1] that effective and timely external communications during a crisis has a significant impact on an organization's reputation, as measured through their share performance. Organizations that communicate quickly, openly and accurately tend to be in a group of businesses that are rewarded with a sustained increase in their share performance post-crisis. By delivering a good crisis response, and communicating rapidly, transparently and honestly, these organizations are building trust and enhancing their reputations.

The communications component of the plan itself should cover:

• who is authorized to sign off on and issue formal communications;

• who is authorized to deliver the message for each platform (live media, recorded interview, radio, etc);

• which platforms will be used to communicate with stakeholders, including internal intranets, email, traditional news media and social media;

• how staff and the public's sentiment towards the organization will be monitored and how the results from this analysis will be used to make adjustments to the communications strategy.

Format and contents

The format of a plan can ultimately come down to personal taste, but there are some basic differences between the various types available that make them more suitable for certain uses than others.

For many the plan will be the first thing they reach for during a disruption or crisis. Without sharp formatting that is appropriate to the need the document is seeking to fill, it is likely to be put to one side and of no use to a member of staff during the response (see Table 11.2).

TABLE 11.2   Summary of plan formats

Traditional (full)	Long-hand document originally intended to be printed and kept in hard copy	✓ Comprehensive in its coverage ✓ All information can be found in one place ✓ Easier to update one document than it is to review multiple plans	✗ Can be too detailed ✗ Harder to navigate and use in an incident ✗ Version control harder to maintain if hard copies have been issued
Traditional (distributed)	This involves breaking a plan down into its constituent parts; each reader is given access to the sections of relevance to them (eg a department, team or function)	✓ Improves usability by only giving readers access to the information they need to perform their role	✗ Suffers from similar issues to other types of traditional plan ✗ Version control issues are amplified with multiple documents in circulation
Process flow	Provides the reader with a graphical sketch-based walkthrough of a response process	✓ Quick and easy to follow ✓ Readily accessible to the reader ✓ Can be used to summarize complex information in a short amount of space	✗ Can provide insufficient detail ✗ Relies upon a degree of inherent knowledge of how a response will be delivered (since much of the detail is not present in the plan itself)

TABLE 11.2   *continued*

System-based	Online BCM planning software tool that generates both an online readable plan and a printable version	✓ Reduces version control issues ✓ Maintains a 'single version of the truth' ✓ Improves efficiency of plan development and updates ✓ Reduces reliance on paper-based plans ✓ Increased resilience, particularly if plans are available in the 'cloud' and not dependent upon the organization's IT systems being available	✗ Costly to implement and maintain ✗ Some systems are inflexible to being tailored to specific organizational needs ✗ Can present data protection issues ✗ Potential to suffer from IT disruption if hosted locally
'Wallet cards'	So called because when folded they fit into a typical-sized wallet Today these documents are typically stored electronically on smartphones	✓ Helpful when summarizing critical information such as contact details	✗ Sensitive information could be lost if not stored securely ✗ Not appropriate for sharing large volumes of data or detailed instructions

Each plan format has individual characteristics that make it suitable for different applications. This is summarized in Figure 11.1. Paper-based plans are quickly becoming obsolete in most settings in favour of online systems capable of storing documentation in secure and resilient environments accessible to all who need it. There are of course occasions where a paper plan is needed, and care should be taken to ensure that any systems relied upon for plan storage and dissemination are resilient so that access can be achieved even if the organization's normal IT systems have been disrupted. This is particularly true in the event of a ransomware attack where access to company systems and data may be blocked and encrypted.

FIGURE 11.1   Summary of plan types, the level of detail they contain, the effort to compile and the circumstances under which to apply them

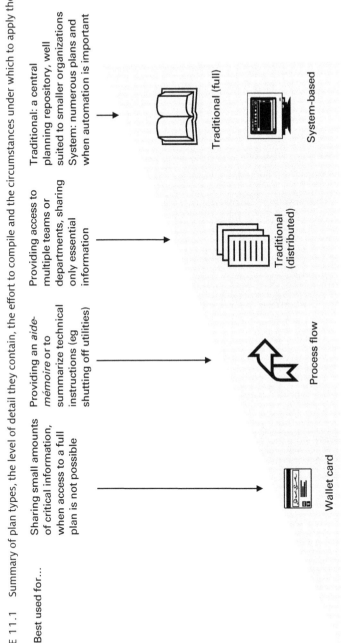

Best used for…

Sharing small amounts of critical information, when access to a full plan is not possible

Providing an *aide-mémoire* or to summarize technical instructions (eg shutting off utilities)

Providing access to multiple teams or departments, sharing only essential information

Traditional: a central planning repository, well suited to smaller organizations
System: numerous plans and when automation is important

Wallet card

Process flow

Traditional (distributed)

Traditional (full)

System-based

Increasing detail
Increasing effort to develop

How many plans are needed?

The answer to this question will be dependent upon the size, structure and risk profile of the organization:

- **Single-location businesses:** may be suited to one single plan, or a single plan that is distributed into separate documents for each critical function, department or team.
- **Multi-site businesses:** would typically either have a suite of plans covering each location, or separate plans written at the value chain level describing the recovery actions for a critical process.
- **Multi-use premises businesses:** for example, a mixture of manufacturing facilities, research and development and office-based premises would likely benefit from separate plans as the characteristics of each of these locations will suit different plan formats and will be aimed at different audiences.
- **High-hazard facilities:** will likely require specific treatment and their own set of focused plans designed around life safety and delivering what is likely to be a highly technical response to an incident or crisis.

If multiple plans are to be developed, it is fundamentally important to ensure they are aligned in their use of consistent command-and-control structures, role descriptions and decision-making authorities. Any misalignment between plans will result in conflicting decision-making and an inefficient response.

Common plan contents

Plans typically share a similar set of contents, the most common of which are set out below.

Purpose

The purpose should clearly explain what the plan is intended for. This may sound obvious, but it is common to find a business continuity plan, which should all be about recovery of critical activities, that focuses on an incident response instead or dedicates the first 10 pages to a description of what business continuity is and why it is important.

Objectives

These should be measurable outcomes that the plan is seeking to achieve – for example, ensuring the safety of people and recovering critical activities within agreed recovery times.

Assumptions

Given the inherent uncertainty associated with responding to a disruption or crisis, plans will always need to make some assumptions about the nature of what might happen and how the organization may respond. Common assumptions refer to an organization's resources being available to implement what is contained within the plan. However, it is important to ensure that any assumptions written into the plan are properly tested. Incorrect assumptions about certain resources being available may undermine the effectiveness of the plan.

Common failures in this section include making assumptions that place demands upon a resource that other plans are also expecting to use in a disruption (for example, a recovery centre with a limited number of desks available). Other failures include seeking to limit the scope of a plan. Pre-Covid-19, many plans would have made assumptions about not expecting a crisis impacting upon all organizational locations at once, or assuming that work area recovery solutions would be appropriate for most scenarios. The pandemic proved these wrong and neatly demonstrates why planning assumptions need to be rigorously tested and validated through regular exercising.

Invocation and notification

This is an often overlooked section of the plan but one that is important in giving guidance on when a response should be triggered and how the invocation and notification processes will work. It should cover who will be notified, and to whom and how the notification will be provided.

The trigger and invocation procedure that is covered in this section should be unambiguous and avoid introducing any single points of failure (for example, by making one person responsible for invoking the plan).

Escalation

This is a natural extension to the section above and should provide the criteria under which higher levels of authority need to be contacted and involved in the decision-making process.

Escalation criteria for moving between operational, tactical and strategic levels of command and control need to reflect the decision-making authorities of each of the teams. Often it is helpful to align the escalation criteria to an organization's existing risk appetite or risk-scoring methodology as these will provide some guidance on the type of impacts the organization considers to be at the more strategic end of the scale.

Teams and roles

The teams and the roles that sit on each team need to provide comprehensive coverage for the risks that may arise in a response but not overlap and cause confusion and conflict. A mixture of technical specialists, corporate function leads (for example finance) and decision-makers with the authority to commit resources will be needed here.

Each team will need a chairperson to direct the conversations and act as the final decision-making authority in the room or on the call.

Tasks

The response and recovery tasks should be linked to achieving the objectives of the plan. They are likely to include:

- instructions on incident response;
- actions to be taken to recover critical activities;
- guidance on when to escalate information, decisions and issues;
- the timing and phasing of actions and how they interrelate with other plans the organization maintains.

Communications

How information flows between each of the response teams, wider staff and other stakeholders can make a big difference to the effectiveness of an organization's response. The interfaces between the teams are likely points of friction, delay and error. Communications arrangements will need to make provision for:

- the type of information that should be routinely shared between response teams;
- the means through which information and decisions should flow between response teams;
- how internal and external communications will be drafted and approved;
- the mechanisms that will be used to deliver internal and external communications;
- alternative means of communication should primary tools become unavailable.

Stand-down

This section will set out the procedures to follow for letting all staff know that an incident has been resolved. The stand-down process should also make provision for:

- the collation of any incident-specific expenditure;
- the collection of action and decision logs kept by each response team;

- the delivery of a post-incident debrief so that lessons can be recorded and used to further improve plans.

Contact details

The storing of contact details in hard copy plans can be a contentious issue.

Some argue that plans must contain all of the contact details needed to deliver an effective response, often resulting in very detailed plans that require significant administration to keep up to date. Others argue that the plans should have no contact details in them at all, with readers relying on other existing forms of storage (such as smartphones and company address books).

A middle ground is likely to be most appropriate for the majority of plans. Contact details that are essential to the delivery of an effective response, particularly for the first few hours of an incident, are likely to be needed in the plan. Multiple pages of contact details are to be avoided on the grounds of the effort of keeping them up to date and the data protection risk this creates. Unless it is essential for teams to hold a paper version of these details, usually the most sensible means to store and disseminate contact information will be via some form of IT-based solution. Today there are plenty of technology-based systems that can be used to store contact information.

Templates

Templates needed to support the response teams should be available in a format that is easy for readers to use and useful in helping to achieve the objectives of the plan. These may include templates for taking meeting minutes and recording actions, conducting impact assessments, performing debriefs and listing pre-agreed communications.

Version control and distribution

A method of recording the plan version and controlling its distribution is needed to ensure that plan users know they are referring to the most up-to-date version of the document.

Plan maintenance

All plans need to be periodically reviewed and updated to ensure they remain fit for purpose. The circumstances likely to drive a need to review a plan include:

- following a significant change to the organization, for example the closure or opening of a building, the acquisition or divestment of a business entity or major personnel changes;
- after experiencing a recent crisis or business disruption;
- following an industry peer experiencing a recent crisis or business disruption;
- changes to the organization's regulatory landscape, or a request from a major customer for evidence of an up-to-date plan;
- after an exercise that has identified areas for improvement.

In the absence of experiencing any of the triggers set out above, the frequency of how often a plan will need to be reviewed will be linked to the organization's risk profile. In organizations that deliver time- and mission-critical activities, or deliver services that are important to life safety, plans are likely to be reviewed very regularly. For some that could mean monthly. The frequent checks and drills undertaken at nuclear power stations for emergency situations are a good example here. In organizations with less time-sensitive activities the frequency will be much lower, averaging between six months and a year.

Following a review, the plan owner and any individual who is expected to use the plan should be retrained in its use so that they are familiar with any changes before having to use the document in a live situation.

TABLE 11.3   Chapter checklist

☐	Choose the right plan for the job – incident, crisis or business recovery.
☐	Keep the plans concise, clearly written and with the reader's needs in mind.
☐	Ensure the right format is chosen for the plan's intended purpose.
☐	Check that the plan provides practical and easily actioned guidance – if in doubt, ask a colleague to peer-review the document.
☐	Ensure plans are aligned and consistent in their use of terminology and follow the same command-and-control structure.
☐	Pay attention to how the plans interact with each other during a response – making sure that information flows freely between teams and that escalation and decision-making requirements are clear.
☐	Be sure to regularly review all plans so that they are kept up to date and are ready for when you need to use them.

Note

1 Knight, RF and Pretty, DJ (2001) Reputation and value: the case of corporate catastrophes, www.oxfordmetrica.com/public/CMS/Files/488/01RepComAIG.pdf (archived at https://perma.cc/RA95-7379)

12

Training and exercising

A business continuity plan on its own will not guarantee a disruption or a crisis will be well managed. The behaviours people display and the decisions they take in a crisis can be the difference between a successful recovery and a disaster for an organization.

Humans are remarkably adaptable and will generally do their best in the face of a disruption or crisis. To improve the chances of a successful recovery, regular training and exercising are needed. A good crisis response does not happen by accident; it takes effort.

The importance of training and exercising is further increased when considering that for many employees, a crisis or major business disruption will not be a common experience. Making sure that employees, particularly those with an active role in responding, are adequately prepared through training and exercising is critical.

However, it is not just employees who need to be given the chance to practise. Plans and any special resources or capabilities that are expected to be deployed in a crisis will need to be properly tested before they are used in anger. Walking into a smoke-filled room is not the best time to find that your fire extinguisher is faulty and the fire escape is blocked.

This chapter explores the reasons why good preparation matters, and why this should include providing plenty of opportunities for staff to receive training and to participate in exercises that validate an organization's plans and recovery capabilities.

Who needs to be trained?

Individuals who require training generally fall into three groups:

1 staff with a role in preparing the business continuity and crisis management plans;

2 staff who have a role in responding to a disruption or a crisis;

3 staff who require a general awareness of the organization's business continuity policy, and their personal role within it.

A training needs analysis can be used to determine the specific requirements of each of these groups. The analysis should define the training outcomes required by each group before selecting the most appropriate delivery method that will achieve it. For example, a detailed understanding of ISO 22301 is not necessary for staff who only require a general awareness of the organization's business continuity policy.

A significant amount of time can be spent performing a detailed training needs analysis. In reality, much of this effort is not needed and delivers little benefit. Instead, the analysis should be focused on those areas where a greater degree of training will be needed and where there will be greater nuance between roles and individuals. This targeted approach allows for investments in training to be focused on the areas that will deliver the best outcomes for individuals and the organization.

A simple two-part training needs analysis can be used to provide a rapid assessment of learning requirements and a means to target a more detailed analysis for those roles that require specialist training or warrant a greater degree of variety in delivery methods.

The first step (Table 12.1) of the analysis is designed to identify high-level training outcomes needed for each group along with potential delivery methods.

Step 2b may not be required for all roles, but for some individuals it will be necessary to conduct a more detailed analysis in order to develop a training programme specific to their needs. Table 12.3 uses the crisis management team as an example.

TABLE 12.1   Step 1: Defining training outcomes and delivery methods

Group	Target training outcome	Delivery method options
1 Staff with a role in preparing business continuity and crisis management plans	Staff hold a sufficient degree of knowledge to execute their responsibilities.	• E-learning and face-to-face briefings • External courses
2 **Staff who have a role in responding to a disruption or a crisis**	Staff have the knowledge, capability and confidence to manage a response to a disruption or crisis.	• Face-to-face briefings • One-to-one coaching • Plan walk-throughs • Exercise participation
3 **Staff who require a general awareness of the organization's business continuity policy**	Staff understand the organization's approach to business continuity and their role in it.	• E-learning package • Intranet pages • Induction training events

TABLE 12.2   Step 2: Roles and delivery plan

Group	Roles	Delivery plan
1 Staff with a role in preparing business continuity and crisis management plans	a Business continuity management team b **Departmental business continuity coordinators**	a ISO 22301 Lead Implementer Course b **In-house-designed classroom-based courses**
2 **Staff who have a role in responding to a disruption or a crisis**	a Crisis management team b **Business recovery team** c **Crisis support roles**	a One-to-one briefing and group role-based training b **Group-based training** c **Targeted role-based training (eg decision log training)**
3 **Staff who require a general awareness of the organization's business continuity policy**	a All remaining members of staff	a Access to e-learning/information on the intranet b **Briefing materials provided at induction**

TABLE 12.3   Step 2b: Refining individual training needs

Group	Roles	Detailed delivery plan
2 Staff who have a role in responding to a disruption or a crisis	Crisis management team	**One-to-one briefings to cover:** • **CEO/chairperson:** leading a crisis team and speaking with the media • **Communications director:** crisis communications principles and practical experience • **HR director:** managing team performance in a crisis

The more significant an individual's role is to the organization's overall resilience capability, the more effort will be needed to carefully define their training needs. For the majority of staff, a detailed individual training plan will be too costly to develop and implement. However, for those individuals who deliver critical roles, for example staff leading the business continuity planning process or key members of the crisis management team, extra effort is needed.

Alongside the steps set out above, it will be necessary for this smaller group of critical individuals to consider how each individual prefers to learn. Learning styles are highly personal. For some individuals, reading and digesting manuals and guidelines will be sufficient, but for others learning will be best achieved in a classroom environment by shadowing others and gaining on-the-job experience. It is worth investing a small amount of time asking these individuals what method they prefer and, if it is possible, accommodating this in the training programme. Some of this information may already have been captured by a human resources department as part of wider training activities delivered by the organization.

Determining the frequency of training

Training needs to be repeated at regular intervals to ensure that staff maintain sufficient knowledge of their roles and remain up to date with current procedures and the latest good practice. One method of determining the frequency of training needed is to establish how often skills will be required to be used during a disruption, and how important they are to the organization's overall response.

Highly intensive and important roles are likely to require an increased frequency of training. For the more important roles this could mean providing refresher training every six months, or even more often in some cases. Some examples are provided in Figure 12.1.

The approach in Figure 12.1, combined with the training needs analysis discussed earlier, can be used to help determine the frequency of training activities for each group and role identified (see Table 12.4).

TABLE 12.4   Establishing the frequency of training

Group	Roles	Delivery plan	Frequency
1	a Business continuity management team **b Departmental business continuity coordinators**	a ISO 22301 Lead Implementer Course **b In-house-designed classroom-based course**	a Refresher every 2 years **b Annual**
2	a Crisis management team **b Business recovery team** **c Crisis support roles**	a One-to-one briefing and group role-based training **b Group-based training** **c Targeted role-based training (eg decision log training)**	a Annual **b Every 6 months** **c Annual (as part of exercise)**
3	a All remaining members of staff	a Access to an e-learning course/information on the intranet **b Briefing on induction**	a Annual refresher **b Once on induction into the organization**

FIGURE 12.1   Relationship between the importance of a response role and how often these skills are used in a disruption with how frequently training may be needed

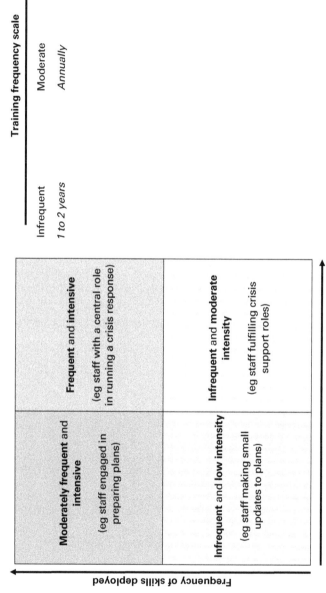

Training frequency scale

Infrequent   Moderate   Frequent
1 to 2 years   *Annually*   *6 months*

Moderately frequent and intensive

(eg staff engaged in preparing plans)

Frequent and intensive

(eg staff with a central role in running a crisis response)

Infrequent and low intensity

(eg staff making small updates to plans)

Infrequent and moderate intensity

(eg staff fulfilling crisis support roles)

Frequency of skills deployed

Criticality of the role to support a crisis response

Training follow-up

At the end of each training session feedback should be collected from participants so that future events can be improved. It will also be necessary to record attendance at training sessions so that a record of attendance is kept – particularly important should an internal audit ask for evidence or if the organization is seeking to achieve accredited certification against ISO 22301.

Measuring training outcomes is also important to check that individuals have achieved the desired learning objectives and to validate the effectiveness of the training programme as a whole. There are a number of methods that can be used to measure training outcomes; all, however, rely upon setting specific and measurable learning outcomes or goals to allow for an assessment to be made at a later date.

Training outcomes can be measured through:

- **Formal tests:** A short post-training questionnaire-based test can be used to validate a participant's understanding of the training content. For some roles it may be appropriate to set a pass mark for the training to be considered successful, particularly in high-hazard environments where a high level of competency matters for safety reasons.

- **External certification:** Individuals who have a significant role in developing plans or responding to crises may benefit from attending externally provided courses that are backed by a formal certification process. These courses typically include an exam that must be passed before a certificate can be awarded. These courses have the additional benefit of giving staff a formal externally recognized qualification that may be recognized by other employers.

- **Formal education:** Formal further education provided through colleges, universities and professional bodies can also be useful for individuals who have a key role to play in plan development and response. Similar to external certification, such training can also act as a helpful motivation for staff as they will be achieving a formal qualification that will help with their career development.

- **Observation:** An individual's understanding of a particular skill or piece of knowledge can be tested by observing its application. This could include reviewing the first business continuity plan that they write, or observing their participation in an exercise and providing targeted feedback to help them improve.

In addition to recording who attends training and when that training has taken place, any objective assessments that are undertaken to establish whether training outcomes have been achieved should also be kept as a record.

Exercising

If training is all about transferring knowledge, exercising is about putting that knowledge into practice.

An exercise involves the simulation of a disruption, incident or crisis event in order to allow individuals and teams to practise a response to it using the plans, tools and other structures that have been previously implemented. Exercises provide an opportunity to validate recovery arrangements, test procedures and recovery solutions, and give teams a chance to become familiar with their role in a disruption event. Crucially, they are performed in a safe environment, meaning the response is delivered as a role-play with no impact on an organization's actual operations.

The delivery of an exercise has five main benefits:

1 increases an organization's preparedness and confidence in dealing with a disruption;

2 provides an effective way to evaluate an organization's response and recovery arrangements and to identify areas for improvement, without having to experience a real event;

3 creates an opportunity for the exchange of views and knowledge between individuals, teams and across the organization;

4 allows senior managers and other responders to rehearse their roles in a safe environment;

5 gives confidence to internal and external stakeholders that the organization's plans are effective and will work when needed.

These benefits can only be realized if an exercise is correctly planned and executed. The following three principles act as a useful starting point when beginning the development of an exercise or exercise programme:

1 The exercise format should reflect the maturity of the plans that are being validated and the experience of the team involved. Delivering an overly complex exercise with a new team with little previous experience in incident management, business continuity and crisis management, or where response procedures have been newly implemented, could be setting individuals up to fail. Similarly, applying a basic exercise to a highly experienced team would undermine the value of the investment. These extremes could damage stakeholder confidence, both in the individuals who are taking part and in the response plans that have been put in place to support them.

2 Exercise complexity should increase as more exercise events are planned. Plans, particularly for critical functions, sites or teams, will need to be subject to increased levels of validation through more complex exercises and a variety of different scenario types. Exercises in these areas of the organization should start at a low base and build over time towards events that are more complex. This approach will help the team, and their plans, mature over time, building confidence as the degree of pressure applied by the exercises increases.

3 Multi-team exercises should be used to validate the relationships between individual functions, locations and teams. These multi-team exercises allow an organization to explore how roles and responsibilities are shared in practice between teams, how information will flow in a real event, and how decision escalation and communication is likely to work. Some of the more vulnerable areas of an organization's response and recovery structures will be in the interfaces between response teams. Practising these hand-offs in a multi-team exercise will help to test assumptions and validate how coordination activities will work in practice.

Who to exercise, and how often

All individuals who will play an active role in responding to a real disruption event should be given the opportunity to participate in exercises.

Some individuals will find the experience exciting, while others will be anxious about the potential to fail in front of their peers or will simply consider it an unwelcome distraction from the day job. In a similar way to the preparation work that is needed to design a training programme, knowing how exercise participants feel towards taking part and what their concerns are will help you correctly communicate the event and prepare individuals for the experience. Some staff will need extra briefings, while others will relish the opportunity to turn up and 'give it a go'. Regardless of how staff feel towards the exercise, it is important to make clear that individuals are not being tested individually and that the main function of an exercise is to validate plans and response structures. An exercise should be considered a learning opportunity – not a test of individuals.

In terms of frequency, plans for critical areas of an organization should be expected to participate in exercises more frequently than others. The minimum is likely to be once per year for these teams, but could be more frequent for highly critical areas or where a team's role involves delivering life safety and security activities. The more these individuals are given the opportunity to participate in exercises, the more automatic and efficient their responses will become in a live event.

In order to give structure to exercises, the development of a programme of exercise events can be helpful. This will help to ensure that exercises are focused in those areas of the business that have the greatest need and will allow teams to plan the resources needed to deliver them.

An exercise programme in an organization with multiple locations would typically run for between one and three years. An example outline of an exercise programme is set out in Table 12.5.

TABLE 12.5   Example outline of an exercise programme

Plan/team	Exercise type	Frequency
Departmental plans	Facilitated discussion	Annual
	Single/multi-team simulation	Every 2 years
Site incident response plans	Table top	Every 6 months
	Live simulation	Annual
		More frequent if the site is high risk
Crisis management team	Table top	Annual
	Single-team simulation	Every 2 years
	Multi-team simulation	Every 3 years

Exercise types

A variety of exercise types are available (Figure 12.2), each appropriate to a discrete set of circumstances and organization and team maturity.

FIGURE 12.2   Exercise formats, their realism, resource needs and the assurance they provide

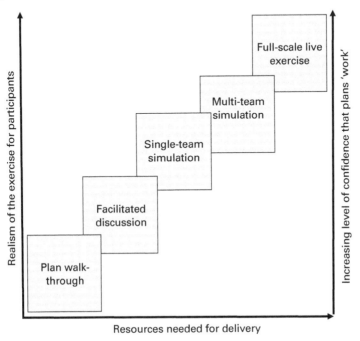

PLAN WALK-THROUGH

A plan walk-through involves a facilitator talking individuals through a plan to familiarize staff with its format, contents and their own individual roles they would be expected to play in a response. This represents the lowest level of exercise maturity – useful with very new teams or when a new plan has been implemented. This exercise format should not be solely relied upon without other forms of exercise that will deliver a more rigorous validation of plans.

FACILITATED DISCUSSION

A facilitated discussion will use a hypothetical disruption scenario or set of scenarios as the basis for a discussion. A trained facilitator will guide participants through the process by presenting the scenario and pausing at key points to ask structured questions designed to explore how the team would respond. When compared with a basic walk-through, discussion-based exercises can help participants better visualize how a plan might be used in a real event without introducing too much pressure on individuals. However, they suffer similar limitations in not providing a sufficient degree of challenge to fully validate a plan.

SINGLE-TEAM SIMULATION

Single-team simulation exercises involve participants responding to a hypothetical scenario as if it were real life. These exercises can be delivered in real time (i.e. with the scenario timeline close to what it would be in a real situation), or time can be elapsed in time-jumps to advance the discussion on to issues that will require debate. During the course of the exercise the team will receive additional pieces of the story to build the exercise – referred to as injects. These injects could be delivered in any form of information that helps to elaborate on the scenario and introduce a new issue or piece of information that the team will need to respond to. This format makes these exercises much more realistic than the two above, but will be much more resource-intensive to deliver.

MULTI-TEAM SIMULATION

The multi-team simulation is an evolution of the single-team exercise but this time involving multiple teams, all responding to the same scenario. This type of exercise is useful to explore how teams would interact with each other in a real event, testing information flows and escalation procedures. These exercises can be very large, involving teams in multiple locations, even different countries participating over several days. Getting the design of these exercises right involves a significant amount of planning and coordination – both in the design of the exercise, to ensure that teams all benefit from the experience, and the facilitation on the day of the event. A 'simulation cell' is often needed to control the release of injects and the development of the scenario across all teams, meaning more resource will be needed to ensure the process runs smoothly. Getting these exercises wrong can be damaging to the business continuity and resilience programme and the careers of the individuals running them, so sufficient time and effort will be needed to plan multi-team simulations thoroughly.

FULL-SCALE EXERCISE

Full-scale exercises are resource-intensive and are usually the preserve of organizations that work in high-hazard environments. This format would involve multiple teams and the physical deployment of staff and assets needed in the response to test the logistics of managing a major crisis event. Here it is common for a significant degree of assurance to be needed to demonstrate that plans will work and individuals know what to do. While this format is sometimes used in other settings, the cost of delivering them, including the significant impact they have on the operations of the business on the day of the exercise, can often be too prohibitive.

Timeline of exercise delivery

A five-stage process can be followed to deliver an exercise, with the complexity of the exercise determining the time needed for each stage (see Figure 12.3).

STAGE 1: SCOPE AND OBJECTIVES

This is a crucial stage of the planning process as this will determine the focus of the exercise and will help drive choices made on who should participate, the scenario, injects and delivery format.

STAGE 2: PLANNING AND DEVELOPMENT

During this stage the materials for the exercise are developed, including the scenario, exercise injects, briefing documentation and any notes needed for facilitators and observers that will be involved on the day.

STAGE 3: FACILITATION

This stage takes place on the day of the exercise and involves the delivery of the scenario to the team that is the subject of the exercise. Commonly an exercise will run for several hours, but can be much longer.

STAGE 4: POST-EXERCISE REPORTING

During this stage the feedback obtained from exercise participants, facilitators and observers is collated and a report is developed to identify any areas for improvement.

STAGE 5: IMPROVEMENT IMPLEMENTATION

Having invested heavily to design and deliver an exercise, further sustained effort is needed to ensure that the improvement recommendations made in the report are tracked until delivery.

Tips on delivering an exercise

The most common mistake made in exercise design is to jump straight to the development of the scenario before defining the scope and objectives for the event. While the scenario might be the more exciting component of the exercise design, starting with its development will narrow the focus of the discussions. Being clear on scope and objectives first will help to inform the development of the scenario itself.

FIGURE 12.3   An example delivery timeline

1. Scope and objectives	2. Planning and development	3. Exercise facilitation	4. Post-exercise reporting	5. Improvement implementation
− 2 weeks	− 1 week	Day zero	+ 1 week	+ 4 weeks
Basic table-top exercise for a single team. Objective to validate a new recovery plan and make the team familiar with how it should be used.	Scenario based upon a building fire with a small number of supporting injects needed.	15-minute pre-briefing, followed by 2 hours of exercise 'play'.	Obtain further feedback from participants and prepare a short report.	Timeline will be dependent upon the number and size of recommendations agreed.

Exercise objectives will fall into four groups:

1 **People:** provide an opportunity for decision-makers to practise their roles in responding to a disruption event and familiarization with the plan.

2 **Plans:** validate recovery plans, exploring areas for further improvement.

3 **Recovery solutions:** validate the effectiveness of recovery solutions.

4 **Relationships:** explore and practise relationships between teams and external stakeholders (for example a key supplier or delivery partner).

The exercise scenario should be plausible so that participants 'believe' in it, but be of sufficient scale and complexity to ensure all exercise participants have a role to play (i.e. there are impacts that all teams can be involved in managing).

In developing the scenario:

- Consider following three broad phases of activity covering the initial response, a consolidation phase and a period of recovery. Sufficient time should be set aside for the recovery phase, as often time runs out before it is possible to cover this crucial phase of the response.

- Give teams that will be more disproportionately impacted by the scenario an opportunity to discuss elements of it prior to the exercise. This will help to avoid any embarrassment of participants who may feel exposed in front of their peers. It also helps to prevent presenting a flawed scenario by ensuring that expert input has been captured as part of the design phase.

- Ensure the scenario covers a broad range of business impacts, including operational disruption issues, people risks, property and asset damage, supply chain disruption, financial impacts, reputational damage, legal, regulatory and customer impacts. Not all exercises will need to cover every impact type, but the scenario should be broad enough to allow the objectives to be achieved and to give all participants a meaningful role in the discussion.

- Develop a range of injects to help develop the scenario, introduce new challenges to the team or help to increase the speed or slow down discussions. If a simulation-type exercise has been chosen, it is often helpful to deliver these injects using communication methods the team would normally expect to be using during a real-life event. This could mean emailing information directly to exercise participants, making telephone calls or building pre-scripted news and social media materials to introduce into the exercise.

- Record the scenario and inject timeline in one document to provide a single version of the truth that will be used to guide the delivery process. This will ensure – particularly for more complex exercises involving multiple teams – that injects are issued at the right time and to the correct teams.

There are a range of internal and external information sources available to help design a realistic scenario and injects. These include:

- enterprise-level, team or site risk registers where operational risks that may result in a disruption are likely to be recorded;

- discussions with management about their previous exercise and real-life incident experience to understand the areas they would like to explore;

- reports from previous exercises and any relevant internal audit reports to provide some insights into disruption risks that will help inform scenario development;

- examples of real-life incidents that competitors, suppliers or other partners have experienced can be useful sources of inspiration;

- risk reports from international, governmental and professional bodies can also be helpful resources to provide additional insights into risks relevant for the organization.

TYPICAL SCENARIO THEMES

The following examples can be scaled to focus on a small geographical area, individual buildings or asset up to a wider-area event impacting upon the entirety of an organization's operations:

1 **Property:** damage or destruction to a key building, or denial of access events that prevent the use of certain sites.

2 **Information technology:** disruption event to a key technology asset, a cyber-attack, data loss or data corruption event.

3 **Utilities:** failure of critical utilities including power, gas and water.

4 **Suppliers:** disruption to a key supply chain partner.

5 **People:** an infectious disease outbreak that reduces the number of staff available for work and limits travel.

6 **Reputation:** an event that threatens to damage the organization's reputation, caused perhaps by an instance of bribery, corruption or fraud.

7 **Strategy:** a more strategic failure (usually slow build) that threatens to undermine an organization's strategy and business plan – since these scenarios rarely include a business continuity component, they are better suited to more strategic-level crisis exercises.

Briefing of participants

Staff who will be participating in an exercise should be fully briefed prior to the event. While staff who have participated in previous exercises are likely not to require a detailed verbal briefing, it is good practice to send a guidance note followed by an offer of a verbal briefing should staff require one.

The briefing should cover:

• the agreed objectives for the exercise;

• logistical arrangements for the event (date, location, timings and guidance on any technology platforms that will be used);

• reminder of the participant's role in the lead-up to, during and after the exercise;

- exercise rules of play;
- reinforcing the message that staff are not being tested personally.

On the day of the exercise

Several hours before the exercise is due to start, it is a good idea to check the final arrangements – is the room(s) still available, does the technology that is due to be used work, and have refreshments been booked?

Immediately prior to the exercise commencing, the facilitator should deliver a final pre-briefing session to reiterate the plan for the exercise and the rules of play. Unless it is an intended part of the exercise, it is worth reminding participants not to make any calls outside the exercise group (i.e. to staff not formally playing in the exercise). This could result in the risk of triggering a full response to a fictitious event should messages be misunderstood. It is also always important to remind participants that should a real incident occur during the session, the exercise will be stopped by the facilitator.

To run the exercise, four main roles will be needed:

1 **Facilitator:** the individual who will introduce the session and run the scenario – this person has an important role to play in making sure the exercise objectives are met.
2 **Observer:** who will monitor the discussions, take notes and record any areas of good practice or areas for improvement identified during the event.
3 **Simulation cell team:** who will manage the issue of scenario injects as planned (such a team may not be needed for less complex exercises);
4 **Time-keeper:** particularly useful for larger exercises but not necessary for all events.

During the delivery process, the facilitator should be ready to:

- **Make adjustments** to exercise timings to ensure sufficient time is spent discussing the issues that need debate.

- **Pause the exercise** and reset the discussion if the group has deviated too far from the plan, or if the exercise scenario or format has not worked as originally anticipated.

- **Make small amendments** to the scenario or injects to ensure exercise objectives are met. On occasion, certain elements of a scenario or individual injects may fail to create the reaction that is expected. The important thing is not to panic, but instead to pause and make small adjustments. Facilitators should avoid knee-jerk reactions that lead to significant changes to the exercise as this could harm the overall effectiveness of the event.

Debrief and post-exercise reporting

For the benefits of exercising to be fully realized, a debrief will be needed along with the development of a lessons learned report. These will help drive the delivery of any improvement actions that have been identified.

The debrief should be performed in two stages:

1 A 'hot' debrief should be performed immediately after the exercise is completed involving all participants that take part in the event. An immediate debrief is an opportunity to record the views of participants while the experience is fresh in their minds. It is usually better to keep these immediate debriefs simple in their structure and take up a minimal amount of time as exercise participants will likely want to move on to other diary commitments.

2 A **full debrief** can take place on the following day, or at least within a week of the exercise. This step allows participants to reflect upon their experience and come prepared with more insightful feedback. These debriefs can be delivered as an open discussion in a group setting or through a survey. An example simple survey-based debrief questionnaire is provided in Table 12.6.

The post-exercise report should be issued quickly after an exercise. Long delays in its publication could result in a loss of interest and commitment from participants to implement the improvement actions that have been identified.

TABLE 12.6   Survey-based debrief questionnaire

1 **To what extent do you feel the exercise was helpful to you in your role?**

☐ Limited usefulness
☐ Provided a useful refresher
☐ Critical in helping me understand my role

2 **Please identify up to 3 things that you felt went well in how the team responded to the exercise scenario.**

1 _____
2 _____
3 _____

3 **Please identify up to 3 things that you would like to improve in your team's response arrangements.** Please consider: your plans, procedures, training, tools and information needs.

1 _____
2 _____
3 _____

4 **Please use the space below to highlight any additional items of feedback.**

_____
_____
_____
_____

The report should include:

- an overview of the exercise, its purpose, scope, objectives, scenario and the participants who were involved;
- a list of observations from the exercise, as captured by the observers and through debrief sessions;
- a clear articulation of the risks and consequences of not addressing any shortcomings set out in the observations;
- a list of clearly defined, realistic and measurable improvement actions;
- an owner and target delivery date for each action.

Following issue of the report, the actions it contains must be tracked to completion. Failing to do so will mean the benefits of the exercise in improving the organization's resilience arrangements will not be fully realized. To achieve this, it may be necessary to deliver a series of working group meetings, involving action owners, to regularly review the progress being made on implementation. Organizations that use an audit or management action tracking tool may find it useful to use these systems to drive delivery.

TABLE 12.7   Chapter checklist

Training	
☐	Undertake a training needs analysis to identify who needs to be trained and what methods to use.
☐	Design a training programme that meets the collective and individual needs of staff involved in preparing plans and responding to disruptions.
☐	Record training attendance and collect feedback from participants to help improve further sessions.
☐	Ensure all training sessions are followed up to establish whether training outcomes have been met (keep a record of any assessments performed).
Exercises	
☐	Define the organization's exercise needs and develop a structured programme of exercise events to meet them.
☐	Identify the purpose of each exercise and establish the scope and objectives that need to be met.
☐	Choose a realistic and credible scenario; validate this with key stakeholders to obtain input if needed (particularly if the scenario is complex or covers topics that are outside the exercise facilitator's area of expertise).
☐	Develop injects to increase the realism of each exercise; use media reports, mock social media feeds, scripted emails and telephone calls.
☐	Be sure to check that all the logistics for the exercise are in place before the event (room, technology, equipment, meeting invites, refreshments).
☐	Run an exercise walk-through with the exercise team to check arrangements are all in place and no further tweaks are needed to the scenario or injects.
☐	Brief exercise participants prior to each event.

TABLE 12.7   *continued*

☐	Encourage participants to participate in the exercise discussions openly.
☐	Conduct a post-exercise debrief and address any identified issues.
☐	Prepare a post-exercise report and ensure that improvement actions are tracked to completion.
☐	Maintain a record of exercises, participants, scenarios and any improvements identified.

13

Supply chain resilience

Every organization relies upon suppliers of some description. Whether through the supply of raw materials, services or other types of resources, third parties play a critical role in supporting the delivery of an organization's key products and services. Most organizations have become so dependent upon suppliers that a disruption to any one of them could result in a major impact on their ability to continue operations. These risks have become particularly acute for organizations that have outsourced technology services to third-party cloud providers; a disruption here could halt operations.

Experience from the Covid-19 pandemic, the global shortage of semi-conductors, the blockage of the Suez Canal by the *Ever Given* cargo ship in 2021 and of course the wars in Ukraine and the Middle East have all cast into sharp relief just how vulnerable supply chains are to disruption. So it is essential that any project to improve the resilience of an organization must ensure suppliers are part of its scope.

The failure to plan for a supply chain disruption will leave an organization significantly exposed, particularly where supplies are of critical importance to the delivery of products and services. The global nature of our supply chains means that organizations have become exposed to disaster and disruption events that they may have in the past had very little or no experience of dealing with themselves. This means that the sources of disruptive events are no longer limited to local risks, but could potentially be caused by a crisis happening anywhere in the world.

The speed of a disruption and how these crisis events can manifest themselves also varies. A disruption can be the result of a slowly emerging series of events involving perhaps a long period of financial warnings about a supplier, eventually resulting in the company filing for bankruptcy. Or it could arrive without much notice at all – sometimes seemingly out of the blue as a result of a natural disaster somewhere or a terrorist attack.

However, when they do manifest themselves, supply chain disruption impacts can be significant, and often far reaching. Examples include:

- A General Motors truck plant in Louisiana, United States had to temporarily close as a result of a shortage of Japanese parts following the 2011 earthquake and tsunami.[1]
- Disruption to active pharmaceutical ingredients (APIs) as a result of the government lockdowns experienced in early 2020 designed to control the spread of Covid-19 in China (the world's largest supplier of APIs[2]). The closure of manufacturing plants and the disruption to local supply chains and labour caused shortages internationally of raw materials needed to develop medicines.
- The UK arm of fast-food chain KFC, whose main product is fried chicken, temporarily ran out of chicken in 2018 as a result of supplier issues, forcing the closure of the majority of their restaurants.[3]
- The blockage for six days of the Suez Canal by the cargo ship the *Ever Given* had a major impact on the 12 per cent of global trade that passes through the canal on a daily basis. One report from Lloyds (the London insurance market) suggested the blockage was holding up $9.6bn of goods a day[4] with alternative routing involving significantly more sailing time around the Cape of Good Hope in South Africa.

There are many more examples that can be quoted, but they all generally follow four themes:

1 An event of such magnitude (like the Covid-19 pandemic or the 2011 Japan earthquake and tsunami) that global disruption is inevitable.

2 The failure of a critical supplier or logistics network with limited immediate alternative options available to the organization (e.g. the KFC chicken experience).

3 A lack of understanding of how an organization's supply chain works and where it is exposed to risk. Most organizations will understand who their primary (or tier 1) suppliers are, but few have a solid understanding of who supplies their suppliers and it is often at this level where there are significant risks.

4 The failure on the organization's part to properly plan for a possible disruption, thereby leaving business continuity risks untreated and the business open to disruption.

This chapter will explore what makes modern organizations more susceptible to feeling the effects of a supply chain disruption and what can be done to prepare for them when they do happen. In doing so, it will also explore methods to plan for disruption to existing suppliers and what should be considered as part of the tendering process when new contracts are being prepared.

Why is supply chain resilience important?

Globalization has made our supply chains more efficient but also more complex, and as a result, our organizations have become dependent upon others to carry out business. There are significant differences between modern organizations and the global context in which they operate and organizations of just 50 years ago, that increase either the complexity of supply chain risks, or the scale of their impact should they materialize.

Cost pressures

The need to manage costs is a constant concern for leaders. Supply chain resilience can mean introducing additional cost to a business through the stockpiling of critical spares or raw materials through to having alternative suppliers contracted to provide support should a primary supplier fail. These measures can all be capital-intensive – they mean boards have to make provision on their balance sheets to pay for this extra resilience. This is money that cannot then be invested elsewhere.

Even writing resilience requirements into a contract with a supplier, a seemingly sensible thing to do, can lead to increased costs for the purchaser. A good example would be an insistence from a purchaser for a specific and aggressive recovery time objective for the services the supplier is providing. This may mean the supplier itself will need to invest in increased production capacity, the stockpiling of certain materials and have extra staff ready to support should a disruption occur. And who will pay for all of this? Typically it will be the organization buying the services.

These additional costs can become a target for efficiency savings. Lean can sometimes mean being less resilient. After all, why pay for something that an organization might not consider will ever happen? To counter this argument, it is essential for resilience professionals to hold a good understanding of supply chain economics so they can challenge these decisions and show the resilience benefits of the investments being made.

Demand has changed

Consumers have become used to having access to quicker, cheaper and at the same time more reliable services. The ease with which consumers can find alternative suppliers that deliver a relevant and reliable set of services, and at prices customers are willing to pay, make it much easier for individuals to move their purchasing loyalties. These demands drive the need for a more efficient business that is able to adapt more rapidly to customer product needs and changes in consumer tastes and spending habits. In the push for greater efficiency and increased competition, supply chains can come under extreme pressure, with operations running with a minimal margin of error. A failure at a critical point along the supply chain, or at a key time for the business (for example in the lead-up to holiday periods for consumer goods), can be catastrophic for the business.

An increased amount of outsourcing

Increased levels of outsourcing have led to discrete processes (for example payroll) or entire functions being contracted to third-party organizations. This changes the dynamic of an organization's risk exposure. First, it decreases the visibility of risks to an organization's management team, since the resources managing a process or a function are now at more of an arm's length to the business. Second, the resources available to do something about these risks are no longer under the immediate and direct control of management – they have to manage the situation through a contract or sometimes via a separate tier of management. The results of these changes mean that in a world of increased outsourcing, disruption risks become less immediately visible and can seemingly appear out of the blue. In addition, the speed of an organization's ability to respond may be less, as it takes more time to direct a response when working through contracts and third-party relationships.

Increase in the frequency and severity of global risk events

Global risk events such as extreme weather (hurricanes, earthquakes, wildfires, etc) or major political and economic disruptions (protests in Hong Kong in 2019 and 2020 or the civil unrest in Chile in the same period, the wars in Ukraine in 2022 and the Middle East in 2023) can have a profound impact on supply chains by physically disrupting trade routes or production processes themselves.

By way of an example: Texas supplies approximately 75 per cent of the US's ethylene needs, an essential chemical building block for the production of plastics. When in 2017 Hurricane Harvey, a category 4 storm, smashed into the state, there were major fears about a national shortage of the chemical.[5] In the short term this led to price rises for the commodity but, more importantly, it demonstrated the potential impact of major climatic events on what have become highly fragile global supply chains.

These characteristics of modern organizations make supply chain disruptions more likely and their speed and impact much more pronounced. The focus on cost reduction and making efficiencies makes responding to supply chain disruptions more challenging.

What is needed is a stronger focus on preparedness through antici-pating [for correct word break] future supply chain risks and developing plans to address them. While this might mean introducing additional costs to an organization, the benefits of paying for increased resilience will generally outweigh the risks of leaving supply chain vulnerabilities unmitigated.

Just-in-time versus depth of supply

The emergence of just-in-time (JIT) manufacturing techniques in the 1960s sought to focus processes on the precise delivery of what customers were demanding. The concept addressed a wide range of measures designed to help organizations increase the quality and effi-ciency of their delivery methods.[6] JIT has since become synonymous with organizations seeking to reduce the amount of inventory they hold on site until the precise moment materials are needed in a production process. This extra capacity is considered by many as 'waste' that needs to be eliminated from a production process. However, this 'waste' can also provide some resilience to the effects of supply chain disruptions, with the extra inventory being useful when supplies have been delayed.

There is a constant trade-off to be made between JIT supply chain techniques and the need for resilience, which will invariably intro-duce extra costs into the system. It is the role of the business continuity and resilience practitioner to ensure that disruption risk exposures presented by JIT techniques are understood by manage-ment and to advocate the case for additional investments in resilience should they be needed.

This can be achieved using a simple equation:

$$(P + L) \times (\% \ probability \ of \ disruption)$$

P = Impact of premium pricing (procuring emergency supplies)

L = Lead times to secure replacement order

Using this equation, the cost of adopting a less-than-optimal JIT approach to sourcing can be compared with the overall cost an unmitigated disruption would cause.

As a worked example, a European bicycle manufacturer is exploring whether holding additional stock of pre-fabricated carbon fibre parts is worth the investment as a means to mitigate the risk of supplier delays of finished parts being shipped from Taiwan.

In this example:

- The organization usually expects to manufacture 1,000 units a day at $200 per unit, generating $1,200,000 of revenue over a six-day-a-week production schedule).

- The organization has one critical supplier supplying the materials needed for production. For each unit $100 is spent on raw materials.

- The risk of a six-week disruption has been calculated with a 30 per cent probability (see Table 13.1).

TABLE 13.1

P	Premium pricing impact (additional cost of ordering 10k units at a 20% increase in unit costs compared to the usual sourcing method):	**$200,000**
L	6 weeks of delay from order to arrival (cost shown is the loss of production):	**$7,200,000**
	Cost of managing disruption without a contingency plan (P+L):	**$7,400,000**
	Total cost assuming risk of disruption is a 30% probability:	**$2,220,000**

When balancing the total cost of the risk against the investments that might be needed to hold six weeks of extra contingency inventory, a more informed discussion exploring cost efficiencies versus resilience can be had. If the overall cost of implementing additional resilience is substantially less than the cost of the unmitigated disruption risk, the balance may be tipped towards holding more inventory.

There are, however, some dangers associated with using such a quantitative-based approach to seeking investments in resilience. The downside to this approach is that a binary calculation of risks might encourage a binary response from management. The purchase of an insurance policy for some of these risks will be highly attractive since it takes minimal effort and should provide a good level of financial protection. However, insurance will leave some risks unmitigated, namely the reputational damage caused by an unscheduled production stoppage, or a competitor seizing the disruption as an opportunity to tempt the organization's normal customers away. In addition, no matter how much the insurance payout that is expected, management would still need to put in place plans to resume production, and it is usually better to do this when the organization and its staff are not under the pressure of a disruption.

Assessing the risk

The first step to understanding the extent of an organization's supply chain risk is to understand the supply chain itself.

This means identifying who an organization's major suppliers are along the value chain. This can generally be achieved through the BIA process. It may also be possible to collect some of this information from an organization's procurement function, which should hold a list of all the major suppliers the organization currently contracts, or is in the process of negotiating with. This list needs to be challenged, however, as it is possible for certain suppliers not to be included here. This could be because no contract is in place with a supplier (which would be a significant concern for any critical third party or where large sums of money are being spent), or the organization's functions and divisions may hold the authority to tender contracts themselves with limited input from a central procurement function. Either way, the simple means to address this is to ask questions of the procurement function to understand how the process works for the on-boarding and ongoing management of a new supplier. It may also be possible to obtain a list from the finance team detailing which third parties are regularly receiving payments.

The next step involves triaging this list of suppliers. For many organizations, particularly those that manufacture or produce something, the list of suppliers will be very large. As an example, Nestlé reportedly works with 165,000 direct suppliers globally.[7] Such a list is far too long to process, so a means of triaging the most important ones will be needed.

Terms such as tier 1 and tier 2 suppliers are often used to describe the organizations that directly supply the business (tier 1) and the organizations that supply the tier 1 suppliers (tier 2). Such a hierarchy is more common in manufacturing organizations but is widely used elsewhere. Most organizations will know who their tier 1 suppliers are, but few solve the challenge of finding out who supplies their tier 1 suppliers. But as discussed earlier, it is at these lower levels (tiers 2, 3 and even 4) where the greatest amount of risk is likely to be found. The challenge, though, is how to obtain information about these suppliers. Asking a tier 1 supplier who supplies them is one approach, but is likely to yield mixed results and will be slow in larger organizations. Instead, many organizations have started to use external data sources such as shipping manifests and customs records information to build a picture of who their tier 1 suppliers trade with without having to actually ask the supplier. Such an approach can yield rapid and extensive results but it can also generate plenty of noise. Knowing where your tier 1 supplier sources its toilet rolls from is unlikely to be useful if you are tracing the component parts of a brake assembly for a motorbike. Getting access to the data is only the beginning – it is not uncommon to go from 100 tier 1 suppliers, to tens of thousands of tier 2 and 3 assets. So it will need to be analysed, cleaned and processed, often in vast quantities, to prove a link between each tier 1 supplier and the organization's own production locations, or other sites.

But once that data has been cleaned, it can then be mined for all sorts of useful information to inform a deeper assessment of risk which can then be ranked and prioritized for treatment.

Assessing criticality for tier 1 suppliers

Before jumping into a detailed analysis of tier 2 and below suppliers, some more basic detective work is needed to categorize, score and prioritize the suppliers that organizations hold a direct relationship with.

Criteria typically fall into five groups:

1 **Critical products and service suppliers:** This group of suppliers provides support to the organization's most critical products and services. The services they provide could be highly specialized and fundamental to the product or service they support. The BIA process, if delivered correctly, should deliver information about who these suppliers are and what the impact would be if they were disrupted.

2 **Highest spending:** These are the suppliers that the organization spends the most with on an annual basis. A supplier receiving large sums of money does not automatically mean they will be critical to the organization's overall objectives. However, it can be used as an indication of a highly important relationship, and one which may be very difficult to replace should there be any kind of disruption.

3 **Accumulation risk:** This is where a single supplier is used in multiple parts of the organization. This might be for the same supply or service, or multiple different services. The latter is important to identify, as while on their own each supply or service may not be that critical, when taken together a disruption to the supplier could have catastrophic effects for the organization as a whole.

4 **Alternatives are not readily available in the market:** Some supplies and services are so niche that only a very small number of organizations can deliver them. Arranging alternatives will likely have long lead times, or be highly costly. Other suppliers in this group would also include those that provide fully outsourced services, where the people, physical assets and critical data are all held and controlled by a third party, making an alternative hard to implement. A good example of this type of supplier could be a fund administrator for an investment bank, where their services are entwined with the bank's internal processes and IT systems. Finding an alternative and implementing their services would take a significant amount of time to plan.

5 **Supplier performance:** Those suppliers that have a track record of poor performance, or perhaps are subject to 'red flags' being raised about the health of their finances, will present an increased risk to an organization, particularly if they also fall into any of the other risk categories set out above. A supplier's performance and their company health can change over time. Regular due diligence exercises will be needed to provide up-to-date intelligence of supplier risks.

The depth of the risk assessment process should be determined by the importance of the supplier to the organization and the level of disruption risk that the supplier may itself be exposed to. It will not be feasible to go into detail below the tier 1 level of suppliers through this process, but for a small number of highly critical suppliers this will be necessary. This process may be relatively easy if the main tier 1 supplier is happy to be transparent and cooperate with the process. This will be highly challenging if they are not. Going deeper for some suppliers will be important, as there could be some substantial disruption risk exposures that are hidden deeper in the supply chain and are currently invisible to the organization and not being actively mitigated.

In organizations with mature procurement processes, it is likely that much of the data needed to triage the long list of tier 1 suppliers against the criteria above will be readily available. However, some level of analysis will still be required, as resilience is unlikely to have been a focus for the original data collection exercise when the contract was first tendered. Much of the emphasis of a procurement function is to ensure that supplies and services are contracted at the most economically advantageous price, balanced against quality and overall service delivery needs.

Resilience is just one of the topics that procurement will be covering as it seeks to strike a balance between the overall cost of a contract and the transfer of risks to a supplier. Few procurement professionals have a substantial background in business continuity and resilience, so it is unusual to find a significant focus on these areas. This means resilience professionals will need to undertake some of the leg work themselves to arrive at a triaged list of critical suppliers. In organizations with thousands of tier 1 suppliers, educating procurement professionals, category managers and contract owners to undertake this process themselves will be the most efficient means of delivery.

The next stage is to perform a risk assessment on the shortlisted group of more critical suppliers. This assessment should seek to understand the organization's exposure to disruption risks present within the supply chain. It is possible that existing risk assessments will provide some of the data needed, but in practice these are usually not undertaken to the depth needed to underpin recovery planning so further work is likely to be needed.

Existing sources of risk information could include:

· **Enterprise-level risk registers,** though these rarely provide a detailed contract-by-contract analysis of supply chain exposures and so will only really be useful to act as a signpost for risks and issues that will need further exploration.

· **Contract-level risk registers,** which will be bespoke to each supplier relationship but generally concentrate on commercial and contractor performance issues rather than scenarios that could give rise to a major disruption. These risk registers can often be the source of emerging supply chain risks, for example in the form of concerns being raised about a general decline in a supplier's overall performance. These could be signs of a more significant disruption risk sitting just below the surface.

· **Internal audit reports,** particularly where a deep-dive audit has been conducted on an individual critical supplier. Depending upon the scope of the audit, this would usually be conducted to a good degree of detail. However, some of the data needed may not be presented in the final report as auditors tend to 'report by exception', only reporting on areas of concern.

· **Anecdotal evidence,** held by contract managers, procurement or other members of staff in the organization that regularly interact with the supplier or depend upon their services. The knowledge held informally by these individuals can provide a richer source of insights into potential risks than any written record often can.

Extending the assessment to tier 2 (and below)

While it is entirely acceptable to place reliance upon the tier 1 suppliers to manage their own supply chains effectively and therefore stop any risk assessment at this point, evidence suggests that supply chain disruptions often begin life as an issue at a deeper level within the supply chain. A failure to understand risk exposures at this level may result in more significant disruptions that seemingly appear with no notice. More mature organizations will therefore want to spend time scrutinizing these risks to ensure resilience and recovery arrangements will be effective. Ultimately, if the tier 1 supplier fails, the effects of the disruption (not withstanding any potential contractual penalties) will sit with the contracting organization to own and manage.

For tier 1 and below, a standard risk assessment process can be followed, like that set out in ISO 31000, the International Standard for Risk Management. This is summarized in Figure 13.1.

Rather than focus on the risk assessment process itself, what is likely to be more helpful here is some guidance on how to approach delivering the assessment and the sort of risk themes to look out for.

Approaching the assessment

Unless the individual conducting the assessment holds a comprehensive understanding of each supplier, why they are important to the organization and what alternatives may be available in the event of a disruption, input will be needed from other internal stakeholders and external sources.

Important stakeholders in this process will include:

- procurement and supply chain professionals;
- contract managers;
- operations (focusing on individuals who are reliant upon the supplier's products or services, including quality management roles where these exist);
- enterprise risk management representatives;

FIGURE 13.1   Summary of the risk assessment process

SOURCE Adapted from ISO 31000

- country managers (useful to help provide input into assessments on local political, economic and environmental risks in the locations where the supplier may be based).
- insurance teams who will have access to a range of risk modelling capabilities including financial risk, natural hazards and climate change.

Open-source information is also available, often providing a rich supply of information to inform the assessment. Sources include:

- industry trade media publications and websites;
- guidance notes and general advice provided by legal advisers;

- audit and accountancy firms;
- insurance brokers and insurance companies;
- risk-modelling companies (for example climate modelling);
- credit and ratings agencies;
- international bodies, such as the World Economic Forum.

The choice of delivery method chosen for the risk assessment will reflect the type of stakeholders that will need to be involved and the internal culture of the organization:

- **Questionnaires** can be a cost-effective means to gather data from a wide range of stakeholders. Such a tool is helpful to obtain some of the basic source information needed to inform interviews or workshops where much of the detailed assessment process will then be undertaken. However, questionnaires on their own will not provide the complete picture needed, particularly when building a picture of the supply chain below the tier 1 level which will involve the collection, collation and analysis of significant amounts of data.

- **Workshops,** if correctly structured and facilitated, will provide a useful forum for a group of stakeholders to collectively feed into a risk assessment process and reach consensus over the results. Taking this approach can save a significant amount of time versus holding one-to-one conversations. In addition, workshop participants will also benefit from the insights and challenge provided in an open forum by colleagues, which will help further strengthen the overall analysis. However, be aware of the risks of 'group think' or an overbearing facilitation process that leaves little room for debate and prevents more novel risks from being discussed.

- **Interviews** are helpful when more detailed qualitative insights are needed. These can be used to either help prepare for a workshop, or as a means to challenge and refine workshop outputs. On occasion it may also be necessary to limit conversations with a very small group of individuals for confidentiality reasons. This could be because of the sensitive nature of the services provided by a supplier (for example in defence) or when a contract is at a key and sensitive stage of negotiation.

- **Data** sources that can be used to deliver a quantitative assessment of risk should be the main focus of attention and act as a key input into the workshops and interviews described above. Not all of these data sources will be readily available, but could include:

  - financial figures of the revenue that would be at risk as a result of a key supplier failing;

  - locations of tier 2 and below assets that support critical tier 1 suppliers;

  - hazard data relating to critical tier 1 and below locations (e.g. flood risk, wildfire, earthquake and geopolitical risk);

  - fraud, bribery and corruption risks (including the potential for child labour in locations where suppliers operate);

  - the financial stability and performance data of critical suppliers.

The specific focus of risk assessment will be driven by the individual context of the suppliers that fall within the scope of the exercise. This will make the outputs highly tailored to individual supplier circumstances. However, there are recurring risk themes that can be used to help structure the risk assessment discussion.

These are summarized in Table 13.2.

TABLE 13.2   Recurring themes in risk assessment discussion

Risk theme	Description	Useful sources of information
Financial stress	Signs of financial stress may indicate a supplier is at risk of defaulting on its contractual obligations, or is, in extreme circumstances, likely to fall into bankruptcy. Warning signs might include negative public reports and a company reporting a supplier asking for advanced payments in lieu of services being delivered, attempts to renegotiate commercial terms of a contract and delays in delivery or quality issues.	• Credit rating agencies • Trade credit data • Supplier performance data • Company external reporting • Share performance

TABLE 13.2   *continued*

Risk theme	Description	Useful sources of information
Geopolitical risk	A supplier that has significant operations in areas subject to major geopolitical risk could be exposed to the impacts of political disruption (e.g. confiscations, nationalization, blockades, civil and labour unrest). Signs of heightened risk might include knowing that supplies are manufactured, managed or transit through countries exposed to heightened geopolitical risk or are operating assets that might be an attractive target during periods of political instability.	• Local government advice/reporting • Credit rating agencies • International humanitarian agencies • Insurance brokers • Legal advisers
Natural catastrophes	A supplier that has significant operations in locations exposed to major natural catastrophe risks could be more vulnerable to physical disruption from earthquakes, hurricanes, mudslides and volcanoes, etc. Mapping supply and logistics locations against regions exposed to heightened natural catastrophe risks will help to identify the extent of any exposures present in this category.	• UN climate change bodies • National meteorological agencies • Insurance brokers and insurance companies • Data modelling vendors
Concentration risk	Suppliers whose sole operation (and perhaps its own supporting supply chain) is concentrated in one small geographical location will be at greater risk of disruption to more widespread events. Similar risks arise where a cluster of critical suppliers might be operating out of the same geographical area. These suppliers would all be exposed to similar external disruption risk events that would have a compound effect on the organization that is buying their services.	• Contract documentation • Publicly available information, including company reports • Insurance data (where key suppliers and their locations have been declared to the insurer) • Tier 2 and below mapping data

TABLE 13.2   *continued*

Risk theme	Description	Useful sources of information
	Mapping key supply and logistics locations will help to identify the extent of any concentration risk, including single points of failure (such as a single port).	
Production/ logistics failures	Suppliers that are operating more complicated production processes or logistics arrangements and are delivering or using untested techniques and technology could be exposed to increased disruption risk. Signs of heightened risk might be evidenced by a history of repeat issues and quality concerns, or the lack of any plausible and scalable alternative available on the open market.	• Supplier investor presentations • Trade media • Original tender documentation used to win the contract
Significant changes at the supplier	Suppliers that undergo substantial changes may be more exposed to increased levels of disruption, either consciously (by changing business processes/products) or unconsciously (where the change acts as a distraction for management). Indications of increased risk could be suggestions of a possible merger or acquisition of the supplier, a significant change in strategy (e.g. entering new markets, or exiting established ones) or significant structural reorganizations, including the purchase or divestment of real estate and assets used to support the supplies and services that are under contract.	• Supplier investor presentations • Trade media

TABLE 13.2   *continued*

Risk theme	Description	Useful sources of information
Structural risk	Lower-tier suppliers that are critical points of failure for multiple tier 1 suppliers could mean that any disruption at this level will be amplified further downstream.	• Tier 2 and below mapping processes • Tier 1 supplier's own data • Trade data (where available)
Cyber risk	Suppliers that operate highly complex technology and/or have a poor grasp on their IT security or perhaps operate in an industry that has a higher risk of cyber-attack. Most suppliers that may have a cyber vulnerability are unlikely to be open about it with their customers. Data sources for this risk are therefore much more limited than other risk categories.	• Media reports relating to recent breaches • Tier 1 supplier's own data/ reports • Industry insights (e.g. some sectors are at higher risk of cyber-attack than others)

Any risks that are identified will need to be evaluated and recorded in a consistent way to allow comparisons to be made when determining investments in resilience controls.

The evaluation and recording method should ideally mirror processes that are already in place within the organization to manage other operational risks. This alignment between scoring mechanisms will help to better position supply chain risks using language that is familiar to decision-makers, and allow broader comparisons to be made with other risks and the investments needed for their treatment. In addition, consistent scoring will also make it easier to transfer the risks into existing risk registers or reporting tools for ongoing management.

An example format for a simple risk register is shown in Table 13.3.

TABLE 13.3   Example simple risk register

Risk theme	Description	Owner	Controls	Rating Pre-controls	Rating Post-controls	Date of last review
Financial	Increasing raw material prices, coupled with fixed price contracts, expose ABC Ltd to unsustainable losses that could result in their bankruptcy.	Supply chain director	• Contract renegotiation • Alternative supplier contracts	HIGH	MEDIUM	December 2020 Audit and Risk Committee

In recording the risks, it is important to ensure that:

- risk descriptions are clear and provide a link between their cause and impact;
- each risk has a suitable senior owner who will be accountable for ensuring mitigation actions are delivered;
- controls are identified for all risks, and their effectiveness is objectively rated in the post-controls rating column;
- the date of the last risk review is captured and indicates at which level this review was undertaken.

Identify recovery options

Suppliers have so far been identified and likely disruption risks are well understood. The next stage is to do something about them. At this point in the process there is an overlap with the BIA method – third-party suppliers are one of the many resource dependencies that the BIA seeks to collect data on to inform recovery strategy development.

Chapter 10 sets out the method to deliver the BIA and define recovery strategies and will not be repeated here. Instead, this section will focus on the potential recovery options available that are specific to supply chain risks, along with their associated delivery challenges. These are summarized in Table 13.4.

TABLE 13.4   Recovery options and likely challenges

Recovery option	Likely challenges	Useful when
New/alternative supplier (under an agreed contract)	Requires some up-front cost and management time to implement. Could also undermine a relationship with the primary supplier.	There is limited capacity in the market but some alternatives are available. Management may be keen to minimize any disruption risks should one materialize (by reducing the time taken to on-board a new supplier).
New/alternative supplier (no contract currently in place)	Will slow down the recovery process as contracts will likely need to be negotiated prior to the delivery of services. This is especially true if the primary supply has abruptly stopped. The organization will also be in a weaker negotiation position to agree a favourable price.	There are plenty of readily available alternatives in the market, keeping prices at competitive levels.
Buy-out of the supplier	Costly exercise, likely requiring a board-level decision and may just transfer the root cause of the problem to the organization rather than solving it.	Supplier is unique and highly critical to the business. It may also be attractive in situations where a competitor is at risk of acquiring the supplier.
Management offer support to the supplier (including resources and advice)	Can be relatively low-cost but could be distracting to the organization and is unlikely to be appropriate for significant or long-term disruptions. Support could include management advice through to pre-purchasing supplies as a means to bolster a supplier's finances.	The supplier relationship is strong and the disruption can be managed with temporary support (eg a busy period, fire or other system failure).

TABLE 13.4   *continued*

Recovery option	Likely challenges	Useful when
In-source	Costly to achieve and will remove the original benefits of outsourcing in the first place (eg risk transfer). The process would also take a substantial amount of time to manage.	The economics of supplier sourced vs insourcing have changed or when there are limited viable alternatives in the market.
Holding more stock	Leads to an increase in the amount of working capital that is tied up and unavailable for other investments. This would also require increased storage space and potential security costs.	An organization is running a lean production process which cannot tolerate much downtime, or to buy time before an alternative supply can be sourced.

Current suppliers versus new suppliers

Much of the subject of this chapter so far has related to an organization's existing suppliers. However, this is only half the issue, as business continuity and resilience also need to be considered for new suppliers, particularly those that will be critical to supporting important areas of the organization.

The earlier into the procurement process a discussion on resilience can be had, the better. That is because it is easier to design resilience into a contract or process before it is finalized than it is to negotiate a contract change later down the line. The latter approach is likely to be costly as it will invariably lead to a requirement to change contract terms.

As a basic example, imagine IT services were being outsourced but the contract agreed made no mention of IT disaster recovery (ITDR) arrangements. Later the organization asks its supplier to put in place ITDR plans to meet the recovery requirements set by their BIA. For the supplier this will likely mean investing in new hardware and support services, and will come at a cost that they will be keen to pass on to the buyer. The better approach would have been to negotiate these services as part of the overall contract tendering process, at a lower price.

The challenge for resilience professionals is to get sufficient warning of a potential major procurement process taking place and to intervene to ensure resilience is at least considered at an early stage. This can be achieved in a number of ways:

- by building strong relationships with the organization's procurement team so that any new significant contracts being considered are flagged to the resilience team prior to their tender;
- through a policy that clearly defines the circumstances under which contracting authorities must consider resilience for certain types of contract, perhaps even requesting an exception from a higher authority where it has been decided that resilience will be taken out of the negotiation process (perhaps to minimize costs);
- by building a formal step into the procurement process for new tender documentation and contracts to be sent to the resilience team for review, allowing the team to establish whether a sufficient degree of resilience has been, or is being, considered.

In all of these approaches the challenge will be in preventing the resilience team from becoming swamped by a large number of tender materials and contracts. In large organizations this could run into the many hundreds per year. A degree of triaging will be needed using some of the criteria discussed earlier in this chapter.

Building resilience requirements into contracts

Any resilience-related requirements placed upon suppliers will need to be carefully thought through to balance their cost against the overall degree of risk protection they will provide. Not all contracts will need resilience clauses built into them – only those that are identified as important by the criteria discussed above, or if the supplier is considered to present a high disruption risk to the organization.

The degree of the resilience requirements placed upon the supplier will also vary, again driven by the criteria described above. Each of

FIGURE 13.2   Example low-effort, low-cost and higher-effort, higher-cost approaches to building resilience requirements into third-party contracts

Low degree of resilience	Higher degrees of resilience
Contract clauses requiring the supplier maintains a business continuity plan. Self-assessment questionnaires to establish existence of plan.	Clauses that require the supplier to follow a specific business continuity process. Contract clauses that place specific RTO and RPO requirements on the supplier. Requirements on: • stockpiling materials; • holding critical spares; • maintaining sufficient staff resources. Extensive and probing supplier audit programme.
Lower cost	Higher cost

the options chosen will sit somewhere on a scale (Figure 13.2) from being relatively easy to implement and offering a low degree of assurance over the resilience of the supplier, through to the other extreme. Each end of the scale will result in different degrees of cost being borne by the contracting authority relative to the effort that will be required by the supplier to implement them.

Seeking assurance from a third party

Just because a contract places a requirement on a supplier to implement and maintain a resilience capability does not mean the third party will actually deliver one. For more important suppliers, a programme of assurance to check the existence and quality of business continuity, ITDR and other resilience measures maintained by the supplier will be needed.

An organization's ability to conduct due-diligence-based assurance will depend upon:

· the willingness of the supplier to be open and transparent;
· the extent to which the contract requires it and gives the organization the authority to ultimately audit the supplier's arrangements.

Options for conducting due diligence and assurance vary – some providing light-touch assurance at low effort and others requiring a more formal and organized programme of auditing. Figure 13.3 sets out some of these options.

FIGURE 13.3   Supplier assurance options

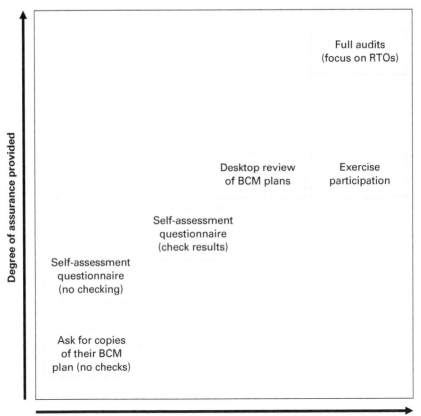

The frequency of assurance activities will again depend upon the criticality of each supplier. More important or higher-risk suppliers may need a greater degree of scrutiny. In larger organizations it will be impossible to conduct detailed assurance on all critical suppliers in one calendar year. A rolling annual assurance programme will be needed to provide a routine high-level assessment of a large number of suppliers (using a questionnaire approach) and a set of deeper-dive

audits focused on the more critical suppliers. Each year the programme will address a different set of supplier relationships with
results being used to feed into the next year's assurance programme
and future contract negotiations. This ensures that lessons learned
are addressed in any new supplier relationships that will be under
future consideration.

A simple starter set of questions to support a supplier review
process can be found in Chapter 18.

Post-incident

Just like in a crisis or a disruption directly impacting the organization,
a post-incident review is used to identify lessons and areas for
improvement. A similar process will be needed in the event of a
supply chain disruption or a near miss. The need for a post-incident
review will remain even if the incident did not lead to any material
disruption impacts being felt by the organization; there will still be
lessons to learn.

The organization's ability to conduct an open and transparent
review will rely upon the strength of the relationship it has with its
suppliers. Partnership-based supplier relationships can be much more
transparent and open than more transactional interactions. Understanding the nature of each supplier relationship will help
practitioners to design the most appropriate due diligence and assurance approach for each critical third party that will be subject to the
extra scrutiny. For some suppliers this could mean placing reliance
upon the internal reviews that are conducted by their own management or internal audit teams or by commissioning joint reviews
involving input from both parties.

Learnings from the post-incident review process will need to be
actioned appropriately. This will include:

- ensuring recovery strategies, options and plans are updated to
  reflect any lessons identified;

- reviewing existing contractual relationships where improvements can be made that will reduce the organization's overall exposure to disruption risks;
- making sure future and live procurement processes take account of any lessons before a new contract is awarded.

TABLE 13.5   Chapter checklist

☐	Ensure consistent and repeatable criteria are used to identify the organization's most critical suppliers.
☐	Start with a small and manageable list of suppliers.
☐	Look for existing sources of risk information already held by the organization that will help inform the analysis.
☐	Seek to map the supply chain that sits below Tier 1 suppliers and feed this into the risk assessment process.
☐	Conduct a risk assessment to identify vulnerabilities in the supply chain and use any existing risk management tools to support the analysis.
☐	Identify and document recovery options for the most critical or high-risk suppliers.
☐	Build a sound business case to secure any investment needed to deliver the recovery options (balancing cost versus the risk improvement it will deliver).
☐	Don't forget to consider new suppliers, ensuring appropriate mechanisms are in place to ensure resilience is 'baked in' to new contracts before they are agreed.
☐	Implement a due diligence and assurance regime balancing the level of scrutiny needed for each supplier (critical versus less critical) against the cost of its implementation.
☐	Don't forget to run post-incident reviews when things go wrong, and act upon the findings.

Notes

1 Lohr, S (2011) Stress test for the global supply chain, 19 March, www.nytimes.com/2011/03/20/business/20supply.html (archived at https://perma.cc/ZCN8-G4BR)

2 Oxford Business Group (2020) The impact of Covid-19 on global supply chains, 24 April, https://oxfordbusinessgroup.com/news/impact-covid-19-global-supply-chains (archived at https://perma.cc/FDQ3-WW56)

3 Weaver, M (2018) Most KFCs in UK remain closed because of chicken shortage, 19 February, www.theguardian.com/business/2018/feb/19/kfc-uk-closed-chicken-shortage-fash-food-contract-delivery-dhl (archived at https://perma.cc/9MNF-XGRD)

4 BBC, 2021, Suez blockage is holding up $9.6bn of goods a day, https://www.bbc.co.uk/news/business-56533250 (archived at https://perma.cc/P4W5-38L5)

5 Kaskey, J (2017) Hurricane Harvey has endangered the supply of the world's most important chemical, 1 September, www.independent.co.uk/news/business/news/hurricane-harvey-ethylene-supply-endanger-chemical-world-most-important-gulf-detroit-car-parts-a7923551.html (archived at https://perma.cc/BLH4-2P4C)

6 University of Cambridge (2016) JIT: Just-in-time manufacturing, https://www.ifm.eng.cam.ac.uk/research/dstools/jit-just-in-time-manufacturing/ (archived at https://perma.cc/H27E-GY8C)

7 Nestlé (2018) Responsible sourcing, www.nestle.com/aboutus/suppliers (archived at https://perma.cc/LNF5-QKFQ)

14

Reviewing, auditing and improving

We are all constantly adapting to change; we do this by living through new experiences and learning from our past mistakes and successes. This is happening all of the time, mostly subconsciously. Every lesson that we learn makes us individually wiser and stronger in the face of further change.

The same is true for organizations. Those that fail to adapt and evolve when confronted with the need for change are likely not to succeed in the long term, left behind by others that have themselves seized the opportunities that all change brings.

Think about when you last purchased a music CD, and now think about where you bought that CD. Most of us at some point in our lives will have visited a record shop, yet the large high street retailers, some with very long histories, have mostly all gone, replaced by a world of online streaming. It could be argued that these organizations did not adapt. This concept of adaptation and evolution in the face of change is at the heart of what makes an organization more resilient. Resilience is not a process that can be run once and then left. Incident response arrangements, business continuity and crisis management plans and procedures all need to be regularly reviewed and updated to ensure that they remain fit for their intended purpose and continue to comply with an ever-changing set of stakeholder and regulatory requirements.

A comprehensive review and auditing process, underpinned by a set of performance metrics, helps to achieve this by checking that an organization's most important recovery arrangements are in place, are being maintained and are likely to be effective when they are most needed.

This chapter explains the different types of review needed to maintain a healthy business continuity regime, who should deliver them and what their intended outcomes should be. It seeks to explain that any type of review, formal or informal, is not something to be feared; instead, they should be embraced as an opportunity to learn and improve. This chapter also explores the performance metrics that will need to be collated to demonstrate business continuity is working as it should be, including measures that seek to understand the completeness of the business continuity delivery process and the health and effectiveness of recovery capabilities themselves.

The benefits of a review, and why not to fear a visit from the auditor

Reviews afford the practitioner an opportunity to improve and get better at what they do. It is, however, human nature to have some degree of scepticism and perhaps fear of a formal audit process. Anxiety about what the auditors might find and report to senior management is natural but can be overcome when you realize that auditors in particular are not there to catch management out or deliberately embarrass colleagues in front of peers.

Their role is one of helping the board to identify areas of weakness in the organization's risk control framework and to position the need for further investment in managing the risk exposures that have been left behind. The auditors can be extremely helpful in giving business continuity and resilience professionals a voice at board level and a platform to pitch for more resources and senior management commitment to support their programme of work.

So rather than take a defensive approach when the auditors come knocking, it is better to see their involvement as an opportunity to learn and improve.

When notified of a potential audit, resilience practitioners should seek to be helpful and supportive. This means:

- Work collaboratively with audit to ensure the scope of the review is focused in the right areas. There may be discrete areas of the programme that are a challenge to deliver and would benefit from an independent view of possible solutions to overcome these challenges. Guiding the scoping process will ensure that the maximum amount of benefit is delivered from the review.

- Open doors for the auditors, making sure they interview the right people and have access to the documentation they need to make informed opinions about the subject of the audit.

- Encourage colleagues to be transparent and helpful in their interactions with the auditors, but ensure they stick to the facts.

- Turn around requests promptly to help the auditors meet their deadlines. Audit committees meet infrequently and so missing deadlines might put the delivery of the report back by three or six months, reducing the effectiveness of the outputs.

- Make a concerted effort not to be defensive and obstructive when the audit report is issued. Remember, this is an opportunity to learn and consider the solutions that would help address anything the auditors have found.

- Ensure that any factual inaccuracies in draft reports are challenged as early as possible so that the final output is an accurate reflection of the situation.

- Take it as an opportunity to learn; it should not be a battle!

Taking the approach set out above will help to make the audit process quicker and a lot less painful. And if significant issues are identified, a good relationship with the auditors may help with the way they position this message to senior management.

Avoiding the self-review threat

There is a general principle of auditing that suggests individuals who have had a significant role in actually delivering what is the subject of the audit are not in the best position to provide an objective review of it.

This is why internal audit teams typically report to the audit committee of a board, working closely with the chair of that committee, who is commonly a non-executive director. This prevents management interference in the design of the annual audit programme and the delivery of audit reviews. After all, they may have a vested interest in ensuring that audit results paint their organization, decisions and actions in a positive light.

While it is important to avoid the self-review trap, this is not to say that a review of a business continuity plan cannot be performed by someone who has had a role in writing it. Two simple questions can be used to help establish who should deliver the review, based on the reason for undertaking the audit:

1 **Is an objective, independent opinion needed to inform, for example, the audit committee and board's assessment of management control?** If yes, someone independent from the delivery process is likely to be a more appropriate choice to perform the review.

2 **Is the output from the review needed by management to inform further developments of their business continuity arrangements (e.g. checking a plan is complete, training has been effective and up to date or actions taken arising from an exercise)?** If yes, it is likely that the review can be undertaken by someone who had a role in delivery. However, there are still circumstances where independent input may be needed, for example if certain expertise is not available from an in-house team, or where individuals may be too close to the subject of the review to be able to spot areas of improvement.

Linking assurance to the three lines of defence

Assurance can take many forms, from an in-depth audit involving a forensic assessment of a subject through to lighter-touch reviews involving an element of self-assessment. In fact, a formal audit is only one type of assurance review available; other, less formal means of assurance will be more widely used in most organizations and so are worthy of consideration here.

So if internal audit is not delivering the bulk of what constitutes an organization's performance management programme, who is?

The three lines of defence model, first discussed in Chapter 9, can be used to describe some of the types of reviews and audits employed at different levels of an organization, and who would typically deliver them (see Table 14.1).

TABLE 14.1   Summary of assurance activities across the three lines of defence

	Typical nature of review focus	Typical delivery methods	Example
First line of defence	Establish the extent to which arrangements owned by first-line teams are in place and complete.	• Management-commissioned reviews delivered either internally, or involving external third parties.	Management review of the completeness of recovery plans maintained by operational teams.
Second line of defence	Checking the completeness or effectiveness of recovery arrangements implemented by the first line against the organization's policy for business continuity.	• Semi-independent audits, usually commissioned by business continuity and resilience teams and delivered internally, or with external third-party support.	Review performed by the central business continuity team over the completeness of recovery plans across the organization, comparing delivery against the requirements set by the organization's policy.
Third line of defence	Providing an independent opinion of compliance against a defined process, policy or regulation.	• Formal internal audits reporting to the audit committee.	Independent audit reporting to the audit committee on compliance with the organization's internal BCM policies.

In addition to internally led reviews, or those being delivered by third-party experts and independent audit teams, peer reviews can also be a useful means through which to gather feedback.

A peer review could be delivered by staff from another part of the same organization or individuals from a similar organization, a major supplier or professional body. These reviews are usually organized under reciprocal arrangements, meaning the receiving organization will return the service in the future. This could potentially introduce a possible conflict of interest, but so long as the outputs are not being used to provide a report that senior management or the audit committee will place reliance on, this risk should be quite small. Confidentiality issues will also need to be addressed, and for many commercial organizations these risks will outweigh the benefit of a peer review. Non-disclosure agreements can be used to prevent information about the organization's recovery arrangements from being leaked.

Performance metrics and maturity models

In order to measure something, some kind of scale is needed to make comparisons against. Without a set of well-designed performance measures and metrics to determine whether outcomes have been achieved and objectives met, we will have limited means to assure ourselves that the effort put into building an organization's resilience arrangements will deliver the capability desired.

Picking the right performance metrics is important – measure the wrong thing and management could be given false confidence over the effectiveness of the organization's plans. Setting the bar too high, too early could set the programme up to fail, resulting in a loss of confidence from senior stakeholders. Maturity models are a useful vehicle to help strike a balance between aiming for an overall outcome versus what is realistic and achievable at any given point in time. In most environments, moving from zero maturity to a fully functioning, industry-leading resilience capability will not happen overnight. Yet many practitioners will come under immense pressure to deliver rapid results. This is where maturity models can help by showing an assessment of capability through time, providing a very simple means to demonstrate the benefits of investments in resilience over a defined period.

Before exploring maturity models in more detail, first it is important to understand the nature of different types of performance metric available to the practitioner.

At the most simplistic level, performance metrics for business continuity can be categorized into three groups:

1 Completeness

2 Compliance

3 Effectiveness

Completeness

Metrics measuring completeness describe the extent to which business continuity capabilities have been implemented against a predefined programme plan. For example, the plan may state that all departments must conduct a table-top exercise at least once annually. In this example the measure would be how many exercises have been completed, and how many remain outstanding.

In summary, these metrics seek to establish whether business continuity deliverables, such as plans, recovery solutions, procedures and policies:

- have been completed;
- are up to date;
- contain no gaps;
- cover the full scope of what is critical to the organization.

Compliance

These metrics are designed to establish whether capabilities comply with the organization's business continuity or resilience policy or some form of external standard. This could be a particular regulation, government or industry guidelines, or a national or international standard such as ISO 22301. Performance against these standards is a means for organizations to measure themselves against codified good practice. This could be achieved through a formal gap analysis against an external standard, or a review using the organization's own internal policies and standards as the benchmark.

Effectiveness

Knowing arrangements arc in place and good practice is being followed in their delivery is important, but this group of metrics goes further to establish whether they will actually work. A performance measurement programme with these metrics missing will likely be giving senior management false assurance over the organization's preparedness for disruption. They are, however, some of the harder metrics to define and measure. As an example, they could be derived from a qualitative assessment of a crisis management team's performance during an exercise, or a set of quantitative measures such as metrics relating to the actual recorded availability of critical IT systems.

This group of metrics typically seek to demonstrate that:

- plans are capable of coping with a range of plausible but significant disruption scenarios, demonstrating that they will work when they are to be used;
- staff with a role to play in overseeing a response have the knowledge and skills needed to deliver an effective recovery;
- recovery strategies and solutions are demonstrated to work.

Maturity models

Maturity models are a tracking and reporting tool used to show the position of the current state of an organization's capability on a maturity scale. The results can then be used to set improvement targets and track progress across an entire organization, or by performing the assessment for individual business lines, functions and sites. While the models themselves can take time to build, as the contents often need to be highly tailored to an organization's specific context, once in place they are a useful vehicle to communicate a complex set of data in a short and simple format.

The models typically use between three and five maturity 'steps' and then explore the quantitative measures or behaviours that would need to be observed at each stage of maturity.

A simple example using a four-stage model is shown in Table 14.2.

TABLE 14.2 Four-stage maturity model

	Incomplete Key capabilities are missing, inadequate or are in the early stages of development.	Developing Some gaps in key capabilities are evident but with some evidence of emerging good practice.	Coordinated A full set of capabilities are in place across the organization and are consistent in their design and implementation.	Optimized There is a culture of resilience, integrated with other risk management activities.
Governance, accountability and responsibility	None in place or highly fragmented	Evidence of a centrally managed programme and/or some structures in place at a function or site level	A planned governance structure drives consistency in delivery across the organization	Full governance regime that is fully integrated into an enterprise approach to managing risks
Business impact and risk analysis	Missing, or in the early stages of design	Evidence that aspects of a BIA and risk assessment process are being delivered in some areas of the organization, but these have not been standardized or are being coordinated	The BIA and risk assessment method is structured and consistently applied to drive local-level recovery planning and the development of enterprise-level recovery strategies and solutions	Outputs from the BIA and risk assessments are used to inform strategic risk planning, and enterprise risk scenarios are used to inform event-based incident response plans and stress-testing
Recovery plan development	None are in place, or are not formally documented	Some plans are in place but do not follow a consistent format and may be missing crucial contents	A consistent set of high-quality plans are in place across the organization	Plans are fully owned by teams. Enterprise, function, site and team-level risks are routinely used to build and further refine recovery arrangements that are capable of managing a full set of disruption risks

TABLE 14.2 *continued*

	Incomplete Key capabilities are missing, inadequate or are in the early stages of development.	Developing Some gaps in key capabilities are evident but with some evidence of emerging good practice.	Coordinated A full set of capabilities are in place across the organization and are consistent in their design and implementation.	Optimized There is a culture of resilience, integrated with other risk management activities.
Exercising, training and awareness	No training or exercises are delivered	Evidence that some training and exercises are taking place in isolated areas of the organization but with no sharing of good practice or consistency in the approaches used for delivery	A full training and exercising programme is in place	Training, exercise and stress-testing activities are built into other risk management programmes. Exercises are a commonly used tool to drive continuous improvement
Review and maintenance	No formal review processes are delivered	Ad hoc review and maintenance activities with limited central coordination or consistency	A structured, planned and coordinated approach to delivering reviews and maintenance activities	Resilience assurance activities form an integral part of the organization's broader assurance regime

Planning versus capability

A comprehensive performance management programme will take elements from all three of the metrics categories set out above (completeness, compliance, effectiveness). No two performance regimes will be the same; with a wide variety of metrics to choose from, there is no one size fits all. Before jumping into finalizing a list of performance metrics, time should be spent understanding what the intended outcome is for the performance management regime.

One of the most common errors for performance regimes is to put too much focus on measuring progress against a project plan and not enough on giving assurance to stakeholders over the level of recovery capability that is actually in place. A report card issued to an executive with lots of green ratings showing how key business continuity project milestones have been met does little to give them any confidence over the level of disruption risk the organization is currently exposed to.

There are four simple questions that can be used to help structure, and then test, the usefulness of any performance regime:

1 Who is the data for?

2 What objective does the data collected need to achieve?

3 Does the data you have access to allow you to achieve that objective?

4 What do I expect the reader to do with the information?

Who is the data for?

Every stakeholder will have a different need. Understanding their interests will help to design the most appropriate performance regime, picking the metrics that give key stakeholders the confidence they need (see Table 14.3).

TABLE 14.3   Defining stakeholder assurance needs

	Typical assurance needs	What this means for performance management
Business continuity or resilience team	• Are the plans in place across the organization in line with the standards and guidelines that have been set? • Are there any gaps in plans, procedures or other capabilities that need to be addressed through improvement? • Will the organization's recovery arrangements work when needed?	A broad range of metrics will be needed, mostly focusing on helping the team to spot and then execute any improvements needed to the organization's recovery arrangements and to help identify any issues that may be systemic across the organization and will therefore require specific treatment.
Board directors	• Are disruption risks properly controlled by management, and within the organization's tolerance for disruption? • Are investments in resilience appropriate? • Are management taking the risks seriously?	A focus on whether resilience arrangements keep the organization within the risk appetite and tolerance set by the board – this generally means board directors are most interested in knowing whether the arrangements are effective rather than receiving a gap analysis against an external standard. However, board directors often ask the extent to which the approach being taken, or the capability that is in place, compares with peer organizations.
Executive	• Will the plans work? • Are all areas of the organization supporting the process?	The executive tend to have a split focus between checking the effectiveness of arrangements and ensuring that plans are in place (complete) across the organization. In more heavily regulated industries, the executive would also ask detailed questions about compliance, particularly where a regulatory failure could lead to a formal investigation, fine or the removal of the organization's operating licence.

TABLE 14.3   *continued*

	Typical assurance needs	What this means for performance management
Audit committee	• Is the control environment working as it should? • Is business continuity being managed in line with other risk management activities?	As the committee of the board that takes an enterprise-wide view of risk management, the audit committee's primary focus will be more of a compliance one. However, in doing so they will also be keen to assure themselves that management have put in place recovery arrangements that will work and are doing so in a joined-up way with other risk management activities.
Departmental heads	• Is my plan in place? • Are plans in place for areas of the organization that I depend upon?	A focus on completeness – for many department heads, business continuity is a major distraction, and so their level of interest tends to limit their focus on whether plans are actually in place and in date.
Regulators	• Are regulatory requirements being met?	A focus on compliance – though more mature regulators are asking harder questions of organizations seeking assurance over the effectiveness of plans that are in place.
Customers (particularly business-to-business)	• Will the organization deliver what it has promised, even in times of disruption?	A focus on effectiveness – how the outcome is achieved may be less of a concern, but knowing that the organization's plans can recover services in line with expectations will be the focus.
Shareholders	• Are investments in resilience appropriate to the risks facing the organization?	Short-term shareholders may see resilience as a cost that needs to be stripped from the business, whereas longer-term investors will take assurance from an effective resilience capability.

What objective does the data collected need to achieve?

In the early developmental stages of a business continuity programme, completeness and compliance metrics are likely to be the main focus. However, once arrangements have been established and bedded in, increased weight is often given to metrics measuring the effectiveness of the organization's recovery capabilities.

The context and culture of the organization, and who is asking for the assurance, can also influence the type of metrics chosen. In highly regulated organizations, an entire assurance programme can be skewed towards demonstrating compliance with an external regulatory regime, often at the expense of a more probing assessment of whether the plans and procedures that have been put in place will actually work. Typically, executive committees are less engaged by discussions about compliance with external standards such as ISO 22301; instead, they are keen to understand whether arrangements will actually work when they are needed and what level of protection is being afforded to the organization from the investments they have previously authorized.

Finally, in an environment where customers are seeking the assurance, the approach can vary quite significantly. Customers with a more mature view of resilience, and typically those with a larger spending power over an organization, will generally be asking questions about the effectiveness of recovery arrangements. For this group the fact the organization has a business continuity plan is a given. What they will want to know is whether that plan recovers the part of the organization that they rely upon in line with their own recovery expectations. While this approach is still relatively rare, where it is used, the effort involved in servicing these requests can be quite significant. However, in most cases the approach is more limited, including asking for a supplier's personal attestation that plans are in place, or simply requesting a copy of their business continuity plan.

Does the data you have access to allow you to achieve your objective?

The collection of project delivery milestone data should be readily available and easy to obtain. This is probably why so many performance regimes focus on reporting these statistics. However, and as discussed above, these metrics do very little to help in satisfying many of the more senior stakeholders receiving the reports, who are often looking for more detailed assurance.

Data pertaining to the effectiveness of resilience arrangements is harder to obtain, but is still possible to collect. One way of addressing this is to explore for each of the key business continuity deliverables what metrics could be captured to demonstrate their effectiveness (see Table 14.4).

TABLE 14.4 Measuring the effectiveness of resilience arrangements

Plans	• Have they passed a test seeking to establish whether the plan is complete? If no, there is little point in further exploring whether the plan will actually work. • Have plans been subject to a variety of regular exercises using different formats? A basic table-top exercise is unlikely to be a sufficient test on its own. • What did these exercises demonstrate – were the plans useful, or were major gaps and shortcomings identified that needed addressing? If there is limited evidence of a meaningful follow-up after each exercise, the plans are likely to be less effective.

Recovery solutions	• Is there objective evidence to demonstrate that the recovery solution is in place (eg a recovery centre contract, a report from a third-party IT provider on an IT DR test of the managed service they supply)?
	• Have the solutions been properly tested, eg:
	   – For remote workers, can they access systems from home?
	   – For secondary office locations, do they have the required number of desks?
	   – For the stockpiling of parts, has a recent stock-take been done?

People (responsible for leading the response)	• Have response personnel been properly trained? • Have they attended a range of different types of exercise simulation? • For the most critical roles, have they undertaken some kind of formal assessment or qualification?

What do I expect the reader to do with the information?

This is the most overlooked step in the process.

Many performance regimes fall at this hurdle in the rush to deliver a report to whatever stakeholder has requested it. Having addressed the questions above, this is the moment to pause and make sure that the finished product actually answers the question and will deliver the results needed.

So if the reader is keen to understand progress against the project plan and sign off on the next phase of the work – does the data show what milestones have been delivered, what is upcoming and what (if any) risks might delay delivery?

And if the reader is expected to make a decision on a proposed investment in resilience – does the report explain why that invest-ment is needed (for example by showing that without it, current recovery arrangements are ineffective)?

This may sound very basic, but it is surprising how many manage-ment reports and performance regimes fail to tell the story they set out to convey.

Different types of review

So far this chapter has discussed why reviews are important, who might deliver them and the different interests of the stakeholders involved. But what form should they take, and what approach should be used to deliver them?

Table 14.5 sets out four of the most common options for deliver-ing a review (self-assessment, quality check, walk-through and a full audit or gap analysis).

Self-assessments are worthy of some additional explanation here as they can provide a highly adaptable, low-cost approach to conduct-ing a review and to identifying areas for further improvement. However, the design of the questionnaire is important – a poorly phrased question will deliver erroneous results.

It is important to:

TABLE 14.5 Types of review

Assurance gained	Self-assessment Low	Quality check	Walk-through	Full audit/gap analysis High
Overview	Usually conducted by individuals who have been involved in the development of what is the subject of the review using a questionnaire built around a pre-agreed scorecard.	A review that seeks to ensure key deliverables (usually business continuity plans) are up to date and contain all the necessary components.	Involving a page-by-page review of a key deliverable. In the case of a plan this may involve using scenarios to explore how the document would respond to various disruption events.	A more forensic assessment of resilience arrangements against a policy, external standard or good practice guidelines.
Useful when	✓ A rapid assessment is needed of an organization's current capability ✓ A simple comparison is required between a large number of teams, locations or business units ✓ An inexpensive delivery option is preferred	✓ Confidence is needed that a deliverable is in place and is complete ✓ A pre-exercise check is needed that a plan is up to date ✓ As a means to re-familiarize team members with a plan	✓ A logical test is needed to determine whether a plan might work during a disruption ✓ Teams need to become more familiar with how a plan works and their roles within it	✓ Detailed and comprehensive assurance is needed ✓ Strong evidence is needed to underpin reporting to senior stakeholders and if investments are needed ✓ An independent opinion is needed
Limitations	✗ Relies upon participants completing the assessment honestly ✗ Can present a self-review threat ✗ Provides limited objective assurance over the effectiveness of arrangements	✗ Provides limited assurance over the effectiveness of the plan ✗ Results are relevant at that moment in time and may quickly become out of date (eg contact details changing, staff moving roles)	✗ May leave some planning assumptions untested (which will be better addressed via a full audit or exercise)	✗ Can be time-consuming and expensive to complete ✗ Can give false assurance if not designed and delivered effectively

- Ensure questions are clear in what they are asking by avoiding too much jargon and can therefore be easily understood by colleagues speaking different languages.

- Avoid asking more than one question per question. This is a common mistake of questionnaire design and will make it impossible to compare the results easily (an example would be 'When was the last time your plan was reviewed, and was the plan then updated?').

- Ensure there is a mix of multiple- and single-choice questions along with free-text options. It is easier to make comparisons and conduct benchmarking using quantitative data, but the qualitative information can also provide a rich source of insights so should not be missed in the design.

- Include response options that leave minimal ambiguity. While a simple scale of 1 = low and 5 = high can be helpful to provide a rapid response, it is often better to be more specific, as one respondent's high might be another person's medium. As an example:

  To what extent have staff named in business continuity plans participated in an exercise in the past 24 months?

  a. *No exercises have been performed in the past 24 months.*

  b. *Exercises have been performed but records of who attended them have not been kept.*

  c. *20 per cent of named individuals have taken part in an exercise.*

  d. *50 per cent of named individuals have taken part in an exercise.*

  e. *100 per cent of named individuals have taken part in an exercise.*

Self-assessment questionnaires can be utilized in a number of helpful ways:

1 in the early stages of a programme, or at key points along it, to provide a baseline assessment of current capability and a rapid check of the progress being made;

2 to quickly capture lessons and feedback arising from a recent exercise or live incident response;

3 as a means to provide benchmarking data to make comparisons between a large number of business units, teams or locations;

4 as a tool to share good practice and encourage less mature areas of the organization to improve.

If a large survey is planned involving multiple locations and teams, it is advisable to pilot the questions with a small group of staff in order to test its design and efficacy before releasing it to a wider group. If a pilot is chosen, it is useful to ensure the group is made up of individuals representative of the overall population that will be asked to complete the survey once it has been launched.

Taking action, making improvements

The main purpose of conducting reviews and measuring progress against performance metrics is to gather the evidence needed to make further improvements to an organization's recovery arrangements. A performance regime is wasted if this final step is not taken.

To achieve the benefits of all the hard work involved in measuring performance, a structured and coordinated approach to tracking improvements will be needed.

There are four steps to achieving this:

1 **Planned:** There should be a centrally managed performance management plan that sets out the methods that will be used to measure performance, the metrics that will be tracked and where reviews will be focused. This would form the basis of an annual performance plan that targets particular functions, teams, locations or even themes (e.g. work area recovery or cyber-risks) so that the outputs from an organization's review activities can be optimized.

2 **Collated:** Data from all performance and review activities should be centrally collected and collated. This will allow trends in data to be more easily identified and addressed where there are recurring weaknesses present in multiple areas across an organization. The repository will also help in organizing and then sharing examples of good practice so less mature areas of the organization are able to benefit.

3 **Actioned:** A means to identify, assign ownership to and track the delivery of improvement actions will ensure the effort spent on identifying areas for improvement is followed through into action that leads to sustainable improvements.

4 **Reviewed:** For some of the more significant improvements identified, a further follow-up review might be needed to provide assurance to stakeholders that a risk or issue has been addressed and closed. This step provides a further opportunity to identify good practice and will help inform the next year's performance management plan.

TABLE 14.6   Chapter checklist

☐	Identify the assurance needs of all key stakeholders.
☐	Establish performance management roles in each of the three lines of defence.
☐	Develop a set of performance metrics that strike a balance between measuring completeness, compliance and effectiveness of resilience arrangements.
☐	Identify the most appropriate means of achieving assurance (methods and tools).
☐	Identify who is best positioned to deliver each of the reviews in the plan.
☐	Run review pilots where they are needed (eg for self-assessment questionnaires).
☐	Build a maturity model to help track progress over time.
☐	Document the work in a performance management plan; communicate this with key stakeholders.
☐	Collect and collate the output from performance reviews and audits.
☐	Track the progress of improvement actions.
☐	Re-perform reviews for the more significant improvements identified.
☐	Remember to consider an audit as an opportunity to learn.

PART THREE

Templates and checklists

15

Plan contents and tips for completion

TABLE 15.1 Typical contents of a plan and tips for its completion

Example contents	Tips
Introduction • Objectives • Scope • Assumptions • Response structure	• The objectives define the focus of the response and the relative priority given to various activities. Many organizations list protecting life as their primary objective, followed by resuming business-critical activities and communicating with stakeholders. • The scope should clearly set out which parts of the organization are covered by the plan. Be careful not to exclude critical parts of the organization. • Assumptions should help guide the reader but not limit the plan's utility. For example, an assumption that suggests the HQ will coordinate the response to a global crisis would be fine, but an assumption suggesting the plan does not cover pandemic scenarios (without a specific pandemic plan being in place) would likely be inappropriate. • The response structure should be very easy to follow and pick up with minimal training needed. It should also, wherever possible, follow existing governance arrangements. • Focus on roles instead of named members of staff – this reduces the need for updates should personnel move on from a role.

TABLE 15.1   *continued*

Example contents	Tips
Incident response phase • Incident response team • Activating the plan • Assembly points • Initial assessment • Escalation process • Incident response team checklists	• Response instructions should be focused and clear, making it easy for readers to quickly follow in an emergency. • Activation criteria should set out the circumstances when a plan will be invoked and (if necessary) who has the authority to do so and who would then be informed (escalation and notification). • Delegations of authority for the incident response team should be clearly defined. • The initial assessment process should be a generic guide that can be applied to any crisis scenario, eg exploring impacts on staff, operations, supply chain, finances and customers. • Escalation processes should not miss any key parts of the business – all individuals who need to be informed should be listed here. • Incident response checklists work best as lists that are easy to follow and check off in an emergency. They should be sufficiently flexible to allow adaptation to individual scenarios.
Crisis management plan • Defining a crisis • Activating the crisis management plan • Crisis management team • The role of the crisis management team • Command centre location and set-up • Crisis management checklists	• How an emergency or business disruption escalates into a full-blown crisis should be clearly defined (eg when X impact on revenue, or Y impact on customers). • Ideally the definition for a crisis should leave little room for interpretation, making it easy to determine when a crisis has actually occurred or has the potential to happen. • The physical location where the crisis team will meet should be set out. • If the team will meet remotely, dedicated conference line details would be helpful, remembering to ensure that any special access codes/PINs to start a call should be available to all who need it rather than in the hands of one individual.

TABLE 15.1   *continued*

Example contents	Tips
Business continuity strategies and solutions • Recovery priorities • Solutions for (staff, site, equipment, IT, data, suppliers)	• Business continuity strategies and solutions should be event-agnostic – this means the plans should be capable of working in any disruptive event. • This section should be focused around the tasks to be delivered in the event of resource X or Y being unavailable (without referring to why it is unavailable). • The recovery solutions should be translated into a set of easy-to-follow actions designed to deliver each solution. • Recovery actions should be assigned to individual roles for implementation.
BCP appendix • Log forms • Impact assessment templates • Standard meeting agendas • Pre-agreed communications templates • Contacts directory	• Contains the useful documentation that the various response teams will need to support a response. • Any templates should be in an easily printable format, or editable to allow tailoring. • Contact details should, wherever possible, be kept on a system where they can be more easily kept up to date. However, for many businesses, having a paper copy of the plan with these numbers listed provides an additional level of resilience should IT systems be disrupted.

16

Response templates

TABLE 16.1   Incident impact analysis template

Date and time of first notification [when did the incident first occur?]	
Summary of the incident (as currently known)	
• Overview of the issue • Expected or actual business impacts • Personnel impacts • Operational impacts	
Summary of actions/decisions taken so far	
Expected decisions needed from response teams	
1.... 2.... 3....	

TABLE 16.1   *continued*

Stakeholders currently involved in the response		
• Incident lead • Operational/tactical teams (including regional/entity CMT) • External stakeholders (including regulators)		
Business impact assessment	Assessment	Notes
1 **People**	Extreme/High/ Medium/Low	
2 **Operations**	Extreme/High/ Medium/Low	
3 **Client and reputation**	Extreme/High/ Medium/Low	
4 **Financial**	Extreme/High/ Medium/Low	
5 **Legal and regulatory**	Extreme/High/ Medium/Low	
6 **Data**	Extreme/High/ Medium/Low	

TABLE 16.2   Decision log form

Ref #	Decision/action	Rationale	Owner	Date/time	Follow-up actions

The standing agenda shown in Table 16.3 can be used by all response teams to help structure their discussions.

TABLE 16.3   Sample response team agenda

1 Roll call	• Confirm who is in attendance • Review roles and responsibilities • Identify any competency gaps
2 Ground rules	• Attendance • Information-handling • Confidentiality • Decision-making principles/cycle

3 Response priorities and objectives	• Set standing priorities, eg:
	  – Safeguard life
	  – Protect assets and reputation
	  – Protect and/or recover critical processes
	  – Manage communications
	• Confirm measurable objectives for the response

4 Incident impact analysis	• Request a status report from other response teams • Perform assessment using template
5 Issues and actions	• Identify issues for management • Agree response options and actions
6 Forward look	• Identify future decision and action requirements
7 Next steps and any other business	• Future meeting schedule • Confirm actions and priorities

17

Assurance scorecard

An example business continuity assurance scorecard

The 13 questions in Table 17.1 are designed as a simple assurance scorecard that can be used and further tailored to inform a self-assessment regime targeted at a business unit/team or site.

The delivery of an enterprise-level review would require an additional focus on the existence of broader governance arrangements and the coordination activities needed to tie business continuity and resilience activities together. The questions in Table 17.1 can be further adapted to support this if needed.

The response to each question is guided by a three-point scoring regime, with the evidence required to meet each stage clearly defined.

TABLE 17.1 Example business continuity assurance scorecard

	Question	Requirements not met 1	Requirements met, with some exceptions 2	Requirements met, well established 3
Governance, accountability and responsibility	1 Has someone been assigned responsibility for business continuity within each business unit?	There is no individual assigned responsibility for business continuity within each business unit.	An individual has been assigned responsibility for business continuity within each business unit.	An individual has been assigned responsibility within each business unit and is fully aware of their responsibilities and has sufficient time to dedicate to their role.
	2 Is ownership of the business continuity plan(s) assigned to an individual?	There is no assigned individual who owns the business continuity plan.	An individual has been assigned ownership of the business continuity plan.	An individual has been assigned ownership of the business continuity plan and they are fully aware of their responsibilities associated with it.
	3 Have business unit staff been assigned responsibility for implementing recovery arrangements and responding to incidents?	Business unit staff have not been assigned responsibility for implementing recovery arrangements and responding to incidents.	Business unit staff have been assigned responsibilities for implementing recovery arrangements and responding to incidents, though there are some gaps/overlap.	Business unit staff have clear roles and responsibilities for implementing recovery arrangements and responding to incidents.

	#	Question			
BIA and risk analysis	4	Has the business unit carried out some form of business impact analysis?	No BIA has been carried out at the business unit level.	A BIA has been carried out in the last 12 months.	A BIA has been undertaken with the outputs reviewed and challenged by senior management.
	5	Based on the BIA, have recovery strategies and solutions been established?	No recovery strategies or solutions have been established.	Recovery strategies and solutions have been established in some areas.	Recovery strategies and solutions have been established for all critical areas identified by the BIA.
Recovery plan development	6	Is a business continuity plan in place for the business unit?	There is no business continuity plan in place within the business unit.	There is a business continuity plan in place within the business unit; some areas have been missed or are not up to date.	There is a business continuity plan in place and this has been recently updated to include all information needed to support a response.
	7	Does the business continuity plan provide guidance on recovering critical activities and ensuring recovery arrangements are implemented appropriately?	The business continuity plan does not provide guidance on recovering key activities.	Generic guidance on recovery is included within the business continuity plan.	Guidance within the business continuity plan is clear and specific with the inclusion of recovery activities/tasks, as required.
	8	Are contact details listed in the business continuity plan, or readily available elsewhere?	Contact details are not easily available.	Contact details are available but have not been kept up to date or are not easy to get access to.	Contact details are readily available and have been reviewed in the last 12 months.

TABLE 17.1 *continued*

	Requirements not met	Requirements met, with some exceptions	Requirements met, well established
Question	**1**	**2**	**3**
9 Have business unit staff received any training or awareness on business continuity?	Business unit staff have not received any training or awareness on business continuity.	Business unit staff have received some training and awareness on business continuity.	Business unit staff have received training and awareness on business continuity within the last 12 months and this is specific to their role or issues they may face.
10 Has the business unit conducted any plan invocation tests?	The business unit has not conducted a test to validate the plan-triggering process.	The business unit has conducted a call tree cascade test.	The business unit has conducted an invocation test involving telephone and automated emergency messaging systems.
11 Has the business unit participated in any exercises?	The business unit has not participated in any exercises.	A small number of staff have participated in an exercise, or the last exercise took place over 12 months ago.	The business unit has participated in an exercise within the past 12 months and shortcomings have been addressed.
Exercising, training and awareness			

Review and maintenance			
12 Is there any evidence of review and maintenance processes taking place?	Business continuity documentation is out of date and has not been reviewed.	Business continuity documentation was last reviewed over 12 months ago.	Business continuity documentation has been thoroughly reviewed and updated in the past 12 months.
13 Is there any evidence of continuous improvement?	There is no evidence of continuous improvement of the business continuity arrangements.	The majority of issues identified through audits, exercises or incidents have been addressed.	All issues identified through audits, exercises or incidents have been addressed; there is clear commitment to improve capability.

18

Supplier assessment

An example set of starter questions to support an assessment of critical supplier BCM

TABLE 18.1   Example supplier assessment questions

Topic	Objective	Question
Regulation	Supplier complies with relevant business continuity and resilience industry standards and regulatory expectations	1 Is your organization covered by any regulation related to business continuity/ resilience?
		2 Do you hold a valid certification against ISO 22301, or comparable Standard? 3 Does the scope of the certification cover the services that are delivered to our organization?
Governance	Supplier has a BCM programme which includes policies, standards and good practice activities including business impact analysis, planning and testing	4 Is there an established business continuity/ resilience programme that has been approved by management and communicated to appropriate stakeholders? 5 Do you have a policy covering BCM with a scope that covers the services you intend to supply to our organization?

TABLE 18.1   *continued*

Topic	Objective	Question
		6 Has senior management assigned the responsibility for the overall management of business continuity?
		7 How often do you update your BCM documentation, including BIAs, BCPs and crisis management plans?
		8 Do you have an agreed schedule of business continuity/crisis management exercises?
		9 Do these exercises include the testing of plans related to the services that are supplied to our organization?
		10 When did you conduct your last BCM exercise?
		11 Did any of your exercises delivered in the last 12 months cover the scope of the services you will deliver to our organization?
Planning	Supplier has a recovery planning capability which meets the requirements of the critical service that they are supporting	12 What recovery time has been successfully validated (i.e. recovered within RTO) for the services you intend to provide to our organization?
		13 IT: Have you validated whether technology resilience arrangements can recover the services provided to our organization within agreed RTOs and RPOs?
		14 People and premises: How long would you be able to sustain remote working/ working from an alternative location without affecting the services delivered to our organization?
		15 Do you have any individuals that present a single point of failure for the services you will deliver to our organization, and how quickly could they be replaced?

TABLE 18.1   *continued*

Topic	Objective	Question
		16 Suppliers: Are your critical third parties that you need to deliver services to our organization capable of recovery within an agreed RTO?
Training	Supplier has implemented a BCM and crisis management training and awareness programme for all staff	17 Do you run a training and awareness programme to ensure staff understand their role in a crisis or business disruption?
		18 How frequently are staff given training covering BCM and crisis management?
Assurance	Supplier ensures continuity procedures and activities are effective	19 When was the last time an independent audit or review on BCM was delivered?
		20 Did the scope of this review cover the BCM capabilities that support the critical processes and resources that you will use to deliver services to our organization?
		21 Did this review identify any high-risk findings that are yet to be addressed?

INDEX

Bold page numbers indicate figures, *italic* numbers indicate tables.

Looking for another book?

Explore our award-winning
books from global business
experts in Human Resources,
Learning and Development

Scan the code to browse

www.koganpage.com/hr-learning-
development

More from Kogan Page

ISBN: 9781789663006

ISBN: 9781398602625

ISBN: 9781398613256

www.koganpage.com

Printed in the USA
CPSIA information can be obtained
at www.ICGtesting.com
JSHW042038270624
65519JS00026B/588